SEPARATION OF CHURCH AND STATE IN VIRGINIA

A Da Capo Press Reprint Series

CIVIL LIBERTIES IN AMERICAN HISTORY

GENERAL EDITOR: LEONARD W. LEVY

Claremont Graduate School

SEPARATION OF CHURCH AND STATE IN VIRGINIA

A Study in the Development of the Revolution

By H. J. Eckenrode

DA CAPO PRESS • NEW YORK • 1971

F
230
·A36
1971

This Da Capo Press edition of
Separation of Church and State in Virginia
is an unabridged republication of the first
edition published in Richmond, Virginia, in 1910.

Library of Congress Catalog Card Number 75-122164
SBN 306-71969-X

Published by Da Capo Press
A Division of Plenum Publishing Corporation
227 West 17th Street, New York, N.Y. 10011

SEPARATION OF CHURCH AND STATE IN VIRGINIA

Virginia State Library

Separation of Church and State
In Virginia

A Study in the Development of the Revolution

Special Report

OF THE

Department of Archives and History

H. J. Eckenrode, Archivist

RICHMOND:

DAVIS BOTTOM, SUPERINTENDENT OF PUBLIC PRINTING,

1910.

PREFACE.

This work, begun shortly after my coming to the library, was at first outlined as a brief monograph on the religious petitions, but it grew inevitably to its present size and scope, as a survey of the whole subject was found requisite for a proper degree of completeness. The first three chapters are introductory in nature. The history of the colonial church cannot be written until the county records and parish registers have been examined in detail. No need exists for a further treatment of the dissenting churches. Foote, McIlwaine, Graham and Johnson have told the story of the Presbyterians, and Semple, Leland, Howell, Benedict, Thom and James have done the like for the Baptists. But there was room and a good deal of available material for a comprehensive study of the politico-religious question as it existed in the Revolutionary period, and the present work is an attempt to deal with this phase of Virginia history.

I am indebted for corrections and suggestions to Dr. H. R. McIlwaine, the Librarian, himself an authority in the same field, and to Mr. William G. Stanard, of the Virginia Historical Society.

H. J. ECKENRODE.

INTRODUCTION.

THE ESTABLISHMENT.

Virginia, unlike New England, was a settlement of average Englishmen who had no political and religious problems to spur them to expatriation. Consequently the colonists who came to Jamestown reproduced the social conditions of England more fully in Virginia than was the case in the other colonies. Innovations were not desired. The Anglican church, as the church of the ruling majority of Englishmen, was set up in Virginia as a matter of course. A minister, Robert Hunt, went with the colonists to Jamestown in 1607 and celebrated divine service under a sail in the midst of the wilderness. "We had daily Common Prayer morning and evening, every Sunday two sermons, and every three moneths the holy Communion, till our minister died." [1]

The English church may be said to have been established from the first in Virginia. The charter of 1606 gave as one of the reasons of the settlement the wish to propagate the faith among the heathen. The king's instructions for the government of the colony contain a clause relating to religion: "Wee doe specially ordaine, charge and require the said president and councells, and the ministers of the said several colonies respectively, within their several limits, and precincts, that they, with all diligence, care, and respect, doe provide, that the true word, and service of God and Christian faith be preached, planted, and used, not only within every of the said several colonies, and plantations, but alsoe as much as they may amongst the salvage people which doe or shall adjoine unto them, or border upon them, according to the doctrine, rights, and religion now professed and established within our realme of England; and that they shall not suffer any person, or persons to withdrawe any of the subjects or people inhabiting, or which shall inhabit within any of the said several colonies and plantations from the same." [2]

The second charter declared in the last article that "because, the principal effect, which we can desire or expect of this action, is the conversion and reduction of the people in those parts unto the true worship of God and Christian religion, in which respect we should be loath, that any person should be permitted to pass, that we suspected to effect the superstitions of the church of Rome: We do hereby declare, that it is our will and pleasure, that none be permitted to pass in any voyage, from time to time to be made unto the said country, but such, as first shall have taken the oath of supremacy." [3]

---

[1] Anderson's History of the Church of England in the Colonies, I, 180, from John Smith's "Advertisements for the Unexperienced Planters of New England," p. 32.

[2] Hening's Statutes, I, 67-75; quoted in Brown's Genesis of the United States, p. 67.

[3] Brown's Genesis of the United States, p. 236.

Hunt, the first clergyman, after a short time disappeared from view. Sir Thomas Gates and Sir George Somers carried another minister, Bucke, with them in their expedition, which sailed in May, 1609.[4] Bucke celebrated service in the Bermudas when the company was ship-wrecked there, and later on in the church at Jamestown upon the arrival of the expedition in Virginia.[5] Other clergymen accompanied the captain-general, Lord de la Warre, in 1610.[6] The church at Jamestown was repaired and improved.[7] These first ministers were maintained by the company from the public store.

The instructions given Gates as governor in 1609 included regulations concerning religion. The council admonished the governor to christianize the Indians and advised him to seize the medicine men in order to destroy the heathen ceremonies.[8] He was also ordered to maintain the worship of the established church and to require the regular attendance of the colonists.

Religious observance occupied a great place in the first code of Virginia laws. Dale's Code, as it is known, went into effect with the arrival of Gates in 1610 and continued to be the law of the colony until Sir George Yeardley became governor in 1619.[9] This rigid and bloody code was probably not enforced to the letter, but narrative and tradition testified to Dale's stern rule.[10]

Dale's Code has been chiefly remembered because of the penalty for blasphemy, which was the thrusting of a bodkin through the blasphemer's tongue. Sabbath observance was enforced by whipping, and speaking against the Trinity or the Christian religion by death.

Dale's foundation of Henrico was accompanied by the building of a church where the missionary, Alexander Whitaker, labored.[11] He was a noble Puritan of the early period who attempted to carry into practice the conversion of the heathen so often proclaimed as a chief reason for the planting of the colony. Whitaker did not succeed in making much impression upon the Indians, but he was an active and useful minister and a good influence in the colony.[12] During Dale's last administration other clergymen came into Virginia and new churches were built.[13]

Captain Argall, who became governor in 1617, among his decrees ordered "That every Person should go to church, Sundays and Holidays, or lye Neck and Heels that Night, and be a Slave to the Colony the following Week: for the second Offence, he should be a Slave for a Month; and for the third, a Year and a Day."[14]

Representative government began in Virginia and in the Americas in 1619, with the arrival in the colony of Sir George Yeardley, the new

---

[4] Anderson's History of the Church of England in the Colonies, I, p. 201.

[5] Anderson's History of the Church of England in the Colonies, I, p. 211.

[6] Anderson's History of the Church of England in the Colonies, I, p. 215.

[7] Purchas His Pilgrimmes, IV, p. 1754.

[8] H. L. Osgood's The American Colonies in the Seventeenth Century, I, p. 63.

[9] First Criminal Code of Virginia. In American Historical Association Report, 1899, I, p. 311.

[10] Osgood, I, 69; Hawks's Contributions to the Ecclesiastical History of the United States. Virginia, p. 24. Stith's History of Virginia, p. 122. Burk's History of Virginia, I, 165.

[11] Anderson, I, 234.

[12] Purchas, IV, 1770.

[13] Hawks, p. 32.

[14] Stith, p. 148.

governor. The church was regularly established by the instructions given him by the London Company in 1618: "And to the intent that Godly, learned and painful Ministers may be placed there for the Service of Almighty God and for the Spiritual Benefit and Comfort of the people, we further will and ordain that in every of those cities or Boroughs the several Quantity of One Hundred Acres of Land be set out in Quality of Glebe Land toward the maintainance of the several ministers of the Parishes to be there limitted. And for a further supply of their maintenance there me raised a yearly standing and certain contribution out of the profits growing or renewing within the several farms of the said Parish and so as to make the living of every minister two hundred pounds sterling per annum or more as hereafter there shall be cause."[15] It was probably within a few years that the tithe of a bushel of corn and ten pounds of tobacco was established for ministerial support. Yeardley's instructions furthermore provided for the foundation of a university at Henrico for the purpose of training Indians in Christianity.

Religion occupied a conspicuous place in the acts of the first Assembly in 1619. A certain number of Indian children were to be educated and trained in Christianity, "for laying a surer foundation of the conversion of the Indians to the Christian Religion."[16] It was enacted that "All ministers shall duely read divine service and exercise their ministerial function according to the Ecclesiastical lawes and orders of the churche of Englande, and every Sunday in the afternoon shall Catechize such as are not yet ripe to come to the Com. And whosoever of them shalbe found negligent or faulty in this kinde shalbe subject to the censure of the Governor and counsell of Estate."

Ministers and churchwardens were required to present persons guilty of adultery and the like offenses, who were subject to suspension from church and excommunication if contumacious. Ministers were to meet four times a year at Jamestown and determine upon the persons to be excommunicated. Church going was required.[17]

When Yeardley reached Jamestown, he found that there were five ministers in Virginia, two of them without orders. "Those in orders were probably Mease, Buck and Thomas Bargrave, a nephew of Dr. Bargrave, Dean of Canterbury, who came in 1618 with Captain John Bargrave, also his uncle, and the first in the colony to establish a private plantation. The Rev. Mr. Bargrave died in 1621, and left his library, valued at 100 marks, to the projected college at Henrico. Those not in orders were Mr. William Wickham and Mr. Samuel Macock, for whom Argall had in 1617 desired ordination."[18]

Clergymen were sent out more frequently in the succeeding years. The Virginia Company sent out Sir Francis Wyatt's brother, the Rev. Haut Wyatt, with him.[19] About the same time Robert Bolton and William Bennett arrived.[20] Other ministers followed.

---

[15] Virginia Magazine of History and Biography, II, 158.
[16] Colonial Records of Virginia, p. 21.
[17] Colonial Records of Virginia, p. 28.
[18] Neill's The English Colonization of America during the Seventeenth Century, p. 319.
[19] Neill, p. 321. Records of Virginia Company, Kingsbury, I, p. 516.
[20] Neill, p. 322.

Wyatt's instructions, which were dated July 24, 1621, directed him to "keep up religion of the church of England as near as may be."[21] According to the instructions, the company complained that "their Endeavours, for the Establishment of the Honour and Rights of the Church and Ministry, had not yet taken due Effect." The Virginia authorities were ordered to advance the worship of the church of England, and "to avoid all factious and needless Novelties which only tended to the Disturbance of Peace and Unity, and to see that ministers were duly respected and maintained."[22]

 The Assembly which met in March 1624 adopted rather elaborate laws for the regulation of the church. In every plantation where the people were accustomed to meet for worship, a room was ordered to be set apart for divine service, and a lot for the burial of the dead. Persons absent from Sunday service without excuse were fined one pound of tobacco, and those absent for a month, fifty pounds. Conformity to the canons of the church of England was required. No minister should absent himself from his church for more than two months upon penalty of forfeiting half his means, and absence for four months carried with it a loss of the cure. Men were forbidden to dispose of their tobacco before the minister was satisfied, and it was directed that one man on every plantation should collect the minister's "means" out of the "first and best tobacco and corn."[23]

The erection of Virginia into a royal colony in 1624 did not affect the condition of the church. For some years there were few changes. The Assembly did not meet and the governor and council apparently exercised legislative power—issuing proclamations on a variety of subjects. One of these decrees, of April 30, 1628, concerned religion, "forbidding to marry without lycence or asking in church."

In 1629, with the arrival of Sir John Harvey as governor, a new spirit was manifested in church affairs. Harvey represented the Laudian ecclesiastical spirit which was becoming paramount in the church of England. Laud had secured a uniformity to his self-imposed ideals in that church but at the cost of a great spiritual decline. The freedom of the Anglican ecclesia was at an end for the time; it became narrow and intolerant, and the early Puritans, who are the chief glory of the English church, were driven into dissent and into a fanaticism born, in considerable part, of oppression.

The October 1629 session of the Assembly passed a Sabbath-observance act, providing a fine of fifty pounds for a month's absence from church, and the profanation of the Sabbath by work or journeying was forbidden. This act is in the Puritan spirit which pervaded the church prior to the inauguration of the Laudian policy. Another act of the same session declared that "It is thought fitt that all those that worke in the ground of what qualitie or condition soever, shall pay tithes to the ministers."[24] Apparently the collection of tithes had not been rigidly enforced.

The Assembly which met in March 1629-30 breathed the new note in English church government, probably as the result of Harvey's activities.

---

[21] Hening, I, 114.
[22] Stith, 194.
[23] Hening, I, 124. Hening, I, 130.
[24] Hening, I, 144.

All ministers were required to conform to the canons of the church of England in all things, and those refusing were subject to canonical censure. All acts formerly passed concerning ministers were continued.[25] The Assembly of 1631-2 again enforced uniformity and with growing emphasis. "It is ordered, That theire bee a uniformitie throughout this colony both in substance and circumstance to the cannons and constitution of the church of England as neere as may bee and that every person yeald readie obedience unto them uppon penaltie of the paynes and forfeitures in that case appoynted."[26]

Ministers and church wardens were ordered to make returns of deaths, marriages, and births; and ministers to preach one sermon each Sunday, to teach children the catechism, comfort the sick, administer the sacraments thrice a year, and to abstain from drinking, dicing and card-playing. The support of ministers received careful consideration, as they had petitioned upon this point. The old allowance of ten pounds of tobacco was continued, and furthermore the twentieth calf, the twentieth kid, and the twentieth pig were granted them.[27] Fees were also allowed for marrying, churching, and burying.

The legislature for some years added nothing further to these acts. New parishes were formed from time to time and old ones were altered.[28]

With the accession of Sir William Berkeley as governor, another chapter of Virginia history began. His instructions directed him to see that the form of religion of the church of England was duly observed. Every congregation should build a parsonage for its minister, to which 200 acres of glebe lands should be attached, and this land should be cleared by the parishioners. Berkeley was further cautioned to "Suffer no invasion in matters of religion and be careful to appoint sufficient and conformable ministers to each congregation."[29]

Berkeley carried out his instructions with ardor, especially the clause requiring uniformity in religion. Puritans had settled in Virginia to some extent, and there was a drift of emigration to this colony as well as to New England. In 1642 a body of dissenters, probably newly settled and not numerous, applied to Boston for Puritan ministers. Three were sent, and they preached for sometime to good crowds.[30] They soon left the colony, however, probably driven from it by an act of the Assembly of March 1642-3, aimed at them. This act required that all ministers should be "conformable to the orders and constitutions of the church of England," and should not otherwise be allowed to preach, and furthermore "that the Governor and Counsel do take care that all nonconformists upon notice of them shall be compelled to depart the collony with all conveniencie."[31]

[25] Hening, I, 149.
[26] Hening, I, 155.
[27] Hening, I, 159.
[28] Anderson, I, 468.
[29] MacDonald Papers, in Virginia State Library, p. 376, and Virginia Magazine of History and Biography, II, 281.
[30] Campbell, p. 202, and Hawks, p. 53.
[31] Hening, I, 277, and Hawks, p. 53.

Trott gives another version of this act, quoted by Hawks, which reads as follows: "that for the preservation of purity and unity of doctrine and discipline in the church, and the right administration of the sacraments, no ministers be admitted to officiate in this country, but such as shall produce to the governor a testimonial that he hath received his ordination from some bishop in England, and shall then subscribe, to be conformable to the orders and constitutions of the church of England, and the laws there established: upon which the governor is hereby requested to induct the said minister into any parish that shall make presentation of him: and if any other person, pretending himself a minister, shall, contrary to this act, presume to teach or preach publicly or privately, the governor and council are hereby desired and empowered to suspend and silence the person so offending; and upon his obstinate persistence, to compel him to depart the country with the first convenience."[32]

In the revision of the laws at this session many acts concerning religion were incorporated, and some changes were made. The former tithe of ten pounds of tobacco and one bushel of corn was continued, and the tax was laid "as well for all youths of sixteen years of age as upwards, as also for all negro women at the age of sixteen years."[33]

An attempt to secure a proper control of ministers inspired the passage of an act requiring a yearly meeting of the ministers and churchwardens "before the commanders and com'rs. of every county court in nature of a visitation."[34]

Regulations for the induction and removal of ministers were provided. Vestries were granted the right of presenting ministers to the governor for induction. Likewise, upon the complaint of vestries, the governor and council were empowered to suspend ministers or inflict other punishment. Removals were left to the Assembly.[35] Hawks states that: "before the passage of this act, it was a matter of dispute whether the parishes, as builders and endowers of all the churches, had not, by the law of England, the right of presentation; and after its enactment, many parishes still contended for the exercise of the right, under the law of England, independent of the statute."[36]

It is probable that the parisnes usually selected ministers before 1642, as Hawks suggests, and that the act legalized a custom. But the question of presentation and induction was not settled and it grew to be a source of conflict between the local authorities and the governor. As a matter of fact the ecclesiastical regulations of 1642 proved inefficient. Instead of providing some practicable plan of church government, supervision of clerical matters was left, in a vague manner, to the county courts and the Assembly. "A minister of the church in Virginia was hereby placed in a position, not only essentially inferior to that retained by his brethren in England, but inferior even to that which any non-conforming minister would have claimed as his own undoubted right."[37]

[32] Hawks, p. 53.
[33] Hening, I, 242.
[34] Hening, I, 240.
[35] Hening, I, 242, and Anderson, I, 470.
[36] Hawks, p. 54.
[37] Anderson, I, 471.

Virginia was quiet during the Civil War in England. Acts were passed from time to time for church regulation as before. Ministers were called upon to reside within their parishes. Elections of vestries were to be made by a majority of parishioners. County courts were empowered to question and fine churchwardens for neglect of duty.[38] By an act of March 1645-6, the commissioners of the county courts were required to fine churchwardens for failure to make presentations to the courts of persons guilty of adultery, fornication, and drunkenness, and the governor and council were in turn empowered to fine the commissioners if they neglected to punish churchwardens.[39] Vestries were given the right to raise the tithe of ten pounds of tobacco for ministers' salaries to such a rate as they found necessary, on account of the losses occasioned by the Indian massacre of 1644.[40]

The Assembly of 1647 attempted to check a growing Puritanism by enacting that in the case of ministers who refused to read the prayers, the parishioners should be exempted from the payment of tithes.[41]

The establishment of the Commonwealth and the surrender of Virginia to the Parliamentary commissioners did not affect the church in the colony greatly. In the articles of surrender, the use of the prayer book was permitted for a year, provided that the part relating to kingship should not be read publicly;[42] ministers were continued in their places and the dues maintained.[43]

The Puritan Revolution, however, at length produced a broadening effect in Virginia. Hening states "that at no former period were the civil and religious rights of the people so well secured or justice and humanity towards our neighbors, the Indians, so sacredly regarded. In the very first act of this session (March 1657-8), for settling the church government, instead of enjoining obedience to the doctrines and discipline of the church of England, as had been invariably the case in all former acts upon this subject, no such injunction appears. On the contrary, all matters relating to the church, the ministers and other parochial affairs, are left at the entire discretion of the people."[44]

This act, entitled "Church Government Settled," gave great power to the people of the parishes; the vestries became quite subordinate.[45] Another act provided for the division into parishes of all counties not so laid out.[46]

The Restoration and the Cavalier triumph brought about a reaction. The

[38] Hening, I, 290, 1644.
[39] Hening, I, 310.
[40] Hening, I, 328. October, 1646.
[41] Hening, I, 341, and Anderson, II, 17.
[42] "It is probable that the latter provision was observed, but there is no evidence that, otherwise, the public use of the regular form of worship of the Church of England was ever abandoned. The Assembly could not (without a conflict with the Parliamentary authorities) uphold the king's religion; but the same end was reached by leaving the parishes to manage their own affairs. This meant that the old faith would be retained." William G. Stanard, in an article on Christ Church, Lancaster, in "Colonial Churches," p. 94.
[43] Hening, I, 364, and Burk, II, 90.
[44] Hening, I, 429.
[45] Hening, I, 433.
[46] Hening, I, 478.

Assembly which met in March, 1660, and elected Sir William Berkeley governor, passed an act for the suppression of Quakers. It imposed a penalty of £100 upon the captain of any ship bringing Quakers into the colony, and all of these who might enter were to be expelled; they were to be proceeded against upon a second entrance and prosecuted as felons for a third entrance.[47]

The Assembly of March, 1661, passed stringent acts for church regulation, sweeping away the popular legislation of 1657. Vestries were limited in number to twelve persons, who were required to take the oaths of supremacy and allegiance and subscribe to the doctrines and discipline of the church of England.[48] They were also given the power to determine the salaries of ministers.[49] In order to encourage clergymen to come to Virginia, all parishes were required to provide glebes, houses, and stock.[50] Vestries were ordered to secure voluntary subscriptions in destitute parishes for the support of ministers.[51] Provision was also made for the appointment of lay readers in vacant parishes. In this way observance of religion was secured,[52] and the substitute system probably proved satisfactory at first, but as time went on a tendency developed to hire lay readers to the exclusion of ministers for reasons of economy.

Measures were indeed necessary to instil some vitality into the church of Virginia. The chief impediment to the growth of religion in the colony was the sparseness of settlement. Virginia was a land of great plantations lying along the main tidal rivers in long narrow strips, with an uncultivated hinterland. The planters consequently tended to neglect religious service because of the distances to be travelled, and to lose, in some part, the religious instinct. Ministers were difficult to obtain, as the work of supervising the immense, thinly-populated parishes was great.[53] At the time of the Restoration about a fifth of the fifty parishes were supplied with ministers, and many parishes still lacked glebes and churches.[54]

Other reasons existed for the difficulty of obtaining ministers besides the great size of the parishes, the isolation of the life, and the small remuneration. The spirit of self-sacrifice was lost in the church of England. The Puritan Revolution, with its excitement and moral strain, acted as a stimulant to the religious temper of the English people, and depression followed stimulation. There were no longer men in Oxford and Cambridge who dreamed of converting the heathen and who were willing to go out into the wilderness, as there had been in the early days of colonization. Good livings were much more desired. The church of England shared inevitably the moral decline of the Restoration. One of the world's greatest idealistic movements had failed and an age of materialism followed as a result.

It was natural that the religious decay in England should influence the most English of the colonies. The intolerance of the Cavalier element in

[47] Hening, I, 533.
[48] Hening, II, 25.
[49] Hening, II, 29.
[50] Hening, II, 30.
[51] Hening, II, 37.
[52] Hening, II, 29.
[53] Virginia's Cure, p. 4. Force's Tracts, III.
[54] Ibid., p. 4.

England, more political than religious, was reflected in Virginia by the Assembly of 1662. All ministers were required to present evidence of ordination by an English bishop, and the governor and council were empowered to silence all other persons teaching or preaching, publicly or privately.[55] The whole liturgy was required to be read in service,[56] a pretty good evidence that the forms had been neglected in some parishes. No other catechism was to be taught than that of the church of England. Attendance on divine service was enforced by fines. Quaker assemblies and conventicles were forbidden on penalty of fines. The anniversary of the execution of Charles I, "of ever blessed and glorious memory," was made a day of fasting, and the date of the Restoration a holiday.

Many important acts concerning the church passed. Chapels of ease were to be built in parishes too poor to build churches.[57] The duties of vestries were defined as the making and proportioning of levies for building churches and chapels, providing for the poor, maintaining the ministers, and, in general, the management of parochial affairs. Two churchwardens were to be selected from the vestrymen, and vacancies in the vestries were to be filled by the vestries themselves. All vestrymen were required to take the oaths of allegiance and supremacy and subscribe to the doctrine and discipline of the Anglican church.[58]

Salaries of ministers were fixed at a value of £80 in commodities of the colony—in tobacco at the rate of twelve shillings a hundred and in corn at ten shilling a barrel.[59] No marriages were to be solemnized except by ministers.

The legislation of this year fixed the character of the church up to the Revolution. The vestries were given all power in parochial matters, and, at the same time, were made irresponsible. A vestry once elected by the people of the parish might fill its own vacancies, and so continue to rule for many years without being called to account. Vestries fixed the amount of the assessment for the minister's salary, church expenses, poor relief, and the individual apportionment. They transacted the parochial business and presented the minister. As a consequence a few leading gentlemen in each neighborhood administered religious matters to suit themselves, and the great mass of parishioners could make no protest. In many cases, however, the vestries doubtless acted in accordance with public sentiment, especially in keeping ministers' salaries as low as possible.

The ministers were generally under the control of a local oligarchy of hard-fisted and often ignorant squires, who were interested in keeping expenses down. Nearly all accounts agree that the system of church government in Virginia was inefficient. Few men of ability would leave England for the colony; those that came were usually inferior in ability and perhaps in character. "The Ministers and publick dispensers of the Gospel which were sent into that Plantation, are for the most part, not only far short of those qualifications required in ministers but men of opposite qualities

---

[55] Hening, II, 46.
[56] Hening, II, 47.
[57] Hening, II, 44.
[58] Hening, II, 45.
[59] Hening, II, 45.

and tempers, such as either by their loose lives, and un-Gospel-becoming conversation, or by their known weakness and unsufficiency of understanding and parts, do not only not gain or win upon those that are without, the Indian heathen, but cause more to go astray, and lose, many, very many of those that pretend to be within, the English Christians."[60] Again: "The Ministers of Virginia, too many of them, are very careless and negligent in dispensing Gods words and sacraments, as also indecent and slovenly in their manner of dispensing them."[61] And also: "There are not a few of the Ministers, whose wicked and prophane lives cause the worship of God, not only to be slighted, but to be little less than abhorred, when they officiate therein." Furthermore, "Those ministers, That are religious and laborious, * * * have scarce that single honour paid them that they deserve, from the most; and are diskonored and despised by too many." [62]

These extracts are taken from a prejudiced arraignment of Virginia and should be treated with great caution. It is to be noted that the pessimistic author acknowledges that there are some worthy ministers, but these, he says, are slighted by the degenerate colonists.

Morgan Godwyn, another witness, wrote a few years later and in a spirit of sympathy with the Indians and negroes. He affirms that the ministers were the slaves of the vestries, "to whom the Hiring (that is the usual word there) and Admission of Ministers is solely left." As the law did not oblige vestries to appoint ministers but allowed them the option of employing lay-readers, two-thirds of the preachers in the colony were these lay-readers.[63] Pluralities were allowed, parishes extended sixty or seventy miles in length, and were often without ministers for years, in order to save charges. Vestries were unfaithful in executing the laws made for the maintenance of ministers. "Laymen were allowed to usurp the office of ministers; and Deacons to undermine and thrust out Presbyters; in a word all things concerning the Church and Religion were left to the mercy of the people."[64]

But the condition of religion in Virginia exhibited nothing abnormal under the circumstances. The people were accustomed to take their religion formally; there were few enthusiasts, few deeply zealous in the colony. Furthermore, the plantation system, by isolating the colonists and depriving them of community interests, weakened their religious instincts. And, besides, the church had no healthy government. It was neither Episcopal, Presbyterian nor Congregational; it was peculiar and colonial. The union of church and state put the church under a political control, and that control took its character from existing political conditions. Vestrymen were usually politicians and frequently burgesses. The church was thoroughly subordinated to the state.

The advisability of a better regulation of the church was recognized early, but the English government for one cause or another did nothing. After 1675 the colony was nominally a part of the diocese of London, but the

---

[60] Public Good Without Private Interest (1657), p. 3.
[61] Public Good Without Private Interest, p. 14.
[62] Public Good Without Private Interest, p. 15.
[63] Negro's and Indian's Advocate, p. 170.
[64] Anderson, II, 352. Godwyn quoted.

bishop in reality made little attempt to exert any authority in Virginia until near the end of the seventeenth century. As a matter of fact, a bishop should have been appointed at this time, when only a bishop's deputy was sent out. Agitation for a colonial bishoprick began early. Alexander Murray was nominated about 1670 but the appointment fell through.[65] Other men from time to time were mentioned for the place, among them Jonathan Swift, but the design was never carried into execution.

In 1673, Charles II bestowed Virginia upon his friends Arlington and Culpeper for a term of years. The patent provided for a system of ecclesiastical patronage upon the same plan as existed in England. The proprietors were to build churches and schools, and to nominate ministers and teachers.[66] The Virginians vainly protested against this rather contemptuous disposition of a royal province to individuals. The church patronage scheme, however, resulted in nothing and matters remained as before.

Culpeper, who came over as governor in 1680, brought with him extraordinary powers in church affairs, but was not able to carry into effect any changes of importance. His report on Virginia to the committee of colonies, states that "The charges of government are maintained: 1. By private levies raised in each parish, for the minister, church, courts of justice, burgesses wages, etc., which are never brought to audit, and yet are high unequal, and burdensome, to the people, as any other; being most commonly managed by sly cheating fellows, that combine to defraud the public, and ought to be supervised by the government."[67] And again: "The ecclesiastical government is under his Majesty's governor, who grants probates of wills, and doth or ought to present to all livings, which ought to be worth threescore pounds a year, and are in number 76 or 7: But that poorness of the country, and the low price of tobacco, have made them of so much less value, scarcely the half; and the parishes, paying the ministers themselves, have used to claim the right of presentation (or rather of not paying,) whether the governor will or not, which must not be allowed, and yet must be managed with great caution."[68]

The unpopularity of the self-perpetuating vestry system was shown by the act passed by Bacon's revolutionary legislature in 1676, providing for an election of vestries every three years. The act, together with many other wise laws, was repealed by the succeeding Assembly. Nevertheless, in order to regulate the power of the vestries somewhat, the Assembly of February 1677 enacted that the voters in each parish should have the liberty of electing six persons to act with the vestry in assessing parish taxes.[69]

Lord Effingham, who became governor in 1684, apparently exerted little influence in church matters. The ecclesiastical policy of James II, however, excited great apprehension in the solidly Protestant province. James Waugh, a minister of the established church, raised a commotion in Stafford county by his speeches against the king.[70] Some of the people of Rappahan-

[65] Anderson, II, 358.
[66] Anderson, II, 374.
[67] Chalmers' Political Annals, p. 355.
[68] Ibid, p. 356.
[69] Hening, II, 396.
[70] Campbell, 341.

nock took up arms. Several persons were prosecuted and imprisoned for treasonable speeches.

The uneasiness of the colonists, however, was removed by the Revolution of 1688, which secured the Protestant religion in England. The new government recognized the need of some system of church regulation, and in 1691, James Blair, who had served some years in Virginia as a missionary, was made the commissary of the bishop of London in that colony. He had, as a bishop's deputy, the right to inquire into and punish ecclesiastical abuses, but his authority was limited and he lacked the power of ordaining to the ministry.[71] Blair consequently did not succeed in doing all that might have been done by authority to build up the church, but he did much. His work, indeed, is a testimonial of what a man of ability and energy may accomplish in a poor and indifferent community. After a long struggle against the inertia of an unenlightened population, Blair succeeded in establishing William and Mary College.[72] Governor Nicholson and the Assembly, when aroused, gave important aid. The college was founded, in large part, for the purpose of educating a native Virginia ministry, and Beverley states that "it was a great satisfaction to the Archbishops and Bishops to see such a nursery of Religion founded in the new world."

The commissary had the power of calling conventions of the clergy and this power he used to make the ministers more self-assertive. Soon after the arrival of Sir Edmund Andros as governor, the clergy petitioned him for an increase in their stipends, which were not large.[73] The house of burgesses, to which the petition was forwarded, refused, alleging that the ministers were well provided for. "Most, if not all, the ministers of the country are in as good a condition in point of livelihood as a gentleman that is well seated, and hath twelve or fourteen servants." The clergy answered that, on the contrary, they were compelled to take tobacco in payment of their salaries at a higher rate than the market price, that in many parishes there were no glebes, and that ministers were liable to ejection at the pleasure of vestries, and, in short, that the circumstances of the clergy were deplorable.[74]

The Assembly acknowledged the justice of the complaint by an act passed at the next session (September 1696) granting ministers a salary of 16,000 pounds of tobacco, besides their perquisites. Vestries were authorized to buy glebes and build houses, or were granted the option of uniting with other parishes.[75]

Blair's labors were in general beneficial to the colony, but his independence and activity demonstrated the fact that the office of commissary was rather out of place in Virginia, and his fate suggests a speculation as to the position a colonial bishop would have occupied. The country was a government of local powers, a land ruled by squires and rural magnates.

The burgesses represented local sentiment in the whole colony and the council represented a certain locality and a small number of leading

---

[71] Anderson, II, 383.
[72] Anderson, II, 387; Hening, III, 122; Burk, II, 312-14; Beverley, 88.
[73] Anderson, II, 388.
[74] Anderson, II, 389.
[75] Hening, III, 151.

families. The governor, who stood for England, held a somewhat anomalous position in the political organization, and the measure of his influence depended chiefly upon his personality. The commissary now came into the colony as a new and disturbing force. He was, like the governor, an outside official, and the somewhat vague extent of his authority brought him into conflict with the governor, who also exercised a certain supervision of church affairs. A weak commissary was only a shadow, but the vigorous and self-confident Blair passed almost his whole term of office in a struggle with a succession of governors.[76]

The rather confused policy of the British government had much to do with the controversy. The instructions given Governor Andros included the powers of an ordinary, the representative of the king and the bishop of London, and thus duplicated Blair's office in fact. In such circumstances, an antagonism between governor and commissary was inevitable. In 1694, Andros suspended the commissary from his seat in the council, whereat Blair retaliated by sending home charges against Andros, as a result of which he was removed from the government.[77] Among other things, Blair declared that Andros allowed negligent vestries to dispense with ministers, by which means they saved the amount of the salaries, and that he also forced ministers to take their allowance in tobacco at double its market value, which reduced the amount one-half.[78]

Blair's controversy with Nicholson, the successor of Andros, was even more protracted and serious. Various reasons existed for the dispute between Blair and Nicholson, but the most important was due to the latter's attempt to present ministers to the parishes[79] when the vestries failed or refused to make presentations. This claim was the result of a favorite colonial practice. The vestries, instead of making presentations, frequently employed ministers by the year. The custom was advantageous to the extent that an unsatisfactory preacher might be ejected with little trouble, but, on the other hand, it tended to put ministers on a very precarious footing. Nicholson wished to check this habit and applied to the English attorney-general, Sir Edward Northey, for his opinion on the Virginia laws governing induction. Northey decided that the right of presentation was subject to the laws of England. Consequently when the parishioners presented a minister for induction, he became the incumbent for life and could not be displaced by them; if the parishioners did not present a minister within six months after a vacancy, the governor as ordinary had the power to collate a minister to such a church by lapse.[80]

This opinion was opposed by the council, and by colonial sentiment in general. Nicholson, however, won over to his side a majority of the ministers, who were partly influenced by gratitude to the governor and partly by jealousy of the commissary. Nicholson held a convocation, in which eleven ministers supported him and only six were opposed. His adherents denied

[76]Anderson, II, 393; Campbell, p. 368; Meade's Old Churches Ministers and Families of Virginia, I, 158; II, 291.
[77] Meade, I, 157; Campbell, p. 357.
[78] Perry's Historical Collections Relating to the American Colonial Church. Virginia, p. 11.
[79] Campbell, p. 367.
[80] Perry, p. 128.

the charges which Blair had made against him.[81] But Blair, with the faithful six, reiterated the charges, and furthermore had the support of the council, for Nicholson had made himself unpopular on various grounds. As a result the governor was recalled in 1705.

The commissary extended his activities in church matters still further. He disapproved of the acts concerning the church included in the revisal of the laws in 1705, and Governor Nott, under his influence, suspended them.[82]

Blair's effort to exercise a genuine ecclesiastical control of the colonial church, however, failed. His attempt at visitations came to nothing, owing to the hostility of ministers, vestries and "the general aversion of the people to everything that looks like a spiritual court."[83] Ministers asserted their want of induction as a valid objection to canonical censure, and at every step technicalities were brought up to hinder procedure. Alexander Spotswood attempted to carry out Nicholson's plan of appointing ministers. Blair resolutely opposed the governor's claim to the right of collation, and the council backed him. The dispute came to a head in 1719 over the question of presentation to St. Anne's parish, Essex, which was vacant. The vestry refused the governor's nominee, one Bagge,[84] and sent another minister, Rainsford, to be inducted. Spotswood declined to induct the latter, but the vestry admitted him to the pulpit, and Blair was said to have advised them to resist.[85] The governor then wrote to the vestry defending his rights, in support of which he pleaded his instructions from home. "His Majesty gives his Governor full power and authority to collate any person or persons to any Churches or Chapels or other ecclesiastical benefices, as often as any of them shall become void; and in his Majesty's instructions, the Governor is particularly directed, as to the qualifications of the persons so to be collated by him; and enjoyned to cause all persons not so qualified to be removed, and immediately to supply the vacancy, without giving notice to the vestries; which is always done in England, where there is a patron."[86] Furthermore Spotswood quoted the grant to Arlington and Culpeper, with the patronage of the churches. Did the king send out ministers at his expense "to depend on popular humour for their livings?" Did the Board of Trade prepare the instructions giving the governor the power to supply vacancies if they had "any imagination that the laws of Virginia gave the right of patronage to the vestries?"[87]

Spotswood took high ground in this letter; he went further than his predecessors and sought to extend the power of the royal government. Consequently, Blair, in maintaining that the governor's right of presentation extended only to those parishes which had lapsed,[88] touched popular sentiment. A convention of the clergy met at Williamsburg in 1719 and considered the claims of the two officials. The convention, as a whole,

[81] Campbell, p. 368.
[82] Campbell, p. 376.
[83] Campbell, p. 402; Meade, I, 160; Manuscript account of a visitation in Virginia Historical Society.
[84] Perry, p. 205.
[85] Perry, p. 204.
[86] Perry, p. 206.
[87] Perry, p. 207.
[88] Perry, p. 216.

sided with Spotswood, who would have relieved the members of local tyranny and made them dependent upon the government. They complained of the difficulty of carrying out the elaborate regulations of the Anglican church in a new country and of their uncertain tenure of position without induction.[89] Only eight out of the twenty-five ministers present sided with Blair; the rest supported Spotswood. But the commissary had the backing of the council and the sympathy of the colony as a whole, and, in the end, he triumphed. It was largely due to the antagonism of the council that Spotswood was recalled in 1722.[90] Blair had proved himself the Virginia Warwick.

The controversies of the first quarter of the century were only a prelude to the more serious struggle of later years, which had far-reaching consequences. The establishment of the commissarial office and the increase in the number of ministers gave the clergy a new self-assertiveness. Their stand for their legal rights against the colonial government and popular sentiment culminated in a controversy which aroused the colony and influenced the growth of dissent, then just beginning to be an important factor in the conservative life of old Virginia.

---

[89] Present State of Virginia, p. 404.
[90] Campbell, p. 404.

CHAPTER II

The Parsons' Cause

The controversy which broke the strength of the establishment arose from the constitutional questions underlying the union of church and state. The civil power, in its attempt to deal with the clergy according to its pleasure, brought on a serious conflict, and the clergy, by appealing for protection to the royal prerogative, became involved in the great dispute as to the extent of British authority in colonial affairs. The "Parsons' Cause" has been treated from several points of view, and it has always and justly received a large share of attention from the historians of Virginia. The political historians, such as Burk, Campbell, and Howison, are against the clergy, while the church annalists, Hawks and Meade, and Wirt, the biographer of Patrick Henry, side with them as to the merits of the case.

The dispute sprang from the Assembly's attempt to commute the ministers' salaries in money, but it is conceivable that differences might have arisen on other grounds, if normal tobacco crops had continued to be raised and if the parsons had received their 16,000 pounds of sweet-scented and other brands. The conflict was probably inevitable on account of the incongruousness of a church establishment dependent, in a final sense, upon a foreign and monarchical power, in a state every day growing more republican and more self-conscious.

Long before Blair's death, the commissary had made for himself a limited place in the governmental scheme. The position, however, was precarious. If the colonial government was jealous of the governor, it was more jealous of the commissary. Blair, in his conflicts with the governor, had astutely sided with and used the council, which was the most influential part of the government. The commissary consequently was able to wield a real influence and to advance the interests of the clergy. His successors were less skilful politicians or were less fortunate. Commissary and council fell apart, and it finally came to pass that the governor, council, and burgesses were arrayed on one side and the clergy on the other, with disastrous consequences to the clergy.

Blair's influence built up the church and strengthened the clergy as a class. After they began to meet in conventions, they were less helpless than when church affairs were purely local questions and when ministers were obliged to deal with vestries in their individual strength. The commissary, as the bishop of London's representative, made reports to the bishop and appealed to him when the clergy were ill-treated. The ministers came to feel that they had a protector against the absolutism of the civil power.

But, conversely, appeals to the bishop of London were not palatable to the civil power. Vestries were accustomed to ruling the ministers and the Assembly to ruling the church in general, and as vestrymen were frequently members of the council and the burgesses, the same set of men controlled the establishment, save to the extent of the governor's interference, which was not great. Consequently, any display of interest in Virginia affairs by the bishop of London was ill-received, and the commissaries who succeeded Blair were frequently unpopular.

The collective power of the clergy enabled them to win one important victory over the vestries. The occasion was the case of William Kay, minister of Lunenburg parish, Richmond, which came up in 1748. A dispute arose between Kay and Landon Carter, a local dignitary of great weight, who brought the vestry to act against the clergyman. The vestry closed the parish church and put other persons in possession of the glebe.[91] Kay preached in the church yard for two or three years without receiving any salary.[92] He then sued for trespass and, in spite of Carter's efforts, received a verdict of £30 damages in the general court.[93] The court also decided that a minister received by a vestry and in possession of glebe land but not inducted had the right of suing for trespass.

Not content with the verdict, Carter secured an appeal to the English courts. At the same time Kay sued for three years' salary in the general court.[94] The committee of the privy council confirmed the decision in Kay's favor,[95] and in 1753 the Virginia general court awarded him £200 damages in lieu of his salary.[96] It was believed that this case decided the ministers' right to continue in possession of the glebes although not inducted,[97] and unquestionably the arbitrary methods of the vestries in dealing with ministers were checked.

The courts now protected the clergy and the Assembly had been led to legislate in their favor. In 1727, an act had been passed providing a better support for ministers,[98] and for the remedying of the old difficulty of collecting their pay. Salaries were fixed again at 16,000 pounds of tobacco. Vestries were directed to appoint collectors to take the tithe, were also required to provide glebes of two hundred acres in each parish, and were authorized to levy taxes for the purpose of building glebe houses. It is true that the Assembly modified this act in certain cases, as in that of the Elizabeth River parish glebe, which was declared, in 1734, to be a sufficient glebe although it contained only 172 acres.[99]

In 1748, probably in view of the Kay incident, another act was passed for the protection of the clergy. The salary of 16,000 pounds of tobacco was continued. Furthermore, every minister received into a parish was entitled to all its benefits and might maintain an action for trespass against anybody who molested him, but at the same time, the vestry was compensated at the governor's expense by a clause declaring that the sole right

[91] Perry, 389 and 395.
[92] Perry, 389-90.
[93] Perry, 390.
[94] Perry, 391.
[95] Perry, 401.
[96] Perry, 410.
[97] Perry, 403, 404.
[98] Hening, IV, 204.
[99] Hening, IV, 440.

of presentation existed in the vestries for the space of a year after the occurrence of a vacancy, instead of six months as before.

The Assembly did not suffer the act of 1748 to stand intact long. In 1753 an act granted the ministers of Frederick and Augusta parishes a salary of £100 instead of the 16,000 pounds of tobacco, which had been compounded at the rate of three farthings a pound and which had proved an insufficient support. Clerical writers professed to find a sinister motive in this exception to the act of 1748, but as a mattter of fact, there seems to be little ground for the suspicion, as the Assembly was constantly experiencing the embarrassments caused by a circulating medium subject to such violent fluctuations in value as tobacco. In the same year, 1753, the people of Halifax, Hampshire and Bedford had to pay public dues and officers' fees in money instead of tobacco.[101] In 1753 and 1754 the burgesses were paid out of the treasury for the purpose of lightening the public levy for the poorer people.[102]

The great clerical controversy began in 1755. In the preceding year, a convention of the clergy, fortified by the Kay case, protested to the governor against an order of council prohibiting clergymen from holding the office of justice of the peace.[103] But worse things than this deprivation were to follow. The Assembly, at the October 1755 session, ventured to violate the statutes it had enacted for the protection of the clergy by passing an "Act to enable the inhabitants of this colony to discharge their tobacco debts in money for this present year."[104] Tobacco due for rents, by bond, in contracts, and for public, county and parish levies and for officers' fees might be compounded at the rate of sixteen shillings, eight pence for every hundred pounds. The operation of the act was limited to ten months.

This law affected all creditors and all officers of the government, but especially the clergy, who were usually not large planters and who consequently received no compensating benefit by the rise in tobacco prices.

The year was a hard one in Virginia. The French and Indian War was beginning and the tobacco crop was short. The act was intended as a relief to creditors and taxpayers. But the clergy determined to appeal to England against this invasion of their rights, and on November 29, 1755, John Camm and a number of other ministers drew up a petition to the bishop of London condemning the act. The paper was a skilful presentation of the clergy's case, advancing the unanswerable argument that a variable currency should not be limited in its fluctuations in only one direction. If salaries were lessened by money compositions when tobacco was high, they ought to be increased in proportion when tobacco was low, so as to provide a fixed salary for ministers. The colonial church could not expect to obtain good ministers from England if salaries were paid "in Tobacco or money or something else, as any of them shall happen to be least profitable."[105] The strongest argument of all against the act was the fact that it provided for the composition of salaries already overdue and consequently was retroactive in

---

[100] Hening, V, 88.
[101] Hening, VI, 372.
[102] Hening, VI, 373 and 440.
[103] Perry, 424.
[104] Hening, VI, 568.
[105] Perry, 434, et seq.

tendency. The petition further argued that the act was in direct opposition to that of 1748, which had obtained the king's sanction. The new law was not, as its defenders had stated, a great benefit to the poor, but rather to the rich, inasmuch as the rich had many more tithables to pay upon than the poor. Clerical salaries were small at best, imported articles were high, and a Virginia rector was no better off than an English curate with £40 a year.

Another set of ministers remonstrated to the bishop in the following February. They denounced the "optional" law and asserted that the clergy received no compensation when the price of tobacco fell low, as had been the case since 1724. Ministers were frequently called upon to wait a year and a half for their salaries, which forced them to go into debt. The Assembly had been so certain that the act of 1755 was illegal and would be repealed that it had made it operative for only ten months. At the same time Thomas Dawson, the commissary succeeding William Dawson, wrote in a milder strain to the bishop, stating that the clergy had asked him to oppose the "optional" act because their salaries for many years had been "very mean and inconsiderable," and that they were now deprived of an opportunity to gain some recompense.[106] The commissary did not think the act would benefit the poor, as they generally paid the levy early and in their own tobacco, while the rich endeavored to pay it in money or in poor tobacco, preferring to sell their own for a profit. He admitted, however, that the price fixed by the act was better than that generally received, but apprehended the bad consequences of violating the act of 1748.

In spite of the appeals of the clergy, nothing was done. The act of 1755 was not disallowed and the ministers had nothing to do but swallow their loss. The Assembly no doubt apprehended a disallowance, but this could only come from England after the act had served its purpose. The British government allowed the matter to pass.

The composition of 1755 had excited no other protests than those of the victims. The Assembly, finding the procedure easy, passed another act in October 1758, compounding tobacco dues in money.[107] The state of the crop was not accurately known, but a shortage was anticipated and prices rose. Burk attributes the advance to "the arts of an extravagant speculator of the name of Dickerson."[108] The war was also probably responsible to some extent for the increase.

The establishment resisted again and this time with more effect. Fauquier, the governor, had approved the act, but the clergy were now fully roused by this second trespass and by a sense of their influence with the British government. A convention denounced the "two-penny" act and sent John Camm to England as the clerical advocate. Camm, an able and insinuating man, gained his point, although the Assembly had employed agents in turn. The bishop of London wrote to the Lords Commissioners of Trade and Plantations, accusing the Assembly of overthrowing the law of 1748, and the council of disingenuous conduct in maintaining that the "two-penny" act was not contrary to that law. The bishop said that the

---

[106] Perry, 447.
[107] Hening, VII, 240.
[108] Burk, III, 302.

governor "boggled at" the act for his own security, and in general he accused the Assembly of treasonable intent in setting aside a law which had received a royal assent.[109] The Board of Trade, in a dispassionate statement, recommended the king in council to disallow the acts of 1755 and 1758, which was accordingly done.

The duty fell to John Camm of conveying the instructions of disallowance to Fauquier. The latter, who was entirely out of sympathy with the clergy in their revolt, received the papers in a violent fit of anger and ordered his negroes to refuse Camm entrance to the Virginia "palace."[110] Fauquier had a reason to be angry, as it was his desire to keep the British government out of disputes with the Assembly.

The veto of that government aroused great bitterness in the colony and a pamphlet and newspaper war followed. Landon Carter began by writing his "Letter to the Bishop of London," a reply to the bishop's letter to the Lords Commissioners. Carter especially resented the charges against the Assembly of disloyalty and of encouraging dissent. He handled the bishop without gloves. Richard Bland, of Prince George, wrote a far abler criticism of the bishop's letter in his "Letter to the Clergy of Virginia." It was an attempt to demonstrate that the Assembly had sought to act from the beginning in a fair and liberal spirit towards the church. He demonstrated from the trend of legislation what was undoubtedly true—that the Assembly intended to limit ministers to a salary of £80 or £100. The year 1757 was a year of suffering, the Assembly had been obliged to issue money from the treasury to keep people from starving, and it had passed a necessary salary act and could not wait for the royal consent under the circumstances. It had indeed dealt generously with the ministers in allowing them a compensation of £144, which was more than they had ever received before. Bland enlarged upon the charge of treason. He admitted that the royal instructions ought to be obeyed, but claimed that there were times when deviation was necessary.

Camm answered Carter and Bland in his "Single and Distinct View of the Two-penny Act," a clever analysis of that measure. Carter responded with the "Rector Detected," a violent and abusive attack upon Camm. Still more bitter was Bland's sardonic rejoinder, "The Colonel Dismounted." This pamphlet is in dialogue, and it assails Camm under the pretense of defending him. Its most important argument is the answer to Camm's charge that the Assembly had restrained the royal prerogative in passing the act and thereby had tended to overthrow the constitution.[112] Bland ably presented the Virginia view of the constitution. Virginians, he claimed, were free, either as Englishmen or as the unsubdued natives, and therefore they had the right to regulate their internal affairs. He agreed that the governor and the king had the power to disallow an act, but he declined to admit that the royal instructions to the governor were law. The "Colonel Dismounted," the last of the pamphlets, differs in tone from the earlier productions. The Assembly is still defended against the charge of disloyalty, but

---

[109] Perry, p. 461.
[110] Perry, p. 476.
[111] Bland's Letter, p. 12.
[112] Colonel Dismounted, p. 20.

there is no evidence of attachment to "the best of kings." As a matter of fact, Camm's pamphlet, able argument as it was, had wrought the clergy harm because it rested upon the basis of the royal authority. In the "Colonel Dismounted" a distinct note of irritation against the royal government appears.

The clergy immediately sought to take advantage of the king's disallowance. Fauquier published the document which he termed a repeal.[113] It was not a repeal, however, and the clergy were right, though rather unwise, in maintaining that a disallowance was a different thing. The council seized upon the term "repeal" as a proof that the disallowance merely stayed the act in the future and had no application to the past. This position was illogical, as the act, by its own terms, was limited to a year, but nothing better illustrates the determination of the Virginians to defeat the king's will than this use of casuistry, in which Fauquier acquiesced.

The clergy would not have it so. Alexander White, rector of St. David's parish, King William, brought suit for the balance of his income.[114] The court stated that the act of 1758 was valid in spite of the disallowance and the jury brought in a verdict for the defendant.[115] It was charged by William Robinson, the commissary, that the court had it entered on record that White had received his salary in tobacco instead of money—a manifest falsehood—in order to prevent an appeal.[116] Thomas Warrington, of Charles parish, York, was awarded damages by a jury,[117] although the court decided the act to be valid.[118] The most noteworthy case of all, and one of the most celebrated law suits in American history, was that of James Maury, rector of Fredericksville parish, which came up in Hanover court in 1763. The court declared the act of 1758 to be invalid.[119] Maury was consequently entitled to recover damages and a jury was summoned to adjudge the amount. A number of clergymen were in attendance, as the precedent was an important one for them. It was at this moment that Patrick Henry appeared as counsel for the vestry and delivered the speech which made him famous. He ignored the law of the case, and appealed directly to the emotions of the jury,[120] especially to the colonial jealousy of English interference, boldly claiming that the king in vetoing a just and necessary law had been guilty of tyranny and so had forfeited the obedience of his subjects. The jury, which was partially composed of Presbyterians,[121] brought in a verdict of one penny damages and the court refused to grant a new trial.

Camm had early brought suit in the general court and, upon an adverse decision, had appealed to England, where the case remained undecided for some time. Warrington appealed to the general court,[122] but it suspended

---

[113] Perry, p. 480.
[114] Perry, pp. 479, 481.
[115] Perry, p. 479.
[116] Perry, p. 497.
[117] Perry, p. 496.
[118] Perry, p. 514.
[119] Perry, p. 497.
[120] Perry, p. 497.
[121] Perry, p. 498.
[122] Perry, p. 514.

judgment, pending the decision in England upon Camm's application. The privy council, however, did not consider the case, as Lord Northington, the president of the council, dismissed the action on the ground of technical errors,[123] As the agitation excited by the Stamp Act had not subsided, it is probable that the British government did not wish to raise a new issue with a colony. The general court, in October 1767, decided against Warrington and an appeal was refused.[124] Camm still wished to push the matter, but James Horrocks, president of William and Mary, advised against further agitation and the "Parsons' Cause" came to an end.

The controversy thus ended triumphantly for the colonial authorities. Patrick Henry's connection with it has been sometimes misunderstood, as he has been represented as the advocate of the popular feeling against the clergy. But as a matter of fact the "Parsons' Cause" was in no sense a class quarrel and should not be so considered. Henry fought the battle of the whole colony, and of the ruling powers more than of any other element. Nor did Henry's wonderful speech, in itself, defeat the clergy. It is not probable, in any case, that they would have succeeded in overcoming the opposition of the council and burgesses, who were in possession of the courts and could have used all the tactics of legal delay to obstruct their cause. But Henry did play a most important part in this crisis. He strongly emphasized the hatefulness of the English overlordship and aroused popular enthusiasm against it. He could not deny that the king had acted constitutionally in vetoing the act of 1758, but he claimed that the king had acted not illegally but unjustly and for so doing ought to be resisted. The popular feeling excited by Henry confirmed the colonial government in its opposition to the establishment, and the excitement over the taxation question prevented the British government from proceeding in such a side issue as the clerical dispute. The "Parsons' Cause" is a proof, if one were needed, that the colonial irritation with England involved more than the question of taxation without representation. At the bottom of it lay the feeling of Virginia nationalism; the colony was humiliated by the exercise of the royal power in opposition to its laws and will. The Virginians valued English institutions, but only as they were modified to suit the practical republicanism of the colony. The governor was an object of jealousy, and the attempt to adapt the Virginia establishment to its monarchical model was regarded as intolerable.

The Anglican clergy, in appealing to the power of the king against the colonial will, had awakened an embittered sentiment. They were unfortunate, too, in invoking royal assistance at the time when the controversy over taxation was rising into importance, and they consequently incurred a double measure of odium. It was in these years, when the civil and ecclesiastical powers were opposed, that dissent flourished all through the colony and began to be formidable.

The right and wrong in the "Parsons' Cause" has been variously estimated. In view of the evidence, it would seem that justice was on the side of the clergy. Ministers were not extravagantly paid, for the Assembly from time to time passed acts for a better provision for them. The salary

---

[123] Perry, p. 525.
[124] Perry, p. 530.

of 16,000 pounds of tobacco had been granted the ministers long enough to become custom as well as law. The Assembly had adopted a very convenient but uncertain medium in tobacco, estimating the ministers' salaries at a time when the weed was at a fairly normal price. In some years the price had fallen very low and ministers received small pay. It was just, therefore, that the ministers should be entitled to the benefit of any rise, unless the circumstances were very exceptional. This they hardly were, and, in any case, the Assembly, if it contemplated an alternative medium for tobacco, should have adopted a maximum and minimum rate of exchange, in order to provide for extraordinary advances and declines in the value of tobacco. It was right to limit the salaries to a certain money value, but it was not right to have this limitation apply only to certain years; justice requires some rule. As a matter of fact, the acts of 1755 and 1758 partook somewhat of the nature of repudiation. Contracting parties·were aware that tobacco might rise or fall in value, just as modern contractors know that the value of money may fluctuate before the obligations are discharged. The "two-penny" act deprived the creditors of a large part of their advantage, as well as the salaried officials.

One strong argument may be advanced in behalf of the Assembly; the "two-penny" act was passed in time of war, and war is taken to justify somewhat unusual methods. War expenses were undoubtedly high and bore upon the people. On the other hand, only the frontiers of the colony were invaded by the enemy and the great advance in the price of tobacco was considered an economic advantage rather outweighing the shortness of the crop.

The clergy ought not to be blamed for seeking to obtain their legal rights. In fact they contended not only for the actual value taken from them, but for a principle. The precedent of constant interference with salaries which the Assembly seemed about to establish was dangerous; it tended to place the ministers on a precarious footing and to make them thoroughly subordinate to the Assembly. The establishment saw this and resisted.

It is a valid question to ask whether the clergy were altogether justified in going to the extent of appealing to England over the heads of the colonial authorities. Acceptance of a wrong was better than the invocation of a power so unpalatable to the colonials. Certainly an appeal to the king against the Assembly after 1765 was unwise if not unjustifiable. The establishment could not expect to live in constant variance with the civil power; it could not expect to use the king as a constant threat against the government, especially in a period when the people were deeply irritated with the king for other reasons. The time was fast coming when loyalty to the king would be treason to the colony, and the establishment paid a heavy price for its attempt to make itself dependent on the crown for its protection. All classes deeply resented the clerical appeal, and the people came to distrust the allegiance of the whole clergy of the establishment to Virginia, a suspicion unjust to probably more than half of the ministers.[125]

The effect of the "Parsons' Cause" was to injure the prestige of the

---

[125] A number of ministers served on committees of safety in the Revolution. Others gave evidence of their loyalty to the American cause, as the Rev. J. B. Dunn of Suffolk has demonstrated.

establishment, shake the confidence of the ministers and encourage the dissenters. Accordingly, the establishment took a rather small part in the agitation for the foundation of an American Episcopate engaged in by the Anglican clergy in the Northern colonies. Nevertheless, some of the Virginia ministers joined their Northern brethren under the leadership of the indomitable John Camm.

The occasion for the movement was an overture from the "United Convention of New York and New Jersey," which delegated Myles Cooper, president of King's college, and Robert McKean to visit the South and secure co-operation for the American episcopate.[126] Commissary James Horrocks, in April 1771, issued a summons for a convention to meet on May 4.

The desire for a bishop may have been prompted in part by the efforts of the general court to extend its jurisdiction over ecclesiastical affairs. The commissary had never possessed sufficient authority to deprive ministers of livings and the government had been chary of interference. The notorious case of John Brunskill, minister of Hamilton parish, Prince William, which occurred in 1757, compelled some action. Brunskill persisted in an immoral life in spite of warning and the vestry complained to Commissary William Dawson, who consulted the governor. Dinwiddie advised him to proceed judicially against Brunskill, but the commissary declared he lacked the requisite powers. The governor then brought the case before the council, which removed Brunskill. This proceeding by Virginia law was, according to Dawson, opposed to canon law. The bishop of London, however, did not interfere.[127] The council had exerted an irregular kind of jurisdiction in church affairs for a long period. In 1739, upon the application of the people of St. Margaret's parish, King William and Caroline, the governor, with the advice of the council, suspended the erection of churches in the parish pending a trial in the general court.[128] In 1741-2 the council tried James Pedin, minister of Nottoway parish, on charges of ill-conduct and recommended the commissary to turn him out of his parish.[129]

In 1767 the case of Ramsay, a clergyman living in Albemarle, was brought before the general court, which declared it had jurisdiction. Fauquier wrote to Bishop Terrick that he would keep him informed of the case, the issue of which is not known.[130] In 1770 and 1771 Governor William Nelson wrote to Lord Hillsborough concerning the anomalous condition of ecclesiastical authority in Virginia and suggesting that if the commissary did not have the power of removing clergymen, the attorney and solicitor generals should prepare opinions as to the general court's jurisdiction in such cases.[131] In view of the absence of any other authority, it seemed likely that jurisdiction would fall to the general court.

The convention did not assemble on May 4, according to the summons.[132] So few ministers appeared on the advertised date that the meeting was post-

[126] Hawks, p. 126 and Cross's Anglican Episcopate and the American Colonies, p. 231.
[127] Cross, p. 137.
[128] Virginia Magazine of History and Biography, XIV, 342.
[129] Virginia Magazine of History and Biography, XV, 377.
[130] Cross, p. 227.
[131] Cross, pp. 228, 229, and Perry, pp. 532, 534.
[132] Cross, p. 231; Hawks, p. 127; and William and Mary College Quarterly, V, 150, Nelson's Letter.

poned until June 4, 1771. On that day twelve of the one hundred Anglican ministers in Virginia met. After a warm discussion a resolution to petition the king for an episcopate was first voted down and then adopted. It was decided to draw up a petition and present it to the king through the bishop of London, provided a majority of the Virginia clergy concurred.[133]

Samuel Henley and Thomas Gwatkin, two of the professors in William and Mary College, published a protest against the resolutions in the Virginia Gazette of June 6. They gave seven reasons for dissenting, the most important of which consisted in the valid argument that an episcopate would weaken the connection between England and the colonies, tend to continue the existing disputes and awaken the fears of dissenters.[134] A warm newspaper controversy followed. John Camm wrote a calm and able reply to Henley and Gwatkin, maintaining that an episcopate could not affect the rights and laws of the colonies, because the latter were modelled on England, and consequently episcopal government was interwoven in their constitution.[135] No tribunal competent to punish unworthy ministers existed, and the clergy were averse "to Episcopal Authority in the Hands of Laymen."

The letters written in reply to Camm exhibit the fear of the monarchical and hierarchical principle in English episcopal government held by all classes of Virginians.[136] Laud's episcopate was cited as a warning and an example.

The controversy between Camm on one side and Gwatkin and Henley on the other continued to fill the pages of the Virginia Gazettes until well through August.[137] Camm argued logically and at length, but he fought in a hopeless cause. Not only was the laity of Virginia, Episcopalians as well as dissenters, unanimously opposed to a bishop, but a great part of the established clergy as well. Richard Bland stated that the appointment of a bishop would have overturned all the acts of Assembly relative to ecclesiastical jurisdiction."[138]

The Assembly considered the dispute of sufficient importance to pass a resolution of thanks to Henley and Gwatkin "for the wise and well-timed Opposition they have made to the pernicious Project of a few mistaken Clergymen, for introducing an American Bishop."[139] The controversy continued for some time. The New York and New Jersey Anglican clergy criticised Gwatkin and Henley in an "Address,"[140] and Gwatkin replied in a pamphlet in which he showed the incompatibility of a bishop with the actual colonial constitution.[141]

---

[133] Cross's Anglican Episcopate and American Colonies, p. 232; Hawks, 127.

[134] Cross's Anglican Episcopate and American Colonies, p. 234.

[135] Dixon and Hunter's Virginia Gazette, June 13, 1771.

[136] Virginia Gazette, June 20, 1771.

[137] Attack on Camm, June 22, 1771; Camm's Letter to Henley, July 11, 1771; Henley to Camm, July 18, 1771; Camm to Gwatkin, August 15 and 22, 1771.

[138] William and Mary College Quarterly, V, 153. "I profess myself a sincere son of the established church, but I can embrace her Doctrines without approving of her Hierarchy, which I know to be a Relick of the Papal Incroachments upon the Common Law." p. 154.

[139] Journal of House of Burgesses (Virginia State Library), 1770-1772, 122; Hawks, 130. Burk, III, 364.

[140] Cross, 238.

[141] Cross, 239.

Possibly this controversy stimulated the house of burgesses to attempt to organize a church court upon the lines of a compromise. In 1772, the house directed the committee for religion to enquire into the state of religion in the colony, and Robert Carter Nicholas, on March 27, 1772, reported for the committee: "That it is the Opinion of this Committee, that for superintending the Conduct of the Clergy a Jurisdiction consisting of the Laymen and Clergymen be established."[142] Benjamin Harrison, Nicholas and Richard Bland were appointed a committee "to establish a Jurisdiction for superintending the Conduct of the Clergy, to be exercised by Clergymen, with an Appeal to a Court of Delegates."[143] Harrison introduced the bill on April 7. It was engrossed two days later and ordered to be read on the first of May, which was after the date of adjournment.[144]

The bill was not introduced at the following session and this mild substitute for episcopal supervision failed. Possibly in a quieter age it would have met with a better fate. In this time of suspicion the establishment of an ecclesiastical court could not be carried through. It is needless to say that the appointment of a bishop in Virginia was impossible. Church and state were united in the colony but in a simple and republican fashion, and the church was subordinate to the state. A bishop, drawing his authority from the king, exercising a jurisdiction over the Virginia church, and living upon the income of the state, would have been an anomaly. The development of republicanism in the colony left no place for monarchical institutions. Furthermore the time was wholly inappropriate for a bishoprick, for the colonies were too irritated with the British government to see anything but Grecian gifts in its offerings, civil or ecclesiastical.

Yet the upper classes in Virginia were sincerely attached to the establishment, and many people doubtless would have accepted such a court as was proposed in the bill of 1772 as the best solution of existing difficulties. But the policy of the clergy in seeking to draw nearer to the Anglican foundation had weakened the devotion of the colonists and had made any action difficult. So church matters remained as before while the colony drifted on to the Revolution.

---

[142] Journal of the House of Burgesses (Virginia State Library) 1770-72, 275.
[143] Journal, p. 300.
[144] Journal, p. 308.

CHAPTER III

The Dissenters

The establishment was destined to come to its end from two main causes—political revolution and the great evangelical revival as represented by the dissenting sects. The tendency of a part of the Virginia clergy to look upon the royal power as an integral element in the union of church and state was contributory.

Dissent did not greatly trouble the establishment until the middle of the eighteenth century. Puritans lived in the colony at an early period, and the Assembly passed legislative measures against them, which were enforced by Sir William Berkeley. In an uncongenial soil and with the authorities hostile, Puritanism failed to obtain a lasting hold.

Quakers came into the colony about 1656[145] They settled in southern Virginia, especially in Nansemond, which was visited by George Fox and long continued to be a Quaker center.[146] An act of Assembly was levelled at them and they were subjected to a considerable persecution at the Restoration.[147] After a time they came to be tolerated by custom and, in 1692, they obtained legal toleration.[148] The Quakers, after their first period, were not aggressive and they never threatened the supremacy of the establishment.

From time to time non-English elements were introduced into the Virginia population, but these were absorbed in a religious, as well as in a political and social sense. The Germans who settled at Germanna in the early years of the eighteenth century set up no really separate church of their own. The Huguenots, who came into the colony in considerable numbers about the end of the seventeenth century, soon conformed to the establishment.

The Anglican church was never seriously disturbed until the rise of Presbyterianism. This sect, however, did not make headway in the colony for many years after its first appearance. Presbyterians were living in eastern Virginia in some numbers in 1683[149] Josias Mackie qualified under the Toleration Act of 1689 and became, as far as is known, the first legal dissenting minister in Virginia.[150] Mackie was the pastor of a congregation on Elizabeth river until about the time of his death in 1716. Francis Mackemie, who came from Ireland to America and settled in Accomac, is

---

145 H. R. McIlwaine's Struggle of Protestant Dissenters for Religious Toleration in Virginia, Johns Hopkins University Studies in Historical and Political Science, 12th series, p. 19; S. B. Weeks's Southern Quakers and Slavery, Johns Hopkins University Studies in Historical and Political Science, p. 13.

146 J. B. Dunn's History of Nansemond County, p. 25.

147 Weeks, p. 14, et seq.

148 Weeks, p. 149.

149 T. C. Johnson's Virginia Presbyterianism and Religious Liberty, p. 13.

150 McIlwaine, 31.

regarded as the real founder of Presbyterianism in the United States. He was licensed to preach in 1699[151] and after living for a time in Virginia, went North, where he fought the battle of religious freedom.

The Assembly of 1699 formally acknowledged the application of the Toleration Act to Virginia. Dissenters, who qualified under the terms of the act, were allowed to be absent from church and to hold their own meetings once in two months.[152] This liberty did not extend to free-thinkers, those who denied the Trinity, the truth of Christianity, or the inspiration of the Scriptures. But advantage was not taken of this concession, and Presbyterianism died out in eastern Virginia after Mackemie.

The creed was next introduced into western Virginia by the Ulster Irishmen who came into the Valley in large numbers after 1730. This immigration was encouraged by the governor, William Gooch, who, in 1738, in reply to an overture from the synod of Philadelphia, assured such Presbyterians as might settle west of the mountains that they would not be disturbed by the Virginia government if they complied with the requirements of the Toleration Act.[153]

Other sects were also represented by the immigrants in the west, who included Germans and English-Lutherans, Quakers, Menonists and Dunkers[154]—but the Presbyterians predominated. Before 1745 there were Presbyterian congregations in the country west of the mountains and a few to the east.[155]

It was not long before Presbyterianism developed in eastern Virginia. The first congregation, which was formed by Samuel Morris in Hanover in 1743, was the result of a spontaneous movement and not of missionary efforts.[156] But Presbyterian ministers soon followed the movement in midland Virginia. William Robinson, sent by New Castle Presbytery, preached in Charlotte, Prince Edward, Campbell and other counties, and John Roan and John Blair came a little later.

The Hanover Presbyterians had not secured a license for a meeting house, but for some time they went unmolested by the authorities, until the fiery evangelist Roan began to attract attention by his denunciation of the Anglican ministers.[157] Roan and Thomas Watkins were presented in the general court in 1745 "for reflecting upon and vilifying the established religion," a legal offense,[158] and Joshua Morris for permitting an unlawful assembly in his house. Other cases followed. Isaac Winston and Samuel Morris were fined twenty shillings for allowing illegal meetings to be held in their houses. But procedure before juries proved unsatisfactory and the Presbyterians were more troubled by fines for non-attendance on church,

---

[151] Johnson, p. 16.

[152] Hening, III, 171. In a few cases licenses were obtained under the act after Makemie's time. One occurred in Richmond county in 1729. Va. Magazine of History and Biography, X, 214.

[153] Johnson, p. 28.

[154] McIlwaine, p. 40.

[155] Johnson, 26; McIlwaine, 42-43. The Planting of the Presbyterian Church in Northern Virginia.—J. R. Graham.

[156] Evangelical and Literary Magazine, II, 113, 186, 201, 329, 353, 474; McIlwaine, p. 45; Johnson, p. 30; Campbell, p. 439.

[157] McIlwaine, p. 46.

[158] Foote, I, 137-140; McIlwaine, p. 48.

inflicted by justices of the peace, than in any other way.[159] Among other preachers, the great Whitefield, visited Hanover, and that county became the center of dissent in the east. In 1746, Gooch issued a proclamation against "Moravians, New Lights and Methodists,"[160] forbidding them to hold meetings under penalty of law. The proclamation was ineffective and the Presbyterian movement received a mighty impetus in 1747 by the arrival of a great man, Samuel Davies, who came to Hanover from Pennsylvania. He applied for a license to preach in three churches in Hanover and one in Henrico.[161] The council hesitated to grant the application, but the license was obtained through the governor's influence.[162] The next year Davies made application for a license for a colleague, John Rodgers, but the council refused. Later on in the same year Davies asked for a license to preach in three new churches, which request was granted. But in 1750, when the New Kent county court ventured to license a meeting-house, the general court revoked the grant. The court claimed the sole right of licensing preaching-places and the council, while admitting that the English Toleration Act extended to Virginia, held the opinion that dissenting ministers should be confined to a limited number of churches. The attorney-general, Peyton Randolph, maintained that the Toleration Act was not law in Virginia, but this contention could not hold good. Davies struggled resolutely for a broad interpretation of the Toleration Act in the face of opposing church and state.

The clergy of the establishment, alarmed by the inroads of dissent, appealed to the bishop of London against Davies,[163] asking that he be limited to one field under the narrow interpretation of the Toleration Act. The latter wrote to Doddridge and Avery, the leading dissenting divines in England, for assistance, and they communicated with the bishop of London on the question of the number of preaching-places allowed non-conformists by law. The bishop of London wrote Doddridge that the Act of Toleration was intended to ease the consciences of non-conformists and not to serve as a dispensation for itinerant preachers.[164] Doddridge replied that the practice in England was to license places of worship wherever required. [165] Commissary William Dawson took the same view as the council and the bishop of London that the Toleration Act bound dissenters rigidly to particular places.

Governor Dinwiddie refused Davies' application for an eighth meeting-house, and the latter met the difficulty by securing an assistant.[167] Undoubtedly dissenting ministers were granted licenses wherever desired in England, but this right was secured by an act supplementing the Toleration Act, that of 10th Queen Anne.[168] This act had not been adopted by the Virginia

[159] McIlwaine, p. 50.
[160] Campbell, p. 442.
[161] Campbell, p. 446.
[162] Campbell, p. 446.
[163] Foote, I, 173.
[164] Perry, 372.
[165] Perry, 374.
[166] Perry, 381.
[167] Perry, 396.
[168] McIlwaine, 55.

Assembly, and the narrower limits of the Toleration Act legally applied. The great point in the issue was the council's wish to differentiate the colonial practice from the English, upholding the power of the general court to decide such cases according to its own interpretation.

The government's objection to licensing a number of preaching-places for one minister was gradually overcome by the increase of Presbyterian ministers in Virginia, so that the accusation of itinerancy could no longer be urged. The growth of Presbyterianism was promoted by other · causes—by the French and Indian War and the "Parsons' Cause." Davies' patriotism during the war did much to reconcile the ruling powers to his creed. When this apostle to the Virginians left the colony in 1759, he left behind him a vigorous and growing church. Numerous accessions from the upper classes gave the Presbyterians a respectable position in the east, while their place as the dominant creed in the west lent them some political influence. Before the Revolution the church had successfully weathered all storms and won a place for itself in the colony; it had gained adherents from all ranks; it had set up an ecclesiastical organization and it was prepared to found a college.

The success of the Presbyterians was a portent of great changes. Church and state had been closely united in Virginia, and the upper class of planters had ruled both. That class was zealous for the supremacy of the establishment, as well as for its own social and political control. The setting-up of a rival sect in the colony, with a form of government responsive to popular wishes, broke in upon the autocracy of the old regime. It is true that in a few years the Presbyterians, with their natural conservatism, ceased actively to antagonize the establishment and settled down to a quiet existence, but they had paved the way for other dissenters who would demand a further extent of liberty. The crust of privilege was broken and democratic ideas in religion and politics spread and strengthened. At the same time the moral and spiritual life of the colony was deeply influenced, and the foundation was laid for the conquest of Virginia to evangelical Christianity.

The sects which followed the Presbyterians into Virginia and whose task it was to widen the spread of evangelical religion were the Methodists and Baptists.

The Methodists came into the colony a few years before the Revolution. Robert Williams, who settled in Norfolk in 1772, established the society in Virginia. Methodism flourished thereafter and within a few years numbered some thousands of adherents.[160] The Methodists counted themselves as members of the Anglican communion and made no effort to oppose the establishment or to play a part in politics. Nevertheless, since their evangelical tenets were very different from the spirit of the establishment, they had much to do with promoting the change in the conception of religion which was coming over Virginia.

Baptists had existed in Virginia from early times, but they left no impression in the unpropitious seventeenth century. In 1714 a colony settled in the southeast but it did not flourish. About the middle of the century Baptists began to enter Virginia in larger numbers. A party of them

---

[160] W. P. Bennett's Memorials of Methodism in Virginia, p. 51.

settled in the Valley in 1743.[170] The earlier comers were known as "Regulars," the conservative branch of the church. The radical element, the "Separates," came into the colony between 1750 and 1760 and within a few years began an agitation which spread through its entire limits. Presbyterians, Methodists and Baptists were all animated by a new spirit, for they all, more or less, represented the great evangelical movement which had resulted from the labors of George Whitefield and John Wesley. They added this impetus to an original Puritanism. They were all at variance with the spirit and practice of the establishment, and the fact of the contrast was one of the strongest weapons wielded by the evangelicals—zeal against apathy, vigorous faith against a claimed decadence. The criticism of the establishment was keen, and of all the critics the Baptists were most trenchant. The Anglican clergy came in for a denunciation which included their lives, their sermons and the performance of their duties.

What manner of men were the parsons of the establishment? The name they have gained in history prompts the question. Tradition and narrative have painted them in black colors, and the peculiar unworthiness of the Virginia clergy is a proverb. The weight of condemnation is not altogether the testimony of enemies. Writers before and after the evangelical movement, Anglicans and others, have testified against them. Jarratt mentions the lack of vital religion in the establishment.[171] Meade has set forth, with painstaking care, the moral deliquencies of a large number of clergymen. The records themselves attest the evil lives of some of the ministers.

But, in spite of all this evidence, the fact is that the unworthiness of the established clergy has been exaggerated.[172] Some of them were, without doubt, evil livers; others were indifferent to their duties; but the majority, from a study of the evidence, appear to have been good, everyday sort of men, and a few were pious. Why then has the whole order come in for condemnation?

The earlier testimony against the worthiness of the Virginia parsons is not wholly trustworthy, as it consists for the most part of the impressions of travellers, who are always looking for flaws. Again, the clergy were more prominent, relatively speaking, in the life of the colony than in England, and their sins were consequently more advertised. It must be remembered, too, that drunkenness, the chief vice attributed to the clergy, was a universal sin in the eighteenth century.

These are minor reasons. The chief cause for the general condemnation of the colonial clergy, and one of the leading causes of the overthrow of the establishment, consisted in the form of religion predominant in Virginia. The Anglican clergy did more than oppose the development of dissent in Virginia—they attempted to controvert the great religious revival which had

[170] A General History of the Baptist Denomination in America, by David Benedict, p. 64.
[171] Life of Devereux Jarratt, 56, 84.
[172] We cannot judge the clergy fairly as long as our knowledge of the colonial church remains defective. I think that the full evidence will put the ministers in a better light than they have yet appeared in. If their lives were as evil as has been alleged, it is strange that presentments were not more common. Grand juries often indicted laymen fearlessly for moral offenses. Why then was a generally depraved clergy tolerated? It is possible that the parsons gained a bad reputation, partly for the very reason that such black sheep as were among them were shown up.

spread from England to the colonies and which had begun to influence even the English church. The evangelical movement, when it reached the colonies, first affected the dissenting churches, awaking internal controversies, dividing them into old and new schools—"old" and "new lights"—but in the end quickening the missionary zeal of the whole bodies and sending them forth prepared to conquer in a world especially prepared for them by the great political controversy between the colonies and England.

The clergy of the establishment were average clergymen of the English church, about on a par with their brethren at home before the beginning of the Wesleyan movement. The Virginia church was still under the influence of that latitudinarianism which had begun to decline in England. The Virginia clergy, true to their training, still continued to preach Tillotson, Sterne and Blair to drowsy audiences. A cold rationalism claimed them. When they were denounced by itinerant evangelists for their lack of ardor, they retorted with denunciations of "enthusiasm" and "fanaticism." It is difficult to estimate the value of the established church and its influence upon the life of the community. Certainly Virginia produced a noble breed of men in this age. The lower classes, however, were not much benefited by the ministrations of the parsons. Ignorance, poverty, and immorality abounded; the records are full of bastardy.[173] But the clergy should not be too greatly blamed for the condition of affairs. It was not according to the traditions of the colonial church to appeal to the emotions. Besides, the lower classes had little voice in church affairs and their interest, therefore, was not much awakened. Furthermore, the parishes were large, sometimes comprising the extent of a modern county and containing some thousands of inhabitants, and the preachers, who were also school teachers, were not able, if they had the will, to look after their scattered parishioners. They contented themselves with preaching on Sunday and administering the ordinances of the church when required. Life was straitly ordered in the colony; duties were a matter of routine, and religious enthusiasm was unknown.

It was into this dull and formal world that the evangelical missionaries came, preaching a new religion. Their sermons were not the rationalistic homilies of Anglican divines, but the burning, moving appeals of enthusiasts. The people, with all of Englishmen's susceptibility to religious feeling, responded powerfully. The awakening of popular emotion in the ordered life of old Virginia was startling in its manifestations because this was the first occasion. The poorer people, hitherto unreached by the establishment, were stirred to the core by the wandering Baptist preachers, who walked the highways and byroads, preaching in season and out and reproducing the apostolic age. The phenomena of the movement were such as mark all great revivals—hysteria, contortions, raptures, and even coma. The contrast between the overpowering sermons of the evangelists and the short prosy moral discourses of the Anglican ministers was great, and between the points of view of the two schools even greater, so that in time, as a result of the evangelical triumph, the "new light" religion came to be considered the only valid form of Christianity, and the unworthiness of the old parsons grew into a sort of legend.

The "Separate" Baptists, as a result of their disturbing influence in

[173] Chiefly found, however, among the indented servants.

the community, were subjected in many places to mob violence, which is a frequent accompaniment of religious agitations. Samuel Harriss, a Baptist minister, was driven out of Culpeper county, and on another occasion he, together with one John Koones, received a beating at the hands of a mob.[174]

Legal prosecution followed. Penalties began to be sharply administered about 1770[175] By this time, the first feeling against dissent as dissent had largely worn away among the upper classes in Virginia, but the Baptists were regarded as a disturbing social element. This they were, since all movements which agitate whole communities and tend to the betterment of large classes of men affect the order of society.

The first known case of the imprisonment of Baptists occurred in Fredericksburg in 1768, when John Waller, Lewis Craig, James Childs, with several others, were arrested by the sheriff on the charge of disturbing the peace.[174] The court offered to release these men if they would promise not to preach in the county for a year, but they refused and suffered an imprisonment.[175] They had not applied for licenses under the Toleration Act, and the judgment of the court in their case was legal. John Blair, president of the council and deputy-governor, wrote to the Spotsylvania king's attorney advising him to allow the imprisoned Baptists to apply for licenses, but they were released without any conditions. Other cases of imprisonment followed. William Webber and Joseph Anthony were jailed in Chesterfield in 1770[176] and John Waller and William Webber, with two others, in Middlesex in 1771. Cases occurred elsewhere, and as late as 1774.[177]

According to Leland, about thirty preachers and a few laymen were imprisoned between 1768 and 1775[178]

The Baptists labored chiefly in the east, the oldest and most thickly settled portion of the colony. Parishes were smaller in this region and ministers were numerous. Consequently the Baptists, in invading the stronghold of the establishment, awakened an inevitable antagonism which resulted in ill-treatment. The preachers might have avoided misuse, in large part, by taking out licenses to preach at certain places, and by discontinuing the practice of wandering through the country agitating against the establishment.[179]

The Presbyterians had been content to keep within the law. That the Baptists were not is significant. The defiance of law was a symptom of the pending political change. The itinerants considered the British laws concerning religion as wholly unjustifiable, and in this spirit they disregarded them although occasionally they applied for licenses and were refused. As a consequence, an inevitable legal prosecution followed which placed the Baptists in the light of sufferers for the cause of religious freedom. This was

---

[174] R. B. Semple's History of the Rise and Progress of the Baptists in Virginia (Beale), p. 20.
[175] Virginia Magazine of History and Biography, XI, 415.
[174] Semple, 29.
[175] According to local tradition the Baptist ministers cursed the town by shaking the dust of it from their feet.
[176] Cambbell, 555; Semple, 20; James, 23.
[177] W. F. Thom's Struggle for Religious Freedom in Virginia. The Baptists, p. 29.
[178] Leland's Writings, p. 107.
[179] Thom, p. 27.

a fact, but the liberty they claimed was incompatible with the existing law. Yet the Baptists could not have done their work if they had strictly complied with the Toleration Act. Itinerancy was a vital feature of their agitation; it was only by going out into the fields and hedges that they could reach a sparse population scattered over a large territory. Their zeal and labors contrasted strongly with the apathy of the Anglican clergy, and their sufferings at the hands of authority in the end gave them a sanctity in the eyes of the populace. Other causes contributed to the marvellous success gained by the Baptists. They were democratic in politics, as well as in religion, and whole-hearted in their sympathy with the colonial cause as against England. But the chief reason for success lay in the fact that the Baptists presented the great evangelical movement in the way which appealed most strongly to the masses; and their preachers, who generally lacked the heavy classical education of the day, possibly for this very reason addressed the ignorant with more effect. The Baptist church grew by leaps and bounds after 1770, and the movement became one of the events of Virginia history. Before the actual beginning of the Revolution, the Baptists had gained thousands of converts.

The spread of the Baptists and their constant conflicts with authority led to the weakening of the legal restraints of dissent. The Baptists, irritated at their ill-treatment, complained, and the Assembly awakened to the fact that some better regulation of dissenters was advisable than the law of 1699, confirming the Toleration Act. "The attempts to prevent the spread of dissent, which fell so heavily on the Baptists from the year 1768 and onwards, but convinced the more thoughtful Episcopalians that some degree of restricted toleration must be granted to the citizens of Virginia, or society must be shaken to its foundation. To appease the agitated community a bill was proposed granting privileges to dissenters." [180]

The movement for a new toleration law began as early as 1769. The house of burgesses, on May 11, 1769, ordered the committee for religion, "to prepare and bring in a Bill for exempting his Majesty's Protestant Dissenters from the Penalties of certain Laws," [181] but the bill was not introduced at this session. At the fall session, on November 11, 1769, the committee for religion was instructed "to prepare and bring in a Bill for granting Toleration to his Majesty's Subjects, being Protestant Dissenters," but apparently the bill for a second time was not introduced.

At the opening session of 1772, a petition from Lunenburg Baptists declared that they "find themselves restricted in the Exercise of their Religion, their Teachers imprisoned under various Pretences, and the Benefit of the Toleration Act denied them, though they are willing to conform to the true Spirit of that Act, and are loyal and quiet Subjects; and therefore praying that they may be treated with the same kind Indulgence, in religious Matters, as Quakers, Presbyterians, and other Protestant Dissenters, enjoy." [183] On February 22, 1772, the same petition was presented by the Mecklenburg Baptists, [184] and on February 24, by the Sussex Baptists, and

[180] Foote, I, 320.
[181] Journals of the House of Burgesses (Virginia State Library), 1766-69, p. 205.
[182] Journals, 1766-69, p. 252.
[183] Journals, 1770-72, p. 161.
[184] Journals, 1770-72, p. 183.

later by the Caroline Baptists. On the same day, the Amelia Baptists declared that they were "restricted in their religious Exercises; that, if the Act of Toleration does not extend to this colony, they are exposed to severe Persecution; and, if it does extend hither, and the Power of granting Licenses to Teachers, be lodged, as is supposed, in the General Court alone, the Petitioners must suffer considerable Inconveniencs, not only because that court sets not oftener than twice in the Year, and then at a Place far remote, but because the said Court will admit a single Meeting-House and no more in one County; and that the Petitioners are loyal and quiet Subjects, whose Tenets in no wise affect the State; and, therefore praying a Redress of their Grievances, and that Liberty of Conscience may be secured to them."[186]

The committee for religion reported that the Baptist petitions "so far as they relate to allowing the petitioners the same Toleration, in Matters of Religion, as is enjoyed by his Majesty's dissenting Protestant Subjects of Great-Britain, under different acts of Parliament is reasonable."[187] The committee was ordered to prepare a bill pursuant to the resolution, and at the same time it was ordered to "enquire into the State of the established Religion in this Colony and Report the same."

Robert Carter Nicholas, on February 27, 1772, presented a "Bill for extending the Benefit of the several Acts of Toleration to his Majesty's Protestant Subjects, in this Colony, dissenting from the Church of England." The bill was re-committed to the committee, which amended it, and it was then engrossed, ordered to be printed, and to be read for the third time in the following July.[190]

This bill did not prove satisfactory to the dissenters. It was a rather illiberal digest of the various English acts of toleration, including the features of that of the 10th Queen Anne, and it did not go far enough to satisfy churches which had gained a pretty substantial measure of liberty. At the May 1774 session of the Assembly, protests against the Toleration Bill began to come in. The Baptists complained that a bill "not admitting public Worship, except in the day time, is inconsistent with the laws of England, as well as the Practice and Usage of the Primitive Churches, and even of the English Church itself; that the night season may sometimes be better spared by the Petitioners from the necessary duties of their callings; and that they wish for no indulgences which may disturb the Peace of Government; and, therefore praying the House to take their Case into Consideration, and to grant them suitable redress."[191] At the same time the committee for religion was directed to bring in a "Bill for allowing a free Toleration to his Majesty's Protestant Subjects in this Colony, who dissent from the Church of England." A petition also came in from the Baptist Association, which met in Loudoun, "praying that an Act of Toleration may be made giving the Petitioners and other Protestant dissenting Ministers liberty to preach in all proper places, and at all Seasons, without restraint."[192]

---

[185] Journals, 1770-72, p. 185.
[186] Journals, 1770-72, p. 186.
[187] Journals, 1770-72, p. 188.
[188] Journals, 1770-72, p. 194.
[189] Journals, 1770-72, p. 197.
[190] Journals, 1770-72, p. 249.
[191] Journals, 1773-76, p. 92.
[192] Journals, 1773-76, p. 102.

In the fall, Hanover Presbytery took action against the Toleration Bill, drawing up a searching and able criticism of the measure. The paper was probably written by Caleb Wallace.[193] The Presbytery objected to the terms of the bill requiring dissenters to confine their ministry to certain designated places because Presbyterian preachers were obliged to itinerate in order to reach the numbers of people included in their communion. The prohibition of night services was inconvenient. The clause requiring dissenters to keep church doors open in all weathers was a reflection upon their loyalty. Furthermore Presbyterians could not refuse to baptize slaves who were qualified to receive baptism; and they desired the liberty to hold property for their churches.[194] The Presbyterian memorial was presented to the house on June 5, 1775.[195] On June 13, the Baptists again petitioned against the bill.[196]

The bill was never passed. The colony was now on the verge of revolution and the great controversy with England drew attention from other subjects. Besides, the time had passed for toleration. The dissenters had practically won toleration before, and, with a revolution on hand, they would be satisfied with nothing short of complete liberty.

---

[193] W. H. Whitsitt's Life and Times of Judge Caleb Wallace, p. 34.
[194] Ms. in Va. State Library. Johnson prints the petition in full, 65-69.
[195] Journals, 1773-76, p. 189.
[196] Journals, 1773-76, p. 225.

CHAPTER IV

The Revolution

The dissenters, even before the Revolution, had gained a place in Virginia which made them dissatisfied with such legal restrictions as were proposed in the Toleration Bill, a system of restraint somewhat similar to that burdening their brethren in England. What they really desired and hoped for was equality before the law with the establishment, although this consummation may have seemed far away in the beginning of 1775. But the Revolution soon gave them the liberty which might not have been secured in decades of peace.

It was inevitable that the evangelical sects, which were Whig in politics, should profit by the struggle with Great Britain. In time of war social and political advances are made in a day, especially when military service is the price paid. The nature of the quarrel with England had, too, a democratic side. The colonies were not, at least in form, contending for the liberties of states imperilled by an overbearing protectorate, as much as for the constitutional right of all Englishmen to tax themselves. Besides, almost all contests with authority lead to a strengthening of democratic forces, particularly in an age when the study of social and political rights engaged the attention of men as almost never before. The dissenters profited largely by the spread of democratic feeling in the colony.

Aside from the arguments used in the controversy with England, a certain nationalist sentiment had developed in Virginia, which played a part in the colony's attitude towards the home government. This feeling had nothing to do with class; it was general. The Revolution in Virginia was not a class or a sectional revolution; it had a political, and not a social, origin. The upper classes in Virginia were almost as strongly opposed to the ministerial policy as the backwoodsmen, although their action tended to be more conservative. Patrick Henry precipitated the Revolution in 1775, just as he had led colonial opinion in opposition to the Stamp Act in 1765, and he received the support of the midland and western elements in his agitation for immediate action, but it must not be thought that he forced the eastern and aristocratic section against its will into an undesired contest. The upper planter class had long been practically united in opposition to England. The majority in the house of burgesses and in the conventions of 1775 and 1776 was composed of this class, and consequently the conservatives, if they had been seriously opposed to revolutionary measures, were in a position to withstand action. It is true that the council at this time was largely under Dunmore's influence, but the council had lost much of its importance in recent years.

The circumstances of life of the planters formed a natural culture medium for the growth of republicanism. In the eastern counties there was substantial wealth without luxury, and a society which had been allowed several generations for development. The men of the leading families were educated largely in a legal and historical direction, and they were trained from youth in legislation and affairs. They managed large estates and controlled numbers of slaves, and they had the leisure and taste for political research and discussion. They ruled church and state and they laid the tax levies. The representative of central power was the royal governor, but his authority was limited. Consequently the planters viewed, with genuine alarm, the desire of the British government to exercise control over the colonies and to curtail their rights and liberties. They recognized the danger to the semi-independent state and they instituted the colonial committee of correspondence to draw the colonies together for resistence. And when the time came for actual war, the upper class was united to such an extent that Toryism existed in Virginia to a smaller degree than in any colony south of New England. The committee of safety appointed in 1775 was wholly composed of men of rank and position.

Two schools of republicanism existed in Virginia when the moment for separation came in 1776. The conservatives were English in sentiment, largely untouched by the political philosophy of the century, and viewing their opposition to England as a defense of the past and as resistance to a policy of innovation. These men deeply regretted the necessity of separation, and they wished the Revolution to end with the actual separation. Their political ideal was the colonial state minus the governor and Parliamentary claims. They regarded social changes with dislike and wished to preserve the establishment intact as the state religion of the new commonwealth. Among the conservatives were Edmund Pendleton, Penjamin Harrison, Robert Carter Nicholas, and Carter Braxton.

The progressive party, led by Patrick Henry, Thomas Jefferson, Richard Henry Lee, and George Mason, fed with Locke and Montesquieu, or representing democratic feeling among the people, looked beyond the English model. This party regarded the Revolution primarily as a development, and, largely because it did so, it led the way and framed the constitution.

The second convention of 1775, which met in Richmond on July 17, made preparations for the war then begun and appointed a committee of safety, with executive powers. The Baptists declared their approval of the convention's measures, in a petition written on August 14, and asked that the liberty be extended four delegated ministers to preach to the colonial troops, which contained many Baptists.[197] The convention immediately granted the request,[198] passing a resolution directing commanding officers "to permit dissenting clergymen to celebrate divine worship, and to preach to the soldiers, or exhort, from time to time * * * for the ease of such scrupulous consciences as may not choose to attend divine service as celebrated by the chaplain."[199]

The convention which met in Williamsburg on May 6, 1776, was probably the most noteworthy assembly ever held in Virginia. It was largely composed of men who had sat in the burgesses and in the earlier conventions, the rulers and picked men of the colony. Among the members were Edmund

---

[197] Ms. in Va. State Library, Religious Petitions. Printed in C. F. James's Documentary History of the Struggle for Religious Liberty in Virginia, p. 218.
[198] Journals of Conventions of 1775, 17.
[199] Journals, p. 17.

Pendleton, Paul Carrington, Archibald Cary, Meriwether Smith, George Mason, Patrick Henry, Robert Carter Nicholas, James Madison, Richard Bland, Richard Henry Lee, Dudley Digges, Thomas Nelson, Joseph Jones, Edmund Randolph, and George Wythe.

On May 15, the convention passed the memorable resolutions instructing the Virginia delegates in the Continental Congress to propose a declaration of independence, and directing the appointment of a committee to prepare a Declaration of Rights and a constitution. This committee included among others, Archibald Cary, Meriwether Smith, George Mercer, Henry Lee, Robert Carter Nicholas, Patrick Henry, Edmund Randolph, Richard Bland, Paul Carrington, Henry Tazewell, and Thomas Ludwell Lee. Strangely enough Patrick Henry wrote, on May 20: "I cannot count upon one coadjutor of talents equal to the task."[200] By this statement Henry probably meant that he had no strong associate on the democratic side.[201] James Madison and George Mason were added to the committee after the appointment, and they furnished Henry with the party support needed.

The Bill of Rights was drawn up in large part, or in its entirety, by Mason, and he also drafted the constitution. Jefferson probably wrote the preamble, and there are those who think he composed the main part of the constitution, but the evidence for this is wanting.

The Bill of Rights and constitution were not accepted without a struggle. The conservative party in the convention advocated an aristocratic model of government drawn up by Carter Braxton.[202] The articles of the Bill of Rights were carried one by one in the face of a stubborn opposition. The story of the conservative resistance to the constitution has never been adequately told. Edmund Randolph, who was in a good position to do it, has given us a slight and unsatisfactory account. Concerning the Declaration of Rights, Thomas Ludwell Lee wrote on June 1, that, "A number of absurd or unmeaning alterations have been proposed. The words as they stand are approved by a very great majority, and yet, by a thousand masterly fetches and stratagems, the business has been so delayed that the first clause stands yet unassented to by the Convention."[203] The core of the conservative opposition, a body of about twenty men, was too small to defeat legislation but large enough to throw obstacles in the way.

The first fifteen articles of the Bill of Rights were adopted without many changes. The sixteenth article, that relating to religion, provoked a discussion which the sources very meagrely illuminate. Indeed, the authorship of the article is in doubt. Tradition credits Mason with the composition of the whole bill. Madison stated in a letter written in 1827 that he retained a perfect impression that Mason "was the author of the 'Declaration' as originally drawn, and with very slight variations, adopted."[204] The copy of the Bill of Rights in Mason's handwriting, which is preserved in the Virginia State Library, contains the fifteenth and sixteenth clauses. Further-

[200] W. W. Henry's Life, Correspondence and Speeches of Patrick Henry, I, 413.
[201] M. C. Tyler's Patrick Henry, 203.
[202] Campbell, 646. Tyler, 203.
[203] M. D. Conway's Edmund Randolph, 34.
[204] W. C. Rives' Life of James Madison, 1, 161.

more, Mason, in a letter of October 2, 1778, enclosing a copy of the Bill, states that it was "just as it was drawn and presented by me."[205]

The only evidence opposing Mason's claim to the authorship of the Bill is a statement in Edmund Randolph's manuscript history, in which he says that "The fifteenth, recommending an adherence and frequent recurrence to fundamental principles, and the sixteenth, unfettering the exercise of religion, were proposed by Mr. Henry. The latter, coming from a gentleman who was supposed to be a dissenter, caused an appeal to him, whether it was designed as a prelude to an attack on the established church, and he disclaimed such an object."[206]

The probability is that Mason wrote the draft of the sixteenth article, and with his liberal views of religion it is hardly likely that he needed any urging; at the same time, if Randolph's statement is worthy of credence, it is evident that Henry gave such a special advocacy to the fifteenth and sixteenth articles as to be considered their originator. And indeed Henry had a peculiar interest in urging the claims of the dissenters. His sympathies were with them, and, besides, his chief political influence lay in the midland region, where dissent and democratic feeling were strong.

The article on religion was not adopted without some amendment. As originally written it contained the phrase, "that all men should enjoy the fullest toleration in the exercise of religion."[207] Madison offered an amendment which declared "That religion, or the duty we owe to our Creator, and the manner of discharging it, being under the direction of reason and conviction only, not of violence or compulsion, all men are equally entitled to the full and free exercise of it, according to the dictates of conscience, and, therefore, that no man or class of men ought, on account of religion, to be invested with peculiar emoluments or privileges, nor subjected to any penalties or disabilities unless, under color of religion, the preservation of equal liberty and the existence of the state be manifestly endangered."[208]

The article as adopted omitted the word "toleration," to which Madison had specifically objected, and affirmed instead "that all men are equally entitled to the free exercise of religion, according to the dictates of conscience." It was certainly a broad declaration of religious liberty, even if the exact extent of its application was not recognized. William Wirt Henry, in writing of it, made the claim that "It is the high honor of Virginia that she was thus the first state in the history of the world to pronounce the decree of absolute divorce between Church and State, and to lay as the chief corner-stone of her fabric of government this precious stone of religious liberty, which had been rejected by the builders."[209] To this statement, Charles J. Stillé, of Philadelphia, took serious exception. He denied that the sixteenth article of the Bill of Rights was a declaration of religious liberty.[210] But if it is not a declaration of religious liberty, it is a grant of toleration. This, however, the article could hardly be, since the word "toleration" was struck out in order to make the article convey the idea of religious liber'

[205] K. M. Rowland's Life of George Mason, I, 237.
[206] Conway's Randolph, 30. Henry's Henry, I, 430.
[207] W. C. Rives' Life and Times of James Madison, I, 142.
[208] W. C. Rives' Life and Times of James Madison, I, 142.
[209] Papers of the American Historical Association, II, 26.
[210] Ibid., III, 205. Henry's reply, same volume, p. 213.

Madison himself left his commentary upon this point in a manuscript copy of the Bill of Rights.

"On the printed paper, here literally copied, is a manuscript variation of this last article making it read"—(Here the amendment proposed by him is incorporated). "This variation," he adds, "is in the handwriting of J. M., and is recollected to have been brought forward by him with a view, more particularly, to substitute for the idea expressed by the term 'toleration,' an 'absolute and equal right' in all the exercise of religion according to the dictates of conscience. The proposal was moulded into the last article in the Declaration as finally established, from which the term 'toleration' is excluded."[211]

Another objection is urged to W. W. Henry's thesis to the effect that the Bill of Rights is not a law but a mere declaration of what the law ought to be when the statute should be subsequently enacted. This statement is followed by an account of the religious struggle in Virginia during the Revolution, including the bill for religious freedom and the act of 1799.[212] As a matter of fact the Bill of Rights has always been considered a part of the organic law of Virginia. It had, too, an immediate effect as law. Prosecution for religious causes ceased. Disabilities on account of religion were removed. Subscription to the declaration against transubstantiation was no longer required of officers of the government. Anglicans, Roman Catholics, Evangelicals, Jews, and unbelievers were placed on the same civil footing. It may be said, then, that Virginia was ahead of the world at the time when the Bill of Rights was adopted, making the first legal statement of the principle of religious liberty.

But W. W. Henry is incorrect in declaring that the sixteenth article effected an "absolute divorce of Church and State." Its action upon the relations of church and state was not clearly understood. 'Dissenters appealed to it as breaking this connection, but Anglicans, on the other hand, interpreted it as sanctioning a broad and liberal union. The Bill of Rights and the act of 1776 suspending for a year the payment of Anglican ministers' salaries did away forever with the taxation of dissenters for the benefit of the establishment, but the question had not been settled as to the compatibility of a tax for the general support of religion with the principle of religious freedom.

This doubt as to the interpretation of the sixteenth article afforded the conservatives an opportunity to rally and to attempt to secure the union of church and state on a broader basis. Another cause contributed to the religious struggle in Virginia after the adoption of the Bill of Rights. Grigsby has pointed out that the limitations of the constitution were not invariably regarded by the Assembly. The house of delegates looked upon itself as occupying much the same position as the house of commons, and consequently as wielding wide and somewhat indefinite powers. The house of delegates claimed a competency to legislate on the question of religion, although this power was felt to be hedged about in a rather undefined way by the Bill of Rights. Practical considerations, too, aided in preventing a

[211] Rives, Madison, I, 145.
[212] Papers of the American Historical Association, III, 205 et seq.

rigid and sweeping interpretation of the sixteenth article. The establishment had always existed as a part of the state; it still continued to be so regarded after the beginning of the Revolution and the adoption of the constitution, even if the existence of an established church in a democratic republic was something of an anomaly. Some years passed before this fact was admitted by the conservative element in the State, but its admission could not be forever postponed.

During the Revolution state and church continued to have a certain connection. Anglican clergymen were still regarded, in a sense, as officers of the state, and as such were alone capable of performing the marriage ceremony. Vestries, too, while bereft of their old power to levy tithes for the support of the establishment, managed the poor relief system and assessed taxes for it.

The act of 1776, "for exempting the different societies of Dissenters from contributing to the support and maintenance of the church as by law established" supplemented the sixteenth article of the Bill of Rights, which did not contain any specific reference, as Madison desired, to the question of clerical dues. It was passed in the recession of the wave of democratic feeling which had moved the Commonwealth in the earlier months of the year.

The first Assembly of the independent state met on October 7, 1776. Edmund Pendleton, former chairman of the committee of safety and president of the convention, was elected speaker of the house of delegates.[213] The committee for religion included Carter Braxton, Richard Lee, Richard Bland, William Fleming, Mann Page, Robert Carter Nicholas, Thomas Jefferson, and other prominent men.[214] On the same day the first dissenter petition came into the house. It was from the largely Presbyterian county of Prince Edward, and the subscribers pledged their allegiance to the new government.[215] Then the plea was made for disestablishment. "The last article of the Bill of Rights we also esteem as the rising Sun of religious Liberty, to relieve us from a long night of ecclesiastic Bondage; and we do most earnestly request and expect that you would go on to complete what is so nobly begun; raise religious as well as civil Liberty to the zenith of Glory, and make Virginia an Asylum for free enquiry, knowledge, and the virtuous of every Denomination. Justice to ourselves and posterity, as well as a regard to the honour of the Common-Wealth, makes it our indespensable Duty, in particular to intreat, That without Delay, you would pull down all Church Establishments; abolish every Tax upon Conscience and private judgment * * * and define accurately between civil and ecclesiastic authority; then leave our Lord Jesus Christ the Honour of being the Sole Law giver and Governor in his Church."

Jefferson, who was a member of nearly all of the important committees, had now begun to launch his great democratic programme, which included religious as well as political, legal, and educational measures. On October 14, 1776, he presented his famous bill "to enable tenants in taille to convey

---

[213] Journal of H. of D., 1776, p. 3.

[214] Journal of the H. of D., 1776, p. 7.

[215] Journal, p.7. The paper is signed by 160 names, many of them Presbyterian—Johnstons, Porters, Cunninghams, Grahams, Caldwells, Morrisons, and many others. It came at a critical moment.

their lands in fee simple,"[216] and on the same day a bill "for the naturalization of foreigners."

Other petitions from the evangelical churches emphasized the Prince Edward memorial. On October 16, a petition was presented asking for the ending of the establishment, that "this as well as every other yoke may be Broken and that the oppressed may go free that so every Religious Denomination being on a Level animosities may cease."[217] On October 22, two petitions, written in the same form and signed by dissenters in Albemarle, Amherst, and Buckingham, advanced the theory that the Bill of Rights had put an end to the establishment and that any laws passed for its maintenance would not be a continuation of an existing institution, but a revival of a dead one.

The establishment was not without its defenders. The Methodists, who seldom interfered as a religious organization in political affairs, asked, on October 28, for the retention of the state church. "We do all in our power to strengthen and support the said Church—And as we conceive that very bad consequences would arise from the abolishment of the establishment— We therefore pray that as the Church of England ever hath been, so it may still continue to be Established." The significant and enlightening words are added: "Signed in Behalf of the whole Body of the people commonly called Methodists in Virginia, consisting of near, if not altogether, three thousand members. Geo. Shadford."[218]

On November 8, the falling establishment spoke for itself in a moderate and well-written paper.[219] The clergy argued that they were educated for a special profession and guarantees were given them of a livelihood and that these guarantees should be fulfilled. Besides, an establishment is conducive to the peace and happiness of a state, as the conduct of men is to some extent dependent upon their opinions, and this being so, "it therefore cannot be improper for the legislative Body of a State to consider how such opinions as are most consonant to Reason and of the best Efficacy in human affairs, may be propogated and supported." Christianity can be best preserved in its purity by an established church, as it supports a learned ministry, and the hardships which an establishment might impose on individuals or bodies of men ought not to be considered as weighing against it. The Virginia church had produced good fruits in the century and a half of its existence and had treated dissenters with charity. This mildness had been acknowledged "by those very dissenters, who now aim at its Ruin, many of whom emigrated from other countries, to settle in this, from motives, we may reasonably suppose, of Interest and Happiness." The petition finally urged that the question of continuing the establishment be deferred until the general sentiment of the people had been consulted.

A large part of the people favored the establishment. A meeting of Accomac people instructed their delegates to oppose the attempt "to subvert altogether the present establishment of the Church of England." A

[216] Journal, p. 12.
[217] Journal, p. 15. Signed by 127 names, apparently of people of several denominations.
[218] Journal, p. 30. This extract and the succeeding quotations of religious petitions, in part or in full, are taken from a manuscript collection in the Virginia State Library, known as "Religious Petitions," and arranged in order by years.
[219] Journal, p. 47. MS. "Religious Petitions," 1776.

petition of Charles City conservatives, not presented to the Assembly but printed in Purdie's 'Gazette, complained of the inroads of dissenters and their night meetings, which attracted large numbers of slaves, and asked "that the Church may be maintained in all its legal rights, 'and that the sectaries may be indulged with such a regulated toleration as to this honorable House shall seem proper."[220]

But these last appeals in behalf of the lost cause were overborne by the demands of the dissenters. Petitioners from Augusta, on November 9, protested against the burden of supporting an establishment while under obligation "to support Gospel Ministers of their own profession." Tuscarora Congregation (Presbyterian), of Berkeley county, argued that laws incompatible with the Bill of Rights ought to be immediately repealed. Human rights, 'and religious liberty as one of them, should have every ground of security which law could assure them. The establishment was inconsistent with the rights of humanity, civil and religious, and it ought therefore to be "suspended or laid aside."

The German congregation in Culpeper asked exemption from parochial taxes on the ground that it supported its share of the expense of the war, while maintaining its own ministers, and yet declared at the same time that it was "not breaking from the established church, as do the Common Dissenders."

The most 'noteworthy petition presented at the session was that of the "Dissenters from the Ecclesiastical Establishment, in the Commonwealth of Virginia." It is, like other petitions, an appeal for the overthrow of the establishment.[221] "Your Petitioners—having long groaned under the Burden of an ecclesiastical Establishment, beg leave to move your Honorable House, that this as well as every other yoke may be broken, and that 'the oppressed may go free."

These petitions were the outside stimuli of a great struggle. It is almost certain that Jefferson would have attacked the establishment, even if no dissenting petitions had come in, but as they came, they were of 'use and strengthened the democratic wing of the Assembly.

The position of the Presbyterian church as the chief dissenting faith was, of course, of great importance. Hanover Presbytery, in its petition to the house, took the ground that the Declaration of Rights had secured religious freedom, and: "Therefore we rely upon this Declaration as well as the justice of our honorable Legislature, to secure us the free exercise of religion according to the dictates of our consciences." Dissenters should no longer be taxed for the benefit of the establishment. Religious liberty should accompany civil liberty. The establishment had injured Virginia by preventing immigration into it of thousands of dissenters. Christianity needed no aid from the state, as it lived by its spiritual power, not by external causes. Presbyterians requested no establishment for themselves; they asked that all churches might be left to the free exercise of their

[220] American Archives, 5th series, III, 1776, Colo. 1092-1093.

[221] MS. "Religious Petitions," 1776. This paper is signed by about 10,000 names. The immense manuscript is made up of segments pasted together and in many cases lists of names are written out by the same hand. No prominent Virginians are included. Most of the names are obscure, although a good many fairly well identified are included. Probably dissenters of all denominations are represented, and possibly persons of no persuasions.

modes of worship and to support themselves by voluntary contributions. The only proper objects of civil government were the happiness and protection of men in this life.

The weight of opinion was against the establishment. Jefferson's activity, also, was very great. He worked constantly in committees and presented bill after bill. Legislation on religion was included in his schedule, and indeed the situation demanded action. The Bill of Rights had made a grant of religious liberty, but the limits of the grant were unknown. Dissenters and Anglicans gave the charter a very different interpretation, and, in the meantime, owing to the confusion of the times, clergymen were experiencing difficulties in collecting their salaries. Adam Smyth, minister of Botetourt parish, had received only one year's salary in three years and a half, and parish affairs had been entirely neglected for two years.[222] Spence Grayson, of Cameron parish, Loudoun, had received no salary for 1775, as his vestry had failed to appoint a collector, and the county court had not even assigned parties to make out a list of tithables for 1776.[223] Other ministers were in the same situation, although their complaints did not reach the Assembly at this time.

The struggle over the establishment was a long and bitter one, beginning in October and lasting until December. On November 9, the religious petitions were referred from the committee for religion to the committee of the whole house,[224] and the fight grew warm. Jefferson's chief opponents were Edmund Pendleton and Robert Carter Nicholas, and both were able and patriotic conservatives. Pendleton had always opposed radical action and he was arrayed against Patrick Henry in 1765. He has been charged by some with Toryism, but the accusation is untrue, since Pendleton served as chairman of the committee of safety and president of the convention, the two most important and dangerous offices in the Revolutionary government. Nicholas was always a zealous upholder of the Anglican church, although he had acted against the clergy in the "Parsons' Cause."

The committee of the whole debated the religious question on November 19, 1776, and finally adopted a set of resolutions providing for the disestablishment of the English church.

"Resolved, As the opinion of this committee, that all and every act or statute, either of the parliament of England or of Great Britain, by whatever title known or distinguished, which renders criminal the maintaining any opinions in matters of religion, forbearing to repair to church, or the exercising any mode of worship whatsoever, or which prescribes punishments for the same, ought to be declared henceforth of no validity or force within this Commonwealth.

"Resolved, That so much of an act of Assembly made in the 4th year of the reign of Queen Anne, intituled an act for the effectual suppression of vice, and restraint and punishment of blasphemous, wicked and dissolute persons, as inflicts certain additional penalties on any person or persons convicted a second time of any of the offenses described in the first clause of the said act, ought to be repealed.

[222] Journal, p. 51.
[223] Journal, p. 60.
[224] Journal, p. 48.

"Resolved, That so much of the petitions of the several dissenters from the church established by law within this Commonwealth, as desires an exemption from all taxes and contributions whatever towards supporting the said church and the ministers thereof, or towards the support of their respective religious societies in any other way than themselves shall voluntarily agree, is reasonable.

"Resolved, That although the maintaining any opinions in matters of religion ought not to be restrained, yet that publick assemblies of societies for divine worship ought to be regulated, and that proper provision should be made for continuing the succession of the clergy, and superintending their conduct.

"Resolved, That the several acts of Assembly, making provision for the support of the clergy, ought to be repealed, securing to the present incumbents all arrears of salary, and to the vestries a power of levying for performance of their contracts.

"Resolved, That a reservation ought to be made to the use of the said church, in all time coming, of the several tracts of glebe lands, already purchased, the churches and chapels already built for the use of the several parishes, and of all plate belonging to or appropriated to the use of the said church, and all arrears of money or tobacco arising from former assessments; and that there should be reserved to such parishes as have received private donations, for the support of the said church and its ministers, the perpetual benefit of such donations."

A committee, which included Bolling Starke, Robert Carter Nicholas, Jefferson, George Mason, Henry Tazewell, James Madison, and William Fleming, was appointed to draw up a bill in conformity with the resolution.[225] The committee, however, was too large for business, and later five members were constituted a quorum.

These instructions were more or less in the nature of a compromise. They provided for a large degree of religious liberty, while, at the same time, they would have maintained a certain connection of the state with the establishment. Jefferson has described the debates on religion as "the severest contests in which I have ever been engaged. Our great opponents were Mr. Pendleton and Robert Carter Nicholas; honest men but zealous churchmen. The petitions were referred to the Committee of the whole House on the state of the country; and after desperate contests in that committee; almost daily from 11th October to the 5th of December, we prevailed so far only as to repeal the laws which rendered criminal the maintenance of any religious opinions, the forbearance of repairing to church, or the exercise of any mode of worship; and further, to exempt dissenters from contributions to the support of the Established Church; and to suspend, only until the next session, levies on the members of that church for the salaries of their own incumbents. For although the majority of our citizens were Dissenters, as has been observed, a majority of the legislature were Churchmen. Among these, however, were some reasonable and liberal men, who enabled us, on some points, to obtain feeble majorities. But our opponents carried, on the general resolutions of the Committee of November

---

[225] Journal, p. 63.

19, a declaration that religious assemblies ought to be regulated and that provision ought to be made for continuing the succession of the Clergy, and superintending their conduct. And in the bill now passed was inserted an express reservation of the question, whether a general assessment should not be established by law, on every one, to the support of the pastor of his Choice; or whether all should be left to voluntary contributions."[226]

The statement of Caleb Wallace, the Presbyterian deputy to the Assembly, is somewhat at variance with Jefferson's account.

"Our Bill of Rights declares that all men are equally entitled to the free exercise of religion according to the dictates of conscience, etc. Yet in some subsequent Acts it is manifest that our Assembly designed to continue the old Church Establishment. * * * And is it not as bad for our Assembly to violate their own Declaration of Rights, as for the British Parliament to break our Charter? The Baptists circulated a Counter Petition which was signed by above 10,000, chiefly Freeholders. Our Transalpian Presbyterians were much chagrined with what was said and done in a more private way against dissenters; and indeed many Dissenters in every part of the country were unwilling any longer to bear the burden of an establishment. These circumstances induced our Presbytery to take the lead, and prepare a memorial on the subject to be presented to our House at the session last fall. * * The result was the Assembly passed an act exempting dissenters for all time to come from supporting the church of England. * * This you may suppose was very pleasing to some, and as ungrateful to others, and still there are many of a certain church, I would rather say craftsmen, who are hoping that something will yet be done in favour of the Great Goddess Diana, and others are fearing that religious liberty and the right of private judgment will be abridged by our assembly's taking upon them to interfere in a case that lies beyond the limits of civil government. Thus has the affair ended, or rather proceeded, without producing any other consequences than a day or two's debating in the House, and a little newspaper bickering."[227]

Wallace's statement that the passage of the bill was effected without any great effort is supported by Edmund Randolph's narrative:

"It has been seen that the friends of the Established Church were apprehensive of the force of their own principles, to which they had assented in the bill of rights, and how they were quieted by the assurances of Mr. Henry. But they were patriots who dreaded nothing so much as a schism among the people, and thought the American principle too pure to be adulterated by religious dissension. They therefore did in truth cast the establishment at the feet of its enemies."[228] It is possible that Jefferson made mistakes as to details, but it is not likely that he erred in his main impression of the incident, which was vivid after a lapse of many years. The controversy on some points at least was warm, even if it is true, as W. W. Henry has pointed out, that the suspensory bill was not debated in the house for any great length of time.

On November 30, the conservatives were more or less successful in the

[226] Henry, I, 495. Writings of Thomas Jefferson (Memorial Association), I, 58.
[227] Historical Magazine, I, 355, quoted by W. W. Henry, I, 493.
[228] Henry, I, 498, from Edmund Randolph's MS. Hist. of Va.

house and passed a resolution "That the committee appointed to prepare and bring in a bill pursuant to the resolution of the whole House on the petitions of the several dissenters to be discharged therefrom, except as to so much of the third resolution as relates to exempting the several dissenters from the established church from contributing to its support, so much of the fifth as saves all arrears of salary to incumbents, and empowers vestries to comply with their contracts, excepting also the sixth resolution; and that it be an instruction to the said Committee to receive a clause, or clauses, to make provision for the poor of the several parishes, to regulate the provision made for the clergy, and to empower the several county courts to appoint some of their members to take lists of tithables where the same 'hath not been already done."[229]

Bolling Starke, from the committee, presented the bill ordered "For exempting the different societies of dissenters from contributing to the support and maintenance of the church as by law established, and its ministers, and for other purposes therein mentioned."[230] On December 3, it passed the second reading and was committed to the committee of the whole house.[231] It was debated on the fourth and fifth and passed.[232] The senate returned the bill with amendments,[233] which the house accepted on December 9.[234]

The first article of the act[235] declared that since "doubts have arisen, and may hereafter arise" whether the acts of Parliament concerning religion are in force or not, every act "which renders criminal the maintaining any opinions in matters of religion, forbearing to repair to church, or the exercising any mode of worship whatsoever," is null and void. This article was an amendment to the original bill, and was probably inserted by the senate.

The first eight lines of the second article, the original preamble of the bill, were struck out, and the lines were inserted to read: "And whereas there are within this commonwealth great numbers of dissenters from the church established by law who have been heretofore taxed for its support, and it is contrary to the principles of reason and justice that any should be compelled to contribute to the maintenance of a church with which their consciences will not permit them to join, and from which they can therefore receive no benefit." The rest of this clause of the act declaring dissenters exempt from all taxes and levies for the support of the church is as in the original bill. It is probable that the first eight lines were a substitute for a more radical declaration.

The third article provided that vestries should assess all salaries and arrears of salaries upon dissenters as well as Anglicans, up to January 1, 1777; and continue making provision for the poor as in the past.

The fourth article reserved the glebes, churches, and chapels and the property in them, together with arrears of money and tobacco, to the use of the Anglican church and ministers.

---

[229] Journal, p. 76.
[230] Journal, p. 76.
[231] Journal, p. 80.
[232] Journal, p. 83.
[233] Journal, p. 89.
[234] Journal, p. 90.
[235] Hening, IX, 164.

The fifth article declared that the question of levying a general assessment for the support of all churches, or of leaving the churches to their own support should be deferred. The original article was extensively amended by suggestion of Robert Carter Nicholas.[236]

The sixth and most important article suspended the levy for support of the Anglican ministers until the end of the next session of the Assembly, that is, until the summer of 1777. This suspension was done on the ground that "by the exemptions allowed dissenters, it may be too burthensome in some parishes to the members of the established church if they are still compelled to support the clergy by certain fixed salaries, and it is judged best that this should be done for the present by voluntary contributions.'

The seventh article directed the method of taking tithables, and the eighth fixed a penalty for the failure to make the lists.

This act, in effect, destroyed the establishment. Many dates have been given for its end, but it really came on January 1, 1777, when the act suspending the payment of tithes became effective. This was not seen at the time. The act of 1776 was intended as both a final and a temporary measure. It was final in supplementing the work of the Bill of Rights and exempting dissenters from the support of the Anglican Church; temporary in suspending the tithes paid by members of that church. But in freeing almost half of the taxpayers from the burden of the state religion, the state religion was at an end. Nobody could be forced to support it, and an attempt to levy tithes upon Anglicans alone would be to recruit the ranks of dissent. In only one way could an establishment be continued and that was by taxing all citizens for the general support of religion. The attempt to do this, in the conservative reaction at the end of the war, failed, thus prostrating the last hope. The fact remains that no taxes for religious purposes were ever paid in Virginia after January 1, 1777.

The overthrow of the establishment had seemed far away in 1774, when the Baptists and Presbyterians had protested against the restrictive Toleration Bill, but two years of revolution had brought great changes. The democratic republic had replaced the royal colony. The conservative element had been forced to make important concessions to progressive feeling. These concessions seemed deplorable sacrifices to such men as Pendleton and Nicholas, who maintained English social and religious ideals. The party they represented was strong and did not suffer definite defeat until 1785, when it became apparent that the progress of democracy could not be checked. Meanwhile, during the war and after, the conservative party[237] struggled hard and was able to stave of a conclusion of the religious question. Jefferson's act of 1779 settled nothing. It merely confirmed what the acts of 1776, 1777, and 1778 had practically perpetuated. The act of 1776 freed dissenters from the obligation to support the old establishment, and this much was accepted as final by all parties. The Anglican church as the exclusive religious branch of the government was no more. What remained

---

[236] MS. in Virginia State Library.

[237] Party terms are not used in a very exact sense. Party organization was not known at this time, and alignments differed on different questions. But there was a consistency of action on certain issues which can only be expressed by the use of descriptive terms, such as "democratic" or "progressive," and "conservative."

unsettled was the attitude of the state towards religion in a general sense as the guardian of morality.

The vestries did not escape wholesale criticism in the progress of the Revolution. Their self-perpetuating powers irritated the people, and, shorn as they were of half their authority by the act of 1776, they still administered the poor relief. Besides, in some parishes vestrymen were not in full sympathy with the Revolution. Consequently, on October 25, 1776, a committee was appointed to prepare a bill "for dissolving the several vestries in this country."[238] The bill was not introduced, however, as the conservatives rallied to oppose a measure they considered so fatal to themselves as a general dissolution of the vestries and the inauguration of a new system of poor relief.

The May Assembly of 1777 continued the suspensory bill. A conservative reaction against the progressive feeling which had passed the Bill of Rights was now under way, and this might have seemed a good time for the revival of the establishment, if such a thing had been possible. A petition from Cumberland protested strongly against the recent innovations in religion and called for a return to pre-revolutionary conditions. A memorial to the same effect came from Mecklenburg.[239]

Nevertheless, on June 2, 1777, the bill "for further suspending the payment of the salaries heretofore given to the clergy of the Church of England" passed the house without amendment.[240] It was brief, merely continuing the suspension of salaries until the end of the next session of the Assembly.[241]

On June 3, the day following, Hanover Presbytery presented another memorial[242] It stated that the Presbyterians were firmly attached to the American cause. "In our former memorial we have expressed our hearty approbation of the Declaration of Rights, which has been made and adopted as the basis of the laws and government of this State; and now we take the opportunity of testifying that nothing has inspired us with greater confidence in our Legislature, than the late act of Assembly declaring that equal liberty, as well religious as civil, shall be universally extended to the good people of this country."

The Presbytery was satisfied with the action of the Assembly, but feared that a general assessment might come. up for discussion, a measure which it considered "contrary to our principles and interest; and, as we think, subversive of religious liberty."

The Assembly, however did not touch upon a general assessment at this time, owing probably to the difficulties of the times. Other legislation concerning church affairs which was enacted by the Assembly was due to local changes wrought by the war and Revolution. The vestries of Newport, Isle of Wight, Christ Church and Stratton Major parishes were dissolved for various reasons.[243] Botetourt vestry was dissolved and the new vestry

[238] Journal, p. 27.
[239] Journal of House of Delegates, May, 1777, p. 36.
[240] Journal, p. 17.
[241] Hening, IX, 312.
[242] Foote, I, 326.
[243] Hening, IX, 317.

to be elected was authorized to sell the old glebe and buy another.[244] Saint Anne's and Cornwall parishes were dissolved.

The fall session of the Assembly simply continued the suspensory act, although conservative petitions were presented as before in support of the establishment. Cumberland protested again at the withdrawal of state support.[245] A petition from Caroline requested the enactment of a general assessment. It approved of the exemption of dissenters from supporting the Church of England, but maintained "that as public worship is a duty we owe, it ought to be enjoined and regulated by the Legislature so as to preserve Public peace, order and decency, without prescribing a Mode or Form of worship to any."[246] A Lunenburg complaint was couched in bitter terms. It indeed charged the dissenters with fraud in getting up the great petition of 1776.[247] "The undue means taken to overthrow the established church, by imposing upon the credulity of the vulgar, and engaging infants to sign petitions handed about dissenters, have so far succeeded as to cause a dissolution of our usual mode of support." In spite of these appeals the house, on January 6, 1778, continued the suspending act of 1776.[248] The May 1778 Assembly continued the suspension,[249] and the October session still further continued it.[250] Unheeded complaints from the conservatives came to the house. Amherst people asked for a general assessment to support religion, which they had seen decline daily for some time owing to the withdrawal of the salaries.

The spring session of 1779 was an important one. The Revolution had now been in progress for four years, and for more than two years the salaries of Anglican ministers had been suspended by law. The establishment was practically at an end, and the parochial system, continued after the church had received a vital wound, was fast going to pieces. Democratic feeling in many counties was opposed to the old vestries. In other parishes, vestrymen had died or gone away or given up the fight. Vestrymen, deprived of half their former power, but still officers of government, continued to perform their duties with difficulty in the face of the criticism of dissenters, who resented this relic of the union of church and state. Many petitions for the dissolution of vestries reached the house. Tillotson parish, Buckingham, complained that there was no vestry and no church in half the county. A request for the dissolution of the vestry of Wicomico parish, Northumberland, on the ground that it had not been elected by the people, showed a growth of democratic feeling in the conservative Northern Neck. Drysdale parish, Caroline, also asked for a dissolution on the same grounds.[251] People of Fluvanna parish, formerly a part of St. Anne's parish, Albemarle, asked that St. Anne's glebe might be sold and a share given to Fluvanna parish, "to be laid out in the purchase of a glebe or in any manner that

[244] Hening, IX, 318.
[245] Journal House of Delegates, Oct. 1777, p. 14.
[246] Journal, p. 57.
[247] Journal, p. 75.
[248] Journal, p. 105.
[249] Hening, IX, 469.
[250] Hening, IX, 578.
[251] Journal of House of Delegates, May, 1779, p. 21.

56

shall seem just." This was the precursor of a host of like requests with spoliation as the object in view.[252]

The Assembly, under the pressure of petitions, appointed a committee composed of Jefferson, Tazewell, William Lee, John Taylor, Jerman Baker, and Anthony Winston, to bring in a bill for the dissolution of the vestries.[253] Baker, on May 28, presented the bill, the terms of which are unknown, but which probably provided for a dissolution of all vestries and the election of a new order of poor officers unconnected with religion.

The progressive party, on June 4, took another stride forward, when the house directed a bill "for religious freedom" should be introduced, and appointed John Harvie, George Mason, and Jerman Baker to prepare it.[254] By way of compensation, the same committee was also ordered to bring in a bill "for saving the property of the church heretofore by law established."[255]

Doubtless Jefferson would have headed this committee but he had ceased to be a member of the house. His great activity had won him an election as the second governor of the commonwealth, succeeding Patrick Henry. He delivered, on June 2, 1779, a short speech of acceptance, in which he uttered the appropriate sentiment: "In a virtuous and free State no rewards can be so pleasing to sensible minds as those which include the approbation of our fellow-citizens."[256]

Although no longer in the house, Jefferson maintained his influence. On June 12 John Harvie presented the bill which will be forever associated with Jefferson's name, the "bill for religious freedom,"[257] and which he probably wrote. At the same time, the accompanying "bill for saving the property of the church heretofore by law established" was introduced. On June 14, the second reading of the bill for saving the church property was deferred until the first of August,[258] and the third reading of the "bill for religious freedom" was put off until the same date. With Jefferson out of the house, the fight had gone against the progressives.

The next day the committee for religion was directed to prepare a bill "for further suspending the payment of salaries heretofore given to the clergy of the church of England," [259] and the house passed it on June 17.[260] The discussion of the bill "for the dissolution of vestries" was postponed until October 10.[261] The session came to an end with the religious question in exactly the same position as before.

The struggle was renewed at the fall session of the Assembly, which began on October 4, 1779. On October 15, petitions from the parishes began to come in. Factions in Drysdale parish indulged in a war of manuscripts; one side asking for the division of the parish because of its size, the other opposing a division on the ground that the crops had failed, the war taxes

---

[252] Journal, p. 34.
[253] Journal, p. 11.
[254] Journal, p. 34.
[255] Journal, p. 34.
[256] Journal, p. 31.
[257] Journal, p. 44.
[258] Journal, p. 46.
[259] Journal, p. 48.
[260] Journal, p. 53.
[261] Journal, p. 59.

were high and much expense had been recently incurred in building two churches and buying a glebe. An Amherst petition called for a redivision of the divided parish; and Antrim parish requested a dissolution of the vestry and a sale of the glebe, as the parish business was neglected and the glebe land worn out.[262]

The committee of courts of justice made its regular report on October 16 on suspended laws, recommending among other things that the act for suspending ministers' salaries be continued.[263] On October 19, a blow was aimed at a section of the Anglican clergy, when the committee of propositions and grievances, which was considering the bill "concerning non-jurors," was directed to add a clause, "to silence non-juring preachers of all denominations, and to deprive of their benefices non-juring clergymen of the Church of England."[264] This clause was intended for the benefit of those Anglican preachers who shrunk from renouncing allegiance to the king because of his position as head of the church.

The "bill for religious freedom" was again brought into discussion by petitions favoring or opposing it. An Augusta memorial called for its passage.[265] A counter-petition from Culpeper protested against it and requested an establishment. Essex presented an ultra-conservative view; "The great confusion and disorder that hath arisen, and likely to continue in this Country on Account of Religion, since the Old Establishment has been interrupted, convinces us of the great and absolute necessity there is for the Legislative Body of this State, to take it under their most serious consideration. And we the Subscribers Freeholders and Inhabitants, of the County of Essex, being much alarmed at the appearance of a Bill entitled Religious Freedom, consider it very injurious to the Christian Religion, and will be attended with the most baneful consequences if permitted to have an existence in this State, and therefore take this method to acquaint the Honble Assembly of it, and do also direct our Representatives to Vote for the destruction of all such Diabolical Schemes. And further pray, that the Honble Assembly, wou'd adopt such regulations as are hereafter expressed to keep up the Public Worship and Teaching of the Christian Religion, and that no person, being a Protestant nor not professing the Christian Religion, and living in conformity to the same, be permitted to hold or exercise any Civil Authority within this State. A general assessment for the support of Religious Worship, wou'd be most agreeable to your Petitioners, that all Licentious and Itinerant Preachers be forbid collecting or Assembling of Negroes and others at unseasonable times. That every Minister of every Christian Denomination have his stated place of Worship. That no Insults, or interruptions be suffered to any Christian Congregation Assembled at proper times for Worship. That no doctrine be permitted to be preached, which may tend to subvert Government or disturb Civil Society. That there be a general Election of Vestry Men in every Parish, and that they may have power to assess or levy upon the Tythables of their respective Parishes, what they may think reasonable

---

[262] Journal of House of Delegates, Oct., 1779, p. 9.
[263] Journal, p. 10.
[264] Journal, p. 14.
[265] Journal, p. 17.

58

for the Support of the Ministers of every Denomination and to be paid
to any profession that the occupiers of such Tythes may think proper."

Petitions from Lunenburg,[266] presented on November 3, and from Amherst on November 10,[267] supported the assessment plan.[268]

The conservatives were ascendant for the time. The "bill for religious
freedom" was not brought up for its third reading, but, on the contrary,
James Henry, of Accomac, on October 25, 1779, presented the conservative
demands in his bill "concerning religion."[269] This bill passed the first reading and was ordered for a second. It marks the great effort of the conservative party to re-establish ecclesiasticism in the State by means of a
general assessment and a regulation of religion. The plan was substantially
the same as that brought forward in 1784. The bill reads:

"For the encouragement of Religion and virtue, and for removing all
restraints on the mind in its inquiries after truth, Be it enacted by the
General Assembly, that all persons and Religious Societies who acknowledge
that there is one God, and a future State of rewards and punishments, and
that God ought to be publickly worshiped, shall be freely tolerated.

"The Christian Religion shall in all times coming be deemed and held
to be the established Religion of this Commonwealth; and all Denominations
of Christians demeaning themselves peaceably and faithfully, shall enjoy
equal privileges, civil and Religious.

"To accomplish this desirable purpose without injury to the property
of those Societies of Christians already incorporated by Law for the purpose of Religious Worship, and to put it fully into the power of every other
Society of Christians, either already formed or to be hereafter formed to
obtain the like incorporation, Be it further enacted, that the respective
Societies of the Church of England already formed in this Commonwealth,
shall be continued Corporate, and hold the Religious property now in their
possession for ever.

"Whenever   free male Persons not under twenty one Years of Age,
professing the Christian Religion, shall agree to unite themselves in a
Society for the purpose of Religious Worship, they shall be constituted a
Church, and esteemed and regarded in Law as of the established Religion
of this Commonwealth, and on their petition to the General Assembly shall
be entitled to be incorporated and shall enjoy equal Privileges with any
other Society of Christians, and all that associate with them for the purpose
of Religious Worship, shall be esteemed as belonging to the Society so
called.

"Every Society so formed shall give themselves a name or denomination by which they shall be called and known in Law. And it is further
enacted, that previous to the establishment and incorporation of the respective Societies of every denomination as aforesaid, and in order to entitle
them thereto, each Society so petitioning shall agree to and subscribe in
a Book the following five Articles, without which no agreement or Union
of men upon pretence of Religious Worship shall entitle them to be incor-

---

[266] Journal, p. 37.
[267] Journal, p. 50.
[268] James, p. 94.
[269] MS. Va. State Library. Collection of Bills, 1779.

porated and esteemed as a Church of the Established Religion of this Commonwealth.

"First, That there is one Eternal God and a future State of Rewards and punishments.

"Secondly, That God is publickly to be Worshiped.

"Thirdly, That the Christian Religion is the true Religion.

"Fourthly, That the Holy Scriptures of the old and new Testament are of divine inspiration, and are the only rule of Faith.

"Fifthly, That it is the duty of every Man, when thereunto called by those who Govern, to bear witness to truth.

"And that the People may forever enjoy the right of electing their own Teachers, Pastors, or Clergy; and at the same time that the State may have Security for the due discharge of the Pastoral office by those who shall be admitted to be Clergymen, Teachers, or Pastors, no person shall officiate as minister of any established Church who shall not have been chosen by a majority of the Society to which he shall be minister, or by the persons appointed by the said majority to choose and procure a minister for them, nor until the Minister so chosen shall have made and subscribed the following declaration, over and above the aforesaid five articles, to be made in some Court of Record in this Commonwealth, viz:

"That he is determined by God's Grace out of the Holy Scriptures to instruct the people committed to his charge, and to teach nothing (as required of necessity to eternal Salvation) but that which he shall be persuaded may be concluded and proved from the Scriptures; that he will use both publick and private admonitions with prudence and discretion, as need shall require, and occasion shall be given; that he will be diligent in prayers and in reading the Holy Scriptures, and in such studies as lead to the knowledge of the same; that he will be diligent to frame and fashion himself and his Family according to the doctrines of Christ, and to make both himself and them, as much as in him lieth, wholesome examples and patterns to the flock of Christ; and that he will maintain and set forward, as much as he can, peace and love among all people, and especially among those that are or shall be committed to his charge.

"No person shall disturb or molest any Religious Assembly nor shall use any reproachful, reviling or abusive language against any Church under the penalty of   a second offence to be deemed a breach of good behaviour. [This clause was struck out.]

"No person whatsoever shall speak anything in their Religious Assemblies disrespectfully or Seditiously of the Government of this State.

"And that permanent encouragement may be given for providing a sufficient number of ministers and teachers to be procured and continued to every part of this Commonwealth,

"Be it further enacted, that the sum of   pounds of Tobacco, or such rate in Money as shall be yearly settled for each County by the Court thereof, according to the Current price, shall be paid annually for each Tithable by the person enlisting the same, for and towards the Support of Religious Teachers and places of Worship in manner following: Within   Months after the passing of this Act every freeholder, Housekeeper, & person possessing Tithables, shall enroll his or her name with the Clerk of the County of which he or she shall be an Inhabitant, at the same time expressing to the Support of what Society or denomination of Christian he or she would choose to contribute; which inrollment shall be binding upon each such person, until he or she shall in like manner cause his or her name to be inrolled in any other Society.

"The Clerk of each County Court shall annually before the day of deliver to the Trustees of each Religious Society, a list of the several names inrolled in his office as members of such Society; with the number of Tithables belonging to each, according to the List taken and returned that Year. Whereupon such Trustees respectively shall meet and determine how the Assessment aforesaid upon such Tithables shall be laid out for the support of their teacher or places of worship, according to the true intent of this Act; and having entered such disposition in a Book to be kept for that purpose, shall deliver a Copy thereof to the Sheriff, together with the List of Tithables so received from the Clerk, and such Sheriff shall on or before the   day of   then next following, Collect, Levy or Distrain for the amount of such Assessment, which he shall account for and pay to the several persons to whom he shall have been directed to pay it by the Trustees of each respective Society, deducting Insolvents and Six per Centum for Collection.

"If any Person shall fail to enlist his Tithables, the Sheriff shall nevertheless Collect or distrain for the Assessment aforesaid in like manner as if he or she had done so, and pay the same to that Religious Society of which he or she shall be inrolled as a member. And should any person liable to this Assessment fail to procure himself to be inrolled according to this Act, or to make his Election at the time of paying his assessment to the Sheriff, the Sheriff shall nevertheless levy in like manner the Assessment aforesaid for his or her Tithables, and lay an Account upon Oath of all Tobacco or Monies so Collected before his Court in the months of   annually; or if no Court be then held, at the next Court which shall be held thereafter, who shall apportion the same between the several Religious Societies in the parish in which such person or persons shall reside, according to the amount of the Assessment for each, to be paid to the Order of such Trustees for the purposes of this Act. And every Sheriff shall annually before the   day of   enter into Bond, with sufficient Security to be approved by the County Court for the faithful Collection and disbursement of all Tobacco or Monies received in consequence of this Act; and the Trustees of any Religious Society, or any Creditor to whom money may by them be Ordered to be paid, on motion in the County Court, having given him ten days previous notice thereof, may have Judgment against any delinquent Sheriff and his Securities, his or their Executors or administrators, for what shall appear to be due from him to such Society or Creditor, or may bring suit on the Bond given him by the Sheriff; and the Bond shall not be discharged by any Judgment had thereon, but shall remain as a Security against him, and may be put in suit as often as any breach shall happen, until the whole penalty shall have been Levied.

"And if any Society or Church so established, shall refuse to appoint some person to receive their Quota of the Assessment from the Sheriff, the money shall remain in his hands for one Year; and if then no person properly appointed shall apply for such money, the same shall by the County Court be equally apportioned between the several Religious Societies in the parish in which such person or persons shall reside, in proportion to the amount of the Assessment for each Society.

"The Clerks of the respetcive County Courts shall be entitled to the same fees for making out and delivering the Lists of Tithables required by this Act as they are entitled to for like Services in other cases.

"And be it farther enacted, that so much of an Act of Assembly passed in the Year 1748, intituled "An Act for the Support of the Clergy, and for the Regular Collecting and paying the parish Levies," as respects the Levying, Collecting and payment of the Salaries of the Clergy of the Church of England which has been suspended by several Acts of the General Assembly; and also so much of an Act intituled "ministers to be inducted," as requires Ordination by a Bishop in England, be and the same are hereby Repealed."

Such a plan for a state church, founded on a basis as broad as orthodox religion, had much to commend it to a people accustomed to an establishment. On October 26, the bill "concerning religion" was read a second time, but failed of a third reading and was committed for a future hearing.[269] On November 5, the house again debated it, but without result. The next day Samuel Goode, of Mecklenburg, presented a bill "for the dissolution of vestries." The crisis came on November 15, when the bill "concerning religion" was again debated. The progressive party was successful and further consideration of the bill was postponed until March 1.[270] The democrats followed up their victory by ordering a bill repealing the act providing for the support of the Anglican clergy, and George Mason, French Strother and Beverley Randolph were assigned the task of preparing it.[271] At the same time, doubtless as a concession to conservative feeling, a bill "for saving and securing the property of the church heretofore by law established" was also ordered, and George Mason, James Henry and Thomas Nelson were the committee appointed for drawing it up.

On November 18, George Mason presented the bill "to repeal so much of the act for the support of the clergy, and for the regular collecting and paying the parish levies."[272] The bill reads: "To remove from the good People of this Commonwealth the Fear of being compelled to contribute to the Support or Maintenance of the former established Church. And that the Members of the said Church may no longer relye upon the Expectation of any re-establishment thereof, & be thereby prevented from adopting proper Measures among themselves, for the Support and Maintenance of their own Religion and Ministers, Be it enacted by the General Assembly, that so much of the Act entitled an Act for the Support of the Clergy, and for the regular collecting and paying the parish Levys and of all and every other Act or Acts providing Salaries for the Ministers and authorizing the Vestrys to levy the same, shall be and the same is hereby repealed, provided nevertheless that the Vestries of the several parishes, where the same hath not been already done, may, and they are hereby authorized and required,

[269] Journal, p. 24.
[270] Journal, p. 56.
[271] Journal, p. 57.
[272] Journal, p. 61. MS. Va. State Library.

at such time as they shall appoint, to levy and assess on all Tithables within their respective parishes, all such Salaries and Arrears of Salaries as were due to the Ministers or Incumbents of their parishes for Services to the first day of January in the year one thousand seven hundred and seventy seven, moreover to make such Assessments on all Tithables as will enable the said Vestries to comply with their legal Engagements entered into before the same Day; and lastly to continue such future provision for the poor in their respective parishes, as they have hitherto by Law been accustomed to make, and levy the same in the Manner heretofore directed by Law; any thing in this Act to the Contrary, or seeming to the Contrary notwithstanding."[273] The bill was read the second time on November 19.[274]

On November 26, George Mason, introduced, according to order, the bill "for saving the property of the church heretofore by law established to the members of the said church for ever."[275] Thus the conservatives hoped to save something from the wreck. The bill states: "Be it enacted by the General Assembly that the several Tracts of Glebe Land with the Appurtenances, the Churches and Chapels, the Books, Vestments, plate and ornaments, all arrears of money and Tobacco, and all property real and personal of private Donation, which on the seventh Day of October in the year one thousand seven hundred and seventy-six were vested in any persons whatever for the use of the English Church until then established by Law, or were due or contracted for bona fide, on that Day, or which since that time have legally become so vested, due or contracted for, shall be saved in all time to come to the Members of the said English Church, by whatsoever Denomination they shall henceforth call themselves, who shall be resident within the several parishes wherein the same shall be; those of each parish to have the separate and legal property of the said Articles belonging to their respective parishes, and to apply them from year to year, or from time to time, by themselves, or by Agents to be appointed by themselves, as they shall hereafter agree, for and towards the Support of their Ministry, and the Exercise of their religious worship; and that no future change in the form of this church Government, ordination of their Ministry, or Rituals of Worship, shall take away or affect the Benefit of this saving.

"And whereas it may be some considerable time before the members of the said English Church will have established the Forms of their future church Government, and in the mean time there may be among the present Incumbents of their parishes, some who are disaffected to the Commonwealth, or immoral characters, or inattentive to the Duties of their Function, who ought to be immediately removed, Be it therefore enacted, that whenever in any parish, any twenty members thereof of the said English Church shall in writing signed by themselves exhibit any Charge or complaint against the Incumbent, and require of either church warden of the said Parish, or if there be no Church warden, then of any vestryman to call a meeting of the parishioners of the English Church, such Church warden or vestryman is hereby impowered and required, within ten Days after the Requisition delivered, to furnish the Incumbent with a true copy of the

[273] Preamble was struck out.
[274] Journal, p. 63.
[275] MS. Va. State Library.

Charge or Complaint against him, and by advertisement to be set up at every church within such parish to call a meeting of the said parishioners at the place where the vestrys have most usually been held; which meeting shall not be within less than three nor more than eight weeks, after the Requisition delivered: the said parishioners, or so many as will, having assembled at the time and place appointed, the warden or vestryman who called the meeting, or if he be not present, then the eldest Vestryman present, or such other person who shall be appointed for that purpose by the said meeting, shall preside in the same, and shall propose the Questions moved, in which every parishioner present of the said English Church qualified by Law to vote for Vestrymen, shall have a Right to vote; and it shall be lawful for the said Meeting, and of all other meetings to be called in like manner, by a majority of Voices, of not less than two thirds of those present and voting, to deprive any Incumbent now holding any such Glebe; and such Vote of Deprivation, attested by the president of the meeting, being delivered to the Sherif of the County, the said Sherif shall proceed to remove the Incumbent from his possession of the said Glebe, and the same to retain and deliver to such other person as shall be authorised to the possession thereof by Vote of any meeting of the parishioners called and qualified as before directed.

"The surviving Vestrymen in every parish shall have authority to carry into Execution all Contracts legally and bona fide made by themselves, or their predecessors, before the first Day of January in the Year one thousand seven hundred and seventy seven, and for that purpose may sue or be sued, as might have been heretofore when Vestries were full.

"Where any parish hath been altered in its Bounds, the Inhabitants thereof shall nevertheless remain liable for their proportionable part of all money or Tobacco due, and all contracts legally made before such Division or alteration, to be apportioned to them, and levied by the Vestry of the respective parish into which they are incorporated by such Division or Alteration. And whereas Vestries, although authorised by Law to levy on their parishioners so much only as was sufficient to answer the legal Demands on this parish actually existing, yet frequently levied more; so that there remained on their Hands a Depositum to be applied to the future uses of their respective parishes, and it may have happened that in some Instances, such Depositums were on Hand on the said first Day of January in the year one thousand seven hundred and seventy seven, after all legal Demands satisfied which were then existing, or which by this Act are made legal, and also Debts may have been owing to some parishes, Be it therefore enacted that such Depositums and Debts shall be applied to the maintenance of the poor of such parish, where it hath not already been done, in Ease of the poor rates to be levied for that purpose in future: and in the Case of any such parish since then divided or altered, or lying in different Counties, such Easement shall be divided and apportioned in the same way as Burthens, in a like case, are herein before directed to be apportioned: But where any parish has no Glebe, such Depositums and Debts, or the proportion thereof belonging to such parish, shall be applied towards purchasing a Glebe, the property and application of which shall be in the same persons, and the the same uses, and according to the same Rules, as wou'd have been by the former part of this Act, had the said Glebe been purchased before the passing hereof."

This bill was presented by Mason and is in his handwriting, so it may be taken as his composition and as his method of solving the religious question. The bill distinctly looked towards a complete separation of church and state, but at a distant date. In the meantime, a somewhat democratic form of government was to be foisted upon the old establishment; parishioners might dismiss their ministers at will. The property rights of the Anglican church were respected. The plan is such a one as a democrat of moderate feelings would devise for a transition from a union of church and state to a complete separation without any jar.

The bill "for saving the property of the church heretofore by law established" was read a second time the next day[276] and came up again on December 11, when it was defeated by postponement to March 3 following. At the same time the repeal bill, reported by Tazewell and amended by the elision of the preamble, was read the third time,[277] and on December 13, it passed.[278]

Jefferson states in his autobiography that "in the bill now passed, (that of 1776) was inserted an express reservation of the question, Whether a general assessment should not be established by law, on every one, to the support of the pastor of his choice; or whether all should be left to voluntary contributions; and on this question, debated at every session, from '76 to '79, (some of our dissenting allies, having now secured their particular object, going over to the advocates of a general assessment,) we could only obtain a suspension from session to session until '79, when the question against a general assessment was finally carried, and the establishment of the Anglican church entirely put down."[279]

Jefferson is rather inaccurate in this account. As a matter of fact, the democrats gained a considerable victory in defeating James Henry's general assessment bill, but the assessment question was by no means ended with this incident. It revived, and with far more strength than ever, in the summer of 1784. The importance of the repeal bill, too, has been somewhat exaggerated. The salaries of Anglican ministers had been suspended by six successive acts, and there was little likelihood of their ever being paid again. Still the act was useful in making permanent in law a policy which before had been limited to temporary legislation, however final in reality that legislation might have been.

The condition of the former establishment was now deplorable. Not only were vestries neglecting their duties, or dying out in many parishes; the ministers, deprived of their salaries and harassed for a living, were leaving their charges. It would have been much better for the Anglican church if separation of church and state had been completed in 1776. It would then have been free to organize itself in accordance with the new conditions. As the case stood, the establishment was still bound to the state while deriving no benefit from that connection. Its polity was still supposed

---

[276] Journal, p. 72.
[277] Journal, p. 85.
[278] Journal, p. 87.
[279] Jefferson's Writings (Memorial Asso.), I, 58.

to be subject to legislative supervision. This condition of semi-anarchy, in connection with the distractions of the war, practically broke up the old establishment.

Ministers grew more and more difficult to retain in the parishes. Precarious subscriptions were raised in some counties. Devereaux Jarratt said in later years: "I never had a scrip or subscription in my favour, nor did I ask for any such thing * * * I called upon him to point out, if he could, a single person, who, from the year 1776 to 1786, ever gave me a six-pence for these services * * * When a subscription was set on foot, in 1785 and 1786, I asked him, if this was done by any solicitation from me? And when about sixty or seventy people had subscribed, and the collection of the money was put into his hand, whether he did not meet with so little encouragement in the business, that, through despair, he gave up all further attempts, after having collected thirty or forty shillings for a whole year?"[280]

Parishes indeed began to advertise for ministers. The vestry of Drysdale parish, Caroline, promised that one would "meet with a very good glebe and a genteel subscription for his support therein."[281] The vestry of Northfarnham parish, Richmond, desired an "Orthodox Divine, of a good moral character, immediately, and if he reads and preaches well, he will give the greater satisfaction. The parsonage or glebe house of brick, with four rooms below, and three above and all necessary offices have been lately put in good repair, a garden newly paled in, and the usual enclosures of cornfields, orchard and pasture under good fences, and agreeable forest situation about a mile from the church * * * and it is not doubted that a handsome subscription will be made for the support of a minister who shall be approved of.[282] A minister was wanted at St. Paul's parish, Hanover.[283] The rector of Lunenburg parish, Richmond, advertised the rent of the glebe.[284] The minister of St. Anne's parish, Albemarle, complained that in spite of the fact that he had espoused the patriot cause the vestry had never made the levy for his salary for 1774; the sale of the glebe as ordered by the Legislature would deprive him of his home. Many other parishes wanted ministers and others of the remaining ministers were in much the same sad condition as the incumbent of St. Anne's.

The year 1780 was a critical one in the history of the war, and internal legislation in Virginia did not receive much attention. Dissenters were protesting at the survivals of the establishment, which were of so little use to the community and yet to which the conservatives clung obstinately. The Baptists sometime before had complained of the narrow marriage law and they continued their complaints through the latter years of the war. Protests from all sides attested the inefficiency of the vestries in the management of the poor. The Presbytery of Hanover, at its meeting in April, 1780, adopted a memorial requesting the Legislature "to abstain from interfering in the government of the church."[285]

[280] Life of Devereaux Jarratt, 187. Mass. Historical Society Proceedings, 42, 341.
[281] Dixon & Hunter's Virginia Gazette, April 16, 1779.
[282] Virginia Gazette, June 19, 1779.
[283] Virginia Gazette, October 30, 1779.
[284] Virginia Gazette, June 26, 1779.
[285] Foote, I, 332 (This paper has not been preserved).

The marriage law and the vestries were discussed at the May, 1780, session of the Assembly. The justices of the new Rockbridge county complained that for want of a vestry no provision could be made for the poor and asked for authority to provide for poor relief.[286] This request indicates the natural tendency of civil officers to assume the duties of the obsolete vestries.

Petitions from Amelia and the Baptist church attacked the exclusive marriage law. "The Memorial of the Baptists by their Ministers Elders and Delegates (at an Association held at Wallers Meeting-House in Spottsylvania County the second Saturday in May 1780) humbly sheweth; that we your Memorialist, heartily approve of the Act that passed in your last Session which partly removes the Vestige of oppression; which 'till then hung over our heads, respecting the Ministers sallary Law: and as we hope to enjoy equal, Religious, as well as civil Liberty: while we demean our Selves as good Citizens, and peaceable Subjects of this Commonwealth—we your Memorilists therefore desire that an Act may pass, Declareing Mariges Solemnized by Dissenting Ministers, either by License, or publication; Valid in Law, for until such an Act shall take place; the Validity of Dissenters rights to officiate in the Same, is much disputed: as the following instances makes manifest of Ministers exacting the exhorbetant Sum of Sixty Pounds for that Service from two very poor people; and two Barrels of Corn from a Baptist, who applyed to his Minister who refused because the Licence was directed to a Minister of the Church of England—Your Memorialists haveing great confidence in the present Honourable Assembly's principals for equal Liberty commit our cause now under God's protection into your consideration hopeing for redress and your Memorialists as in duty bound shall ever pray.

Signed by Order and in behalf of the Association
JOHN WALLER MODERATOR
JOSEPH ANTHONY CLERK."

George Carrington, chairman of the committee for religion, on June 27, presented a bill "for the dissolution of the vestries and appointing overseers of the poor."[287] On June 29, the alternative and less comprehensive bill "for dissolving several vestries and electing overseers of the poor"[288] was introduced. This bill was read the third time and passed on July 6, 1780.[289] The senate also passed it with amendments, which the house accepted.

On July 4, George Carrington presented the bill "declaring what shall be a lawful marriage."[290] It was put through the house rapidly, passing on July 7,[291] but the conservative senate failed to pass it, and the question as to the legality of marriages performed by non-Anglican ministers remained open.

The act "for dissolving several vestries and electing overseers of the poor" completed the separation of church and state in certain of the western counties—Rockbridge, Botetourt, Montgomery, Washington, Greenbrier,

[286] Journal House of Delegates, May, 1780, p. 16.
[287] Journal, p. 64.
[288] Journal, p. 67.
[289] Journal, p. 78.
[290] Journal, p. 73.
[291] Journal, p. 79.

Augusta and Frederick.[292] Vestries had long been an anachronism in those counties, and the appointment of civil poor officers in their place was a matter of necessity. The act directed the sheriffs of the counties to proceed to the election of five freeholders in each county, to serve five years; they were constituted a corporation and invested with the powers of the former vestrymen and churchwardens. Elections were to be conducted as in the case of the vestrymen.

At the fall session of 1780, petitions concerning vestries came in again in large numbers, and the marriage bill, which had failed to pass in the spring, was revived.

The passions engendered by the war were curiously illustrated in the McRea case, which attracted much attention in the Southside. McRea was a non-juring clergyman of Cumberland, and perhaps others of his kind were involved with him. Petitions came in from Buckingham and Prince Edward asking that all non-juring ministers be silenced and deprived of their benefices and that the learned professions should be closed to men refusing to take the oath of alligiance to Virginia. A counter-petition from Cumberland accused the Presbyterians of organizing an agitation for the purpose of driving Christopher McRea, a non-juror, from his glebe and breaking up the church of England in that region. The incident well illustrates the prejudice created amongst the English-hating population against the old establishment by a few ministers too scrupulous or too unwise to identify themselves with the republic.

Petitions came in from St. Stephen's, Stratton Major and Drysdale parishes asking for a consolidation of the three into two parishes.[293] St. Margaret's parish requested a dissolution of its vestry; the vestry of Nottoway parish, Amelia, asked for power to remove the minister, Thomas Wilkinson, from the glebe. This clergyman, since the suppression of his salary, had refused to perform any of his clerical offices, such as baptizing or marrying, without charging exhorbitant fees, and he had besides destroyed all the wood on the glebe.

The bill "declaring what shall be a lawful marriage" was passed. The Baptist church had again asked for an adequate marriage law in a petition presented on November 8, 1780[294] "The Memorial of the Baptist Association met at Sandy Creek in Charlotte * * * humbly sheweth that a due Regard to the Liberty and Rights of the People is of the highest Importance to the Welfare of the State—That this heaven born Freedom, which belongs equally to every good citizen, is the Palladium which the Legislature is particularly intrusted with the Guardianship of, and on which the Safety and Happiness of the State depend. Your Memorialists therefore look upon every Law or Usage now existing among us, which does not accord with that Republican Spirit which breathes in our Constitution and Bill of Rights, to be extremely pernicious and detrimental, and that such Law or Usage should immediately be abolished.

"As Religious Oppression, or the interfering with the Rights of Conscience, which God has made accountable to none but himself, is of all

[292] Hening, X, 288.
[293] Journal of the House of Delegates, Oct., 1780, p. 48.
[294] Journal, p. 11.

Oppression the most inhuman and insupportable, and as Partiality to any Religious Denomination is its genuine Offspring, your Memorialists have with Grief observed that Religious Liberty has not made a single Advance, in this Commonwealth, without some Opposition—They have been much surprized to hear it said of Things indisputably right and necessary 'It is not now a proper Time to proceed to such Affairs, let us first think of defending ourselves &c.,' when there cannot, surely, be a more suitable Time to allow ourselves the Blessings of Liberty, which we have in our own Power, than when contending with those who endeavour to tyrannize over us.

"As the Completion of Religious Liberty is what, as a Religious Community, your Memorialists are particularly interested in, they would humbly call the Attention of your Honourable House to a few Particulars, viz. First the Vestry-Law which disqualifies any person to officiate who will not subscribe to be conformable to the Doctrine and Discipline of the Church of England; by which Means Dissenters are not only precluded, but also not represented, they not having a free voice, whose Property is nevertheless subject to be taxed by the Vestry, and whose Poor are provided for at the Discretion of those who may possibly be under the Influence of Party-Motives—And what renders the said Law a Greater Grievance is, that in some Parishes, so much Time has elapsed since an Election, that there is scarcely one who was originally chosen by the People, the Vacancies having been filled up by the remaining Vestrymen—Secondly, the Solemnization of Marriage, concerning which it is insinuated by some, and taken for granted by others that to render it legal it must be performed by a Church Clergyman, according to the Rites and Ceremonies of the Church of England; conformably to which Sentiment Marriage-Licenses are usually worded and directed.—Now, if this should in Reality be the Case, your Memorialists conceive that the ill Consequences resulting from thence, which are too obvious to need mentioning, render it absolutely necessary for the Legislature to endeavour their Removal—This is an Affair of so tender a Nature, and of such Importance, that after the Restoration, one of the first Matters which the British Parliament proceeded to, was the Confirmation of the Marriages solemnized according to the Mode in Use during the Interregnum, and the Protectorship of Cromwell—And the Propriety of such a Measure, in Virginia, evidently appears from the vast Numbers of Dissenters, who having Objections against the Form and Manner prescribed in the Book of Common Prayer proceed to marry otherwise; and also that in many Places, especially over the Ridge there are no Church Parsons to officiate—On the other Hand if Marriages otherwise solemnized are equally valid, a Declaratory Act to that Purport, appears to your Memorialists to be highly expedient, because they can see no Reason why any of the free Inhabitants of this State, should be terrified by a mere Mormo from their just Rights and Privileges; or censured by others on Suspicion of their acting contrary to Law—To these Considerations your Memorialists would just beg leave to add that those who claim this Province of officiating at Marriage-Solemnities as their sole Right, undertake at the same Time to be the sole Judges of what they are to receive for the same.

"Your Memorialists humbly hope that your Honourable House will take effectual Measures to redress these Grievances, in such a Way as may mani-

fest an equal Regard to all the good People of this Commonwealth, however, diversyfied by Appellations or Religious Sentiments—and that as it is
your Glory to represent a free People, you will be as forward to remove every
just Cause of Offence, as your Constituents are to complain of them—and in
particular that you will consign to Oblivion all the Relicks of Religious
Oppression, and make a public Sacrifice of Partiality at the glorious Altar
of Freedom.

Signed by order

SAML. HARRIS, Modr.

JOHN WILLIAMS, Clk."[296]

The ably written request was complied with. George Carrington, on
December 2, 1780, presented a bill from the committee for religion "declaring
what shall be a lawful marriage."[296] This bill, amended in several particulars, was read the third time on December 15,[297] and passed on December
18. The act, wrung from a reluctant Assembly by the insistence of the
Baptists, should have been passed long before. The lack of a definite legal
statement of marriage was an encouragement to immorality and could in no
way benefit the state. The act passed declared that any minister of a
Christian society might perform the marriage ceremony, provided that the
ceremony was accompanied by a license or a publication of banns, except
in the case of Quakers or Menonists, for whom a somewhat modified provision was made. Judges of courts were authorized to issue licenses to four
ministers of each sect in a county to perform the marriage ceremony within
the bounds of that county alone. Ministers might demand a fee of twenty-
five pounds of tobacco and no more.[298]

The year 1781 was taken up largely with military affairs, as the State
was invaded, and the religious question was not debated in the Assembly.

In 1782, with peace in sight, the old problems were revived. The marriage act of 1780 had not entirely satisfied the Baptists, and on June 3, 1782,
they petitioned the Assembly for a repeal of the clause which limited non-
Anglican ministers to performing the marriage ceremony in only one county,
and for a change in the poor relief system: "Your Memorialists firmly
believe as they are taught in the Declaration of Rights 'that no Man or set
of Men are entituled to exclusive or separate Emoluments of Privileges from
the Community, but in Consideration of public Services.' That they cannot
see that for a Person to call himself a Church-Man and to conform to the
Rites and Ceremonies of the Church of England, is doing the State any
publick Service—That it is evident that Dissenters are not on an equal
Footing with Churchmen as they are subject to taxation without a fair and
Equal Representation by the Vestry Law, and their Ministers so ignom-
iniously distinguished from Episcopal Ministers in the latter Clause of the
Act declaring what shall be a lawfull Marriage. Your Memorialists therefore hope that your wisdom and Justice will suggest to you the Expediency
of removing the Ground of Animosity, which will remain while Preference

[295] James.
[296] Journal, p. 35.
[297] Journal, p. 53.
[298] Hening, X, 361.

is given, or peculiar Favours are granted in our Laws to any particular Religious Denomination.

ELIJAH CRAIG MODERATOR
REUBEN FORD, Clk."

On the same day some of the frontiersmen of Louisville petitioned for a legalizing of marriages performed by civil magistrates, because of the scarcity of ministers in the western country.

. The Assembly, however, took no action on these petitions. It dissolved the vestries of Shenandoah, Henry, Monongalia, Ohio, and Berkeley counties and ordered the election of overseers of the poor for these counties, thus practically completing the separation of church and state in the west.[299] The vestries of Antrim and Westover parishes were dissolved and new elections ordered. They had not been held, however, when the Assembly re-assembled in the fall,[300] and the fact shows how relatively unimportant the vestries had become. The glebe of Antrim parish had not been sold according to the terms of the act, as the minister declared that he regarded it as his freehold and would return to it upon proper encouragement.

The marriage law was considered at the fall session of 1782. The committee for religion, which now included Richard Henry Lee and Charles Mynn Thruston, on November 22, 1782, reported upon a petition protesting against the limitations still imposed upon non-Anglican ministers by the marriage act of 1780. It recommended the repeal of the clause limiting ministers to marry in only one county, but reported adversely to changing that which confined the grant of licenses to marry to a certain number of preachers in each county.[301] No further action was taken at this session.

By the summer of 1783, the country had begun to settle down from the war and to consider in earnest the many financial and political problems to be solved. The Assembly at its May session displayed a reviving interest in religion by electing a chaplain, Benjamin Blagrove, and directing him "to compose a form of prayer, to be approved by the committee for religion, fit and proper to be used in this House; and that it be a standing order, that divine service be performed every day, by using the said form or any other as the House may from time to time direct."[302]

Many vexatious parish questions came before the house. Lynhaven parish, Princess Anne, petitioned for a dissolution of the vestry.[303] Elizabeth River parish, Norfolk, asked for authority to hold a lottery to raise money to build a church and glebe-house, which had been destroyed. The parish had suffered greatly in the war, and its number of tithables had fallen from 1800 to 500. Lower Nansemond parish asked for relief in a typical case arising from the depreciation of the currency. It had loaned out £600 of

---

[299] Hening, XI, 62.

[300] Journal of House of Delegates, Oct., 1782, p. 16.

[301] Journal, p. 31.

[302] Journal of House of Delegates, May, 1783, p. 7. Edmund Randolph commented humorously on this procedure in a letter to Madison of May 15, 1783: "Religion, which has hitherto been treated with little respect by the Assembly, was yesterday incorporated into their proceedings. Mr. Hay moved for a chaplain, and that a prayer should be composed adapted to all persuasions. The prayer has not been reported, though several trials, I am told, have been made."

[303] Journal, p. 11.

poor funds and the debtors tended in payment paper worth one-half the amount. Similar petitions came to the fall session. Adam Smyth, the former minister of Botetourt parish, asked for the enforcement of the act securing him his arrears of salary. No list of tithables had been furnished the sheriff, and besides the people considered themselves oppressed by the levy and refused to pay it. People of Botetourt parish requested a sale of the glebe, and also an apportionment of a part of Smyth's salary to Green-brier county, which had once formed a part of Botetourt parish. Fairfax parish desired a biennial election of vestrymen by freeholders, as the existing vestry contained only one member who had been elected.[304]

The Baptists renewed their appeals for a completely liberalized marriage act at the May 1783 session. A petition to this effect was presented on May 30.[305] On the following day a memorial was presented from the Baptists of Amelia requesting that all denominations be placed upon the same footing, without any distinctions whatever. "We do not ask this, Gentlemen, as a Favour which you have a Privilege either to grant or withhold at Pleasure, but as what we have a just Claim to as Freemen of the Commonwealth, and we trust it is your Glory to consider yourselves not as the Masters but servants of the People whom you have the Honour to represent, and that you will not fail in any Instance, to recognize the Natural Rights of all your Constituents."[306]

The committee for religion reported favorably upon this petition[307] and William Cabell presented a bill "to amend the several acts concerning vestries," on June 9.[308] On June 19, Cabell introduced the measure desired by Baptists, the bill "to amend the several acts concerning marriages," which was read once and then referred to the next Assembly.[309] The vestry bill suffered the same fate by a vote of 52 to 28.[310] Most of the progressives, including George Nicholas, Archibald Stuart, William Cabell, French Strother and Isaac Zane, voted for the bill.

A modified marriage bill "to authorize and confirm marriages in certain cases," was passed.[311] This act permitted the licensing of laymen in the sparsely-settled western districts to marry people according to the forms of their respective churches, at the same time requiring a marriage license or the publication of banns. It allowed fees of three shillings for certificates of publication and of six shillings for marrying. Marriages performed by magistrates prior to the act and other marriages not authorized by law were legalized.[312]

Notwithstanding this act, the Baptists again complained at the October, 1783, session of the Assembly of the restrictions remaining upon non-Anglican ministers in marrying, and of taxation by vestries. Besides, the penalty for failure to make returns of marriages was excessive and the

[304] Journal House of Delegates, Oct., 1783, p. 28.
[305] Journal House of Delegates, May, 1783, p. 26.
[306] Journal, p. 29.
[307] Journal, p. 30.
[308] Journal, p. 43.
[309] Journal, p. 67.
[310] Journal, p. 78.
[311] Journal, p. 81.
[312] Hening, XI, 281.

72

publication of banns was undesirable. But requests for a complete separation of church and state were countered by the inevitable conservative reaction against the liberalism of the war which now began to make itself felt. The Revolution had produced a modified religious liberty, but it had not settled the relations of church and state in a broad sense. The plan for a general system of taxation for the support of all Christian denominations, which had been temporarily defeated by the failure of James Henry's bill in 1779, now revived. On November 8, 1783, a petition was presented to the house from Lunenburg asking for a general assessment.[313] "The humble petition and remonstrance of all Sects and Denominations of Christians within the State: sheweth That soon after the Declaration of Indepency the General Assembly, with a view to the promotion of religious Liberty and free Toleration, thought proper, by Act to suspend the collection and payment of the salaries formerly allowed by Law to Inducted ministers of the Gospel: whereby all the Citizens of the state became emancipated & free from contributions to any Church revenue.

"That from that period we have with pain and regrett, seen the propogation of the Gospel die away in many parts of the country; and its diligent and faithful Ministers neglected; through a want of that Holy zeal in their adherents as Christians to support their respective Churches with the Dignity becoming their profession: and public Virtue as Citizens, to propogate and cherish the Sacred test of truth; as a necessary and indespensable branch of Civil Government.

"That the indifference and impiety of those who are careless of their own Salvation, and equally deaf and negligent to all religions; must greatly encrease the burdens of the people of God who would wish to support the Cause of Christianity, (as they have done that of freedom) even with their last mite.

"That Confined to Christianity alone; we wish for the establishment of a free and universal Toleration Subject to the Constitution; we would have no Sect or Denomination of Christians privileged to encroach upon the rights of another. For the accomplishment of these desirable purposes we wish to see the reform'd Christian religion supported and maintained by a General and equal contribution of the whole State upon the most equitable footing that is possible to place it.

"We therefore pray that you our Representatives in General Assembly taking the matter into Consideration will adopt such Mode as your Wisdom shall suggest to raise Just, equitable and adequate Contribution for the support of the Christian Churches, to be collected or distrained for as other Taxes, but with Liberty nevertheless reserved to each of the Contributers respectively, at the time he gives in his list, or otherwise becomes liable to the payment of such Contribution; to direct for whose benefit it is Contributed. The framers of this Petition and remonstrance; will not presume to decend further into particulars: Intending only by this to tell you their Complaints & wishes and to trust your wisdom and Justice for the address."[314]

---

[313] Journal House of Delegates, Oct., 1783, p. 12.

[314] Signed by John Ragsdale, D. A. Stokes, Joshua Ragsdale, Anthony Street, The. Buford, N. Hobson, Wm. Hardy, Edwd. Jordan, Robt. Dixon, James Hamlett, Mich'l McKie, William

George Carrington reported resolutions from the committee for religion declaring that since the Baptist petitions concerning vestries and marriages were reasonable the vestries should be dissolved and overseers of the poor appointed in each parish in the State, and the marriage law amended; also that the Lunenburg petition for a general assessment should be referred to the next Assembly.[315] The first two resolutions passed; the third was tabled.

A petition, however, from Amherst, also asking for a general assessment, was presented on November 27, and the report of the committee on the Lunenburg petition was referred to the committee of the whole.[316]

Carrington, on December 16, presented bills "for the election of overseers of the poor," and "to amend the several acts concerning marriages."[317] The bills were read twice, but conservative feeling then referred them to the limbo of the following March.[318] The Assembly of 1783, like so many others, adjourned without having taken any important action on religious questions, although those questions were even more in the public eye than formerly.

A new era was left to decide whether the Revolution should be pushed to its logical conclusion and the separation of church and state completed, or whether the progress of liberalism should be checked by such a state connection with religion as yet remained possible.

Tysdale, Fran. DeGraffenreid, Josiah Whitlock, Benja. Estis, Thos. Edwards, Joseph Smith, Daniel McKie, Will. Glenn, Drury Murrell, Elisha Winn, John Hix, Isaac Brigandine, Joel Farguson, Wm. Stokes, Ths. Winn, Jur., John Gooch, Gab. Fowlkes, Peter Lamkin, Rawleigh Carter, Bowler Hall, Sterling Wallington, Thos. Mitchell, Ambrose Jeter, Stith Bolling, Charles Bailey, Henry Buford, Josiah Jackson, Asa Davis, L. Royal, John Jennings, William Gooch, John Winn, Gabl. Fowlke Sen, John L. Crutz, Robert Crutz, Ste. Cocke, Richd. Jones, Junr., Wm. Cross Craddock, Hch. Bland, Christn. Ford, Edmd. Booker, Jnr., Jan Wills, Abram Green, Jnr., Isham Clay, Jas. Jenkins, John Jones, Edwd. Munford, Wm. Greenhill.

[315] Journal, p. 19.
[316] Journal, p. 37.
[317] Journal, p. 66.
[318] Journal, p. 73.

CHAPTER V

Assessment and Incorporation

Edmund Randolph, in a letter to Jefferson of May 15, 1784, stated that the following questions would occupy the debates of the spring session of the Assembly: "1. a general assessment; 2. restitution of British property; 3. payment of British debts; 4. the introduction of a stamp-act, under a less offensive name; 5. the making of Norfolk, the only port of entry and clearance."[319] He added: "The first has Henry for its patron in private; but whether he will hazard himself in public cannot be yet ascertained."

It will be observed that Randolph put the assessment scheme first in the list of legislative topics. It was, in fact, the most important of the subjects agitating the public mind, although it had just begun to come into prominence in the early part of 1784. The year was a memorable one in the annals of Virginia, but the only subject of controversy now well remembered at all is the religious struggle.

The question of the payment of British debts according to the terms of the treaty of 1783 engrossed the attention of the people in general, because it is said that the Virginia planters were in debt to Englishmen to the amount of ten millions, and the country was very poor. The two chief parties in the house of delegates, the followings of Richard Henry Lee and Patrick Henry, opposed each other more openly and strongly in this than in any other issue; the Lee party favored the payment of the debts and Henry successfully fought off the settlement. Madison, with a thoughtful eye for the future of Virginia in commerce, succeeded in putting through a bill restricting foreign trade to a few ports. Resolutions were passed favoring a prompter and better method of complying with the requisitions of Congress, and in this legislation the hand of Madison is also evident.[320]

Commissioners were appointed to treat with Maryland concerning a State boundary line through the Potomac river. Madison advocated a plan for the revision of the constitution and gained Richard Henry Lee's support, but Patrick Henry killed the plan.

Henry was the leading advocate of a general assessment for the support of religion. He and Richard Henry Lee sunk their differences and agreed on this issue. Lee was one of the chief promoters of the assessment. "He, with Mr. Henry, were advocates of a proposition to make every man contribute something to the support of the Christian religion, as the only sure basis of public and private morality. Both these gentlemen were utterly opposed, however, to any established State religion. On the contrary, they were strenuous advocates of an entire freedom of religious belief."[321]

---

[319] Conway's Edmund Randolph, p. 56.
[320] Rives's Madison, I, 563.

The reasons for Henry's advocacy of assessment are not altogether known. The sentiment which led to a demand for it grew out of the conservative reaction from the Revolution, which began to be felt at the close of the war. The war had brought about a great deal of license and radical changes of opinion, such as are inevitable in all revolutionary struggles, especially in those involving the principle of liberty. These effects must have been obvious, for a variety of witnesses testified to the decline of morals and religion. "Justice and virtue are the vital principles of republican government," George Mason wrote to Henry in 1783, "but among us a depravity of manners and morals prevails, to the destruction of all confidence between man and man." [322] Presbyterians and Baptists gave evidence as to the low state of religion. Dr. William Hill said: "The demoralizing effects of the war left religion and the church in a most deplorable condition." [323]

Semple states that "The war, though very propitious to the liberty of the Baptists, had an opposite effect upon the life of religion among them." [324] And again: "With some few exceptions, the declension was general throughout the State." [325] Richard Henry Lee said that "Refiners may weave reason into as fine a web as they please, but the experience of all times shows religion to be the guardian of morals; and he must be a very inattentive observer in our country who does not see that avarice is accomplishing the destruction of religion for want of legal obligation to contribute something to its support." [326] The petitions asking for a religious assessment asserted in strong terms that religion and morals had declined during the war.

This opinion was most strongly held by the real conservatives, the old advocates of the establishment, who had been overborne by the weight of events, but who had never become reconciled to the separation of church and state and who welcomed the return of peace as affording an opportunity to once more place religion under governmental protection. Religion, indeed, seemed to be menaced. The Anglican church had nearly gone to wreck during the war; the few ministers who continued to serve existed precariously on the voluntary contributions of their diminished congregations. The Presbyterian ministers lived in the same way, and their congregations were poor. The Baptists and Methodists received little or no hire for preaching and eked out a living by following secular employments. An unprecedented freedom of opinion prevailed in all classes and a certain slackness of responsibility. The church appeared to lack the support of that organized social sentiment which is its strongest bulwark; men feared that religion would not be able to oppose successfully the inroads of skepticism and license of manners without some authoritative aid, and this the Legislature seemed best able to afford. The spirit of pessimism was particularly pronounced in those who had been brought up in the regulated life of colonial Virginia and who looked back upon this life as ideal. The social progress of the Revolution was distasteful to them; they had aimed merely at separation from

[321] Lee's Life of Richard Henry Lee, I, 237.
[322] Rowland's Mason, II, 44.
[323] Foote, I, 412.
[324] Semple, p. 55.
[325] Semple, p. 56, and Henry's Henry, II, 203.
[326] Lee's Richard Henry Lee, II, 51.

England and they had little sympathy with the democratic opinions and practices which had gained strength during the war.

The conservatives had behind them the weight of wealth, intelligence, and influence, but their cause tended to decline and they knew it. Consequently, the accession of Patrick Henry was a great gain to them, for Henry was the most popular leader in the State; he, more than any other man, stood for the Revolution, and he was a power with the masses. Patrick Henry had begun life as an agitator, but, as a matter of fact, he was a conservative at bottom. Time and experience had cooled the revolutionary ardor of his youth, and in his maturity he fought on the defensive, laboring to preserve the State from the encroachments of the Federal constitution and society from the insidious effects of unrestrained liberalism.[327]

Henry took the lead of the conservative forces in the beginning of 1784, and soon made himself felt. A quorum was obtained in the house of delegates on May 12, 1784, and John Tyler was elected speaker.[328] The committee for religion, appointed the next day, was a strong one, including Wilson Miles Cary, the future governor, James Madison, William Norvell, a colleague of Jefferson's in the convention of 1776, Joseph Jones, of King George, French Strother, William White, Garland Anderson, John Ward, Nathaniel Wilkinson, Samuel Sherwin, the veteran George Wray, William Walker and Edmund Byne.[329] The committee was further strengthened by the addition of James Hubard, of Gloucester, John Berryman, of Lancaster, Patrick Henry,[330] Mann Page, of Spotsylvania, Thomas Matthews, of Norfolk, John Bowyer, of Rockbridge, Joseph Prentis, of York, Thomas Towles, of Spotsylvania, Adam Craig, John Breckinridge, Archibald Stuart, and finally Richard Henry Lee, William Grayson, the future senator, and Alexander White. The eastern and conservative element predominated in the committee, but it included such leaders of the opposition as Madison, Wilson Miles Cary, French Strother, and Alexander White.

The advocates of assessment presented a petition three days after the beginning of the session, on May 15, 1784. This memorial, which came from Warwick, declared "that it is essentially necessary for the good government of all free States that some legislative attention shou'd be paid to religious duties" and called for a general assessment upon tithables. No plan of distribution was given.[331]

At the same time the evangelical elements in the State made them-

---

[327] Henry's Henry II, 211.
[328] Journal House of Delegates, May, 1784, p. 4.
[329] Journal, p. 5.
[330] Journal, p. 8.
[331] Journal, p. 8. The names are: John Dunn, Francis Lee, Thomas C. Amory, William Amory, John Jones, James Lewelling, Miles Wills, Richd. McIntosh, Josiah Massenburg, Thos. Mallicote, Wm. Liveley, Mattw. Gibbs, Thos. C. Amory, Jr., Cole Diggs, David Jons,, James Crandol, Richd. Cary, Mattw. Wills, John Picket, Johnson Drewry, Thos. Allen, Wm. Mallicote, Wm. Allan, Robert Brown, Jon Crandol, Aaron Barney, John Drewry, William Gibbs, Junr., Dixon Brown, Gimima V. Noblin, Matthew Noblin, Thomas Pope, Will Jones, Everard Downing, Henry Scasbrooke, Thomas Jordan, Chr. Haynes, Humphr. Harwood, Saml. Blard, Miles Cary, Saml. Thos., John Houghton, Morey Mallicote, John Needham, Jams. Dunn, John Burnham, James Drewry, John R. Jones, Moses Watson, Wm. Gibbs, Peter Pierce, William Harwood, Richard Noblin, Edwd. Charles, Richd. Harrison, Thos. Charles, Thoms. B. Dunn, Samuel C. Dunn, Richd. Smith, Wm. Langhorne, Wm. Morrow. Several names are repeated.

selves felt. On May 26, 1784, the Baptist association presented a memorial. reiterating the complaint that the Baptist appeals had received no attention from the Legislature. "And with respect to the Vestry laws," the paper continues, "which confines the election to the members of one society, and subjects the property of the whole to their taxation, and even the ministers of other denominations appointed by them to possession their neighbours' lands—We therefore hope that as the Episcopal church, to which they belong, have equal right as a church, without your honourable house, to appoint elders, and call them by what names they please, that law will be considered as unequal and be repealed." And with respect to the marriage laws, "We hope you will regulate the Ministers of every Denomination perfectly by one law, and to have neither publication of Banns, nor returning to the Court Clerks." [332]

The Presbyterian clergy of Virginia introduced a memorial on the same day.[333] It was a clearly expressed, a vigorous and even radical document, written by John Blair Smith,[334] and breathing the spirit of the Revolution. The Presbyterians declared that they expected liberty and equality in the eyes of the government. "An entire and everlasting freedom from every species of ecclesiastical domination, a full and permanent security of the inalienable rights of conscience and private judgment, and an equal share of the protection and favor of government to all denominations of Christians were particular objects of our expectation." Members of other churches had the right to expect that distinctions, preferences and emoluments from the hand of the State should be abolished. It was consequently with dissatisfaction that Presbyterians viewed the failure of the Legislature to fulfill these expectations. Religious rights had been left to common law and the caprices of the Legislature instead of being inserted in the constitution, with the result that the Episcopal church had continued to style itself the established church until 1778, and the title had never been formally disclaimed.

Other inequalities existed. The estate of the old established church, worth several hundred thousand pounds, was appropriated to the Episcopal church, although this property was the result of the taxation of the members of all denominations. The Episcopal church was incorporated. The Episcopal clergy enjoyed the right of performing the marriage ceremony anywhere in the State, while other ministers were restricted to their particular counties, Vestries, required by law to be composed of Episcopalians, levied taxes for poor relief upon the members of all denominations. The Presbyterian clergy, therefore, in the interests of justice and contentment, called for the remedy of these grievances. "You will remove every real ground of contention and allay every jealous commotion on the score of religion."

Neither the Baptist nor the Presbyterian petition mentioned the subject of assessment, but the agitation was just beginning in May, 1784, and it had hardly gained sufficient prominence as yet to call for an expression of opinion from those opposed to it.

On May 27th Wilson Miles Cary delivered the resolution of the committee for religion on the Warwick petition, that "it is the Opinion of this committee, That the petition of sundry Inhabitants of the county of Warwick

---

[332] Journal, p. 20.
[333] Journal, p. 21, and Foote, I, 333.
[334] Foote, I, 332.

78

whose names are thereunto subscribed praying that an act may pass for a general Assessment upon all tithables of this Commonwealth, for the support of the christian religion within the same, is reasonable." The resolution was referred to the committee of the whole.[335]

The religious struggle fairly began on June 4, 1784, when the Protestant Episcopal church asked for an act of incorporation by way of adjusting its condition to the existing state of affairs. The Episcopal convention met in Richmond on June 3, 1784, with Samuel Shield as president, and drew up the memorial.[336] The paper states that the Revolution had rendered alterations necessary in the government and liturgy of the church, as the legal requirements as to forms of worship and qualifications of ministers had become obsolete after the separation from England. The church asked for the repeal of that part of the act concerning induction which required that "No minister be admitted to officiate in any parish church except such as present ordination from some English bishop and shall subscribe to orders of the Church of England." And that "being by the late happy revolution, loosed from those obligations which bound us to our former spiritual as well as temporal rulers, we wish to be indulged also with the liberty of introducing into our church a system of order and government suited to our religious principles—or directing a form of public worship hereafter to be used in the Episcopal Churches within this Commonwealth and of regulating all the spiritual concerns of that Church." An act was asked which would give the Episcopal clergy the power to regulate the spiritual concerns of the church, alter forms, institute canons and make rules for its government.

An important feature was the clause dealing with vestries. The petition requested that the direction of the poor should be taken from the vestries, and thus, in fact, that the last feature of the old establishment should be done away with. The reason given for the request was that in the election of vestrymen dissenters voted in large numbers, which resulted in the choice of dissenters as vestrymen. The Episcopal church, in its reorganization, wished the vestries to be elected by and from the Episcopal body exclusively.

An act was desired which should secure the perpetual title of the Episcopal church in the glebes and other property of the old establishment. As a conclusion, the memorial recommended to the assembly the "patronage and care of the Christian religion, which, from the moderation and gentleness of its principles, must merit the encouragement of all public bodies instituted for the government of mankind." This clause was not a direct request for an assessment, but it leaned that way. Perhaps the Episcopalians thought that they had asked enough in presenting their comprehensive scheme for reorganization.

It will be noted that eight years after 1776 the Assembly was still supposed to have the power to fix church doctrines and regulations, for the petition expressly requested the grant of this power to the clergy. The ecclesiastical laws existing prior to the Revolution were still supposed to be in force, in spite of the Bill of Rights, which might reasonably be interpreted as leaving to each sect the regulation of its own doctrine and affairs. The

[335] Journal, p. 23.
[336] Journal, p. 36.

"act to induct ministers" must be revised before new ministers could legally officiate, although they were no longer supported by the state and although no state religion existed. The force of custom prevailed over the spirit of the laws brought into existence by the Revolution. And, as a matter of fact, in the retention of the glebes, in the taxing power wielded by the vestry, and in the marriage laws survivals of the old connection between church and state certainly existed, although they hardly warranted the belief that the state still possessed the right to legislate concerning the creed and government of the church.

On the same day of the presentation of the Episcopal memorial, a petition came in from Powhatan county asking for a legal contribution for the support of ministers.[337] The committee for religion proceeded to digest these various petitions and on June 8th Cary appeared before the house with the committee's recommendations.[338] These were framed in a spirit of general accommodation. The Episcopal memorial praying for a change in the laws "which restrain the said church from the like power of self-government, as is enjoyed by all other religious societies; and which prescribe the mode of appointing vestries and the qualifications of vestrymen may be changed, and that the churches, glebe lands, donations and all property belonging to the said church may forever be secured to them is reasonable."

Further, that such part of the Presbyterian and Baptist memorials "as prays that the laws regulating the celebration of marriage and relating to the constitution of vestries may be altered, and that in general all legal distinctions in favor of any particular religious society may be abolished is reasonable." And lastly, that such part of the Episcopal and Presbyterian memorials "as relates to an incorporation of their societies is reasonable, and that a like incorporation ought to be extended to all other religious societies within this Commonwealth which may apply for the same." The house ordered the committee for religion to prepare bills pursuant to these resolutions.

The committee had outlined its report on a broad plan, but it had gone too far in coupling the Episcopal and Presbyterian churches as asking for incorporation. The spirit of the two bodies was very different, and, as a matter of fact, the Presbyterians had not asked for the right of incorporation, but had complained that the right was confined solely to the Episcopal church. "The episcopal church is actually incorporated, and known in law as a body, so that it can receive and possess property for ecclesiatical purposes, without trouble or risk in securing it, while other Christian communities are obliged to trust to the precarious fidelity of trustees chosen for the purpose." [339]

The chief question before the committee for religion was the incorporation of the Episcopal church, and circumstances made it a momentous one. The Protestant Episcopal church in America, the successor of the church of England, had framed a liturgy and canons which dispensed with the king of England and was now about to launch out upon its new career. The Anglican branch in Virginia wished to become connected formally with

[337] Journal, p. 36.
[338] Journal, p. 43.
[339] May 1784 Memorial.

the new communion. It was now time for the Legislature to abandon its make-shift policy and recognize the position of the Episcopal church as the successor to the properties of the established church. An act was needed, or was supposed to be needed, to secure the property to the church and to make it independent of legislative control.

Joseph Jones, of King George, presented a bill from the committee for religion, on June 16th, "for incorporating the Protestant Episcopal Church and for other purposes," drawn up along the lines of the Episcopal petition. The bill met with no opposition apparently and was read the first and second times and ordered to be committed to the committee of the whole for the following day.[340] It was not debated the next day, but on June 25th, shortly before adjournment, the committee of the whole considered it. After a discussion of some length, Thomas Matthews reported to the house that the committee of the whole had not had time to go through the bill and asked for another consideration.[341] The house, however, shelved the bill until "the second Monday in November next," and the incorporation question came up no more in the spring session. Assessment, too, was allowed to drop; the sentiment for it had not yet been worked up sufficiently. Madison wrote that "The friends of the measure did not chuse to try their strength in the House." [342]

According to the resolution of the committee for religion, a bill "to amend the several acts concerning marriages" was brought into the house. The bill was draughted by a special committee composed of William Ronald, William White, Isaac Zane, Thomas Towles and Madison.[343] It was introduced on June 23, 1784,[344] and was read the second time the next day and passed on June 28th by a vote of 50 to 30.[345] This vote was without special significance. Wilson Cary Nicholas, Archibald Stuart, French Strother, John Breckinridge were among the prominent men who voted in the affirmative. Against the bill were Carter Henry Harrison, George Wray, Spencer Roane, William Pickett, William Grayson, Isaac Zane, Henry Tazewell and Alexander White. Spencer Roane, William Pickett, Isaac Zane and Alexander White were afterwards strong advocates of the progressive religious policy, opposed to assessment and incorporation. The senate did not pass the bill and the regulation of marriages waited over till the next session.

The incorporation bill, so far from meeting with the approval of the Presbyterians, had awakened their fears. The bill was altered before it became a law in the fall session of 1784. In its earlier form it granted extensive powers to the clergy and perhaps justified the Presbyterian criticism that the Assembly aimed at making them a separate caste. "The Episcopal Clergy," Madison wrote, "introduced a notable project for re-establishing their independence of the laity. The foundation of it was that the whole body should be legally incorporated, invested with the present property of the Church, made capable of acquiring indefinitely—empowered to make canons & bye-laws not contrary to the laws of the land, and incum-

[340] Journal, p. 79.
[341] Journal, p. 79.
[342] Madison's Works (Hunt) II, 58.
[343] Journal, p. 71.
[344] Journal, p. 76.
[345] Journal, p. 81.

bents when once chosen by vestries, to be immovable otherwise than by sentence of the Convocation. Extraordinary as such a project was, it was preserved from a dishonorable death by the talents of Mr. Henry."[346]

John Blair Smith, the president of Hampden-Sidney college and the leader of Presbyterian thought, wrote to Madison, on June 21, 1784, asking him to lend his influence against incorporation. He especially resented the demands made by the Episcopal clergy in their petition. "I should expect that such an Idea of spiritual domination, would be resented & opposed by every adherent to that Society (Episcopal). I should suppose that every one of them who felt the spirit of his station would regard the attempt, as an indefensible remains of Star-chamber tyranny & resist it accordingly. However, if the Gentlemen of that communion are so used to Dictators, that they either have not observed the Jure divino pretension to dominion over them, or have no inclination or spirit to oppose it, perhaps it may be thought proper for one so little interested in the matter as myself to be silent. * * * But that part of the petition, which concerns me most as well as every non-Episcopalian in the State, is, where these clergymen pray for an act of the Assembly to Enable them to regulate all the spiritual concerns of that Church &c. This is an express attempt to draw the State into an illicit connection & commerce with them, which is already the ground of that uneasiness which at present prevails thro' a great part of the State. According to the spirit of that prayer, the Legislature is to consider itself as the head of that Party, & consequently they as members are to be fostered with particular care. * * * I am sorry that Christian ministers should virtually declare their Church a mere political machine, which the State may regulate at present; but I shall be surprized if the Assembly shall assume the improper office. * * * It would be to give leave to do what every class of Citizens has a natural, inalienable right to do without any such leave; every religious society in the State possesses full power to regulate their internal police; without depending upon the Assembly for leave to do so. Surely we are not again to be irritated & harrassed with the heavy weight of a State Church, that is to sit as sovereign over the rest, by depending in a more particular manner for direction in spirituals, upon that antiquated fountain head of influences, the secular power."[347]

This was the chief ground of the Presbyterian objection to the incorporation. Smith outlined the point clearly; he protested against the act granting the Anglican clergy the privilege of making the canons and regulations of their church as an assertion of the Assembly's right to legislate concerning religion. Madison held the same views of incorporation; it is impossible to know whether he was influenced in this by Smith or not.

In the summer of 1784, however, Madison was of the minority. The incorporation bill met with the general approval of the conservatives, and the assessment plan gained ground rapidly under the patronage of Patrick Henry. The great orator's advocacy of assessment went a long way towards reconciling to it many people of moderate opinions, who might otherwise have considered the movement somewhat reactionary.

The power of the conservatives lay chiefly in their ascendency in the

[346] Madison's Works, II, 59. Hunt.
[347] Letters to Madison, Vol. XIII, MS., Library of Congress, and Madison Calendar, p. 624.

Assembly, which, according to the system of equal representation of counties, contained a majority of members from the east. But prominent men from all sections sat in the house of delegates, making it probably the most talented legislative body in America. The fall session of 1784 was noteworthy both in the personnel of the members and in the importance of the questions under consideration.

Few members of the house were obscure; many who are not remembered now were men of prominence in their own times, when the limits of a single state were considered broad enough for a generous ambition. Some of the delegates became known in both State and Federal politics, as Wilson Cary Nichclas, a son of Robert Carter Nicholas, who represented Albemarle in the house, and sat for that county, together with his greater brother, George Nicholas, in the convention of 1788. He was elected to the United States senate in 1799 and became governor of Virginia in 1814. Nicholas was one of Jefferson's most devoted and useful lieutenants. Archibald Stuart, cf Augusta, was another Jeffersonian democrat, a judge and a man of great influence in the west. Andrew Moore, of Rockbridge, was likewise a democrat and an advocate of religious freedom in the broadest sense. He became a member of the house of representatives and United States senator. Isaac Vanmeter, of Hardy, Isaac Zane, of Shenandoah, and Zachariah Johnston, of Augusta, were three westerners who strongly opposed the conservative propaganda. Alexander White, of Frederick, was the leading westerner in the house. He was a chairman of a committee and took an important part in the discussions of the house for several terms. John Breckinridge, of Montgomery, was an able lawyer and later became attorney-general of the United States. Spencer Roane was cne of the leading easterners of liberal ideas. His reputation was confined to the State, but it was a great one. He became chief judge of the Virginia court of appeals and ranks as one of Virginia's greatest jurists. John Taylor, of Caroline, the doctrinaire, grew to be the leading democrat in the State politics of a decade later. He entered the United States senate and was a senator of great powers and of uncompromising republican virtue. William Grayson left a deep impression upon his State, although he died shortly after becoming a United States senator and in his prime.

Among the conservative leaders in the church controversy, the names of John Tyler, Benjamin Harrison, Miles King, George Wray, John Marshall, John Scarsborough Wills, Joseph Jones, of King George, Richard Lee, Francis Corbin, Littleton Eyre, Patrick Henry, Carter Henry Harrison, Henry Tazewell, William Norvell, and Willis Riddick are best remembered. John Tyler was the speaker of the house. Benjamin Harrison had become well known as a member of the continental congress, governor and speaker of the house of delegates—few men in the State held a higher position. Joseph Jones, of King George, served in the continental congress for several years as an influential member. Miles King and Willis Riddick were members of the house of delegates for many terms. Francis Corbin and Littleton Eyre enjoyed the reputation of men with great futures before them. The veteran Henry Tazewell had sat in the house of burgesses and the Revolutionary conventions, and he was destined to become the chief judge of the court of appeals and United States senator. Carter Henry Harrison was a typical conservative country gentleman who once outraged John Blair Smith by declaring that "The greatest curse which heaven sent at any time into this Country, was sending Dissenters into it."[348] John Scarsborough Wills and Richard Lee sat in the house for many sessions.

Patrick Henry was the great strength of the party, for he was at once a power in the house and in the State at large. His reputation for patriotism was above question, and his character and popularity gained a respectful consideration for any measure he advocated. Comment upon John Marshall, the chief justice, is unnecessary. His conservative temper and his taste for strong government led him to espouse the policy of a state support of religion.

James Madison, Henry's antagonist in the religious controversy, was destined to become the controlling figure in the Assembly. He had grown quickly into a position of influence and honor by his industrious and successful career in the continental congress. Madison was young, and his mind looked to the future. He had seasoned a thorough education with liberal ideas, and he had entered the service of the State as a democratic leader and the advocate of progressive policies. Even in 1784 he held a high place in politics. Washington and Jefferson overshadowed him with their greater personalities, but Madison yields to none in brains. He was a deep and eager student and the ablest of American political thinkers, with possibly one or two exceptions. Yet he lacked somewhat in charm and force of character—cold-blooded, clear-headed, and far-sighted, but colorless. Madison possessed the virtues of the philosophic temperament. He had no vanity; he was a Saxon without bile, content to rest in the shadow of his great and good friend Jefferson, and to serve him loyally forever. A cool debater in an age of oratory, his logic proved a match for the greatest of orators. He was a successful politician in a time when personal attractions had great weight in politics. His life is a proof that a man may be a scholar and hold his own in the field of action. The measure of his success came as the result of labor, care, and unsparing service. Madison was well prepared for a controversy over the relations of church and state, for, in his characteristic fashion, he had made a profound study of religion and knew more divinity than a seminary professor.

The Assembly met on October 19th, but a quorum was not obtained until October 30, 1784.[349] The committee for religion was appointed on November 1, 1784. It consisted of William Norvell, of James City, Zachariah Johnston, of Augusta, Carter Henry Harrison, of Cumberland, James Madison, of Orange, William Watkins, of Dinwiddie, Garland Anderson, of Hanover, French Strother, of Culpeper, Wilson Cary Nicholas, of Albemarle, Edmund Ruffin, of Prince George, Bernard Markham, of Chesterfield, Samuel Sherwin, of Amelia, John Ward, of Campbell, George Wray, of Elizabeth City, and Robert Clarke of Bedford.[350] Charles Hay and Joseph Jones, of King George, were added later. Consideration of the religious question began on November 4th with the presentation of a petition from Isle of Wight, "setting forth, that they are much concerned to see the countenance of the civil

[348] Smith's Letter. Letters to Madison. Vol. XIV, ms. Library of Congress.
[349] Journal, House of Delegates, Oct., 1784.
[350] Journal, p. 6.

84

power wholly withdrawn from religion, and the people left without the smallest coercion to contribute to its support; that they consider it as the duty of a wise Legislature to encourage its progress, and diffuse its influence; that being thoroughly convinced that the prosperity and happiness of this country essentially depends on the progress of religion, they beg leave to call the attention of the Legislature to a principle, old as society itself, that whatever is to conduce equally to the advantage of all, should be borne equally by all, and praying that an act may pass to compel every one to contribute something, in proportion to his property, to the support of religion." [351]

Four days later a similar memorial was presented from Amelia. It declared "that your Petitioners have with much concern observed a general Declension of Religion for a number of Years past, occasioned in Part, we conceive by the late War, but chiefly by its not being duly aided and patronized by the civil Power; that should it decline with nearly the same rapidity in Future, your Petitioners apprehend Consequences dangerous, if not fatal to the Strength and Stability of Civil Government." * * * "Were all Sense of Religion rooted out of the Minds of Men, scarce any thing would be left on which human Laws would take hold. * * * Your Petitioners therefore think that those who legislate, not only have a Right, founded upon the principle of public utility, but as they wish to promote the Virtue and Happiness of their Constituents & the good People of the State in general; as they wish well to the Strength and Stability of Government, they ought to aid & patronize Religion."

In these ponderous sentences the Amelia conservatives laid down their reasons for state support of religion. "As every Man in the State partakes of the Blessings of Peace and Order," which results no less from religion than the operation of the laws, so "every Man should be obliged to contribute as well to the Support of Religion, as that of Civil Government; nor has he any Reason to complain of this, as an Encroachment upon his religious Liberty, if he is permitted to worship God according to the Dictates of his Conscience."

The memorial further calls for the protection of the Episcopal church in its possession of the glebes and the grant to it of the right of self-government, and for a general assessment in order to encourage men of learning to enter the ministry. [352]

On November 11, 1784, the Baptist petition came into the house. The general committee had met at Dover meeting-house on October 9, 1784, and had considered the religious question and drawn up a memorial to the Legislature. "The law for the solemnization of marriage and the vestry law" were considered political grievances. They also resolved to oppose the law for a general assessment and that for the incorporation of religious societies, which were now in agitation."

A memorial to the General Assembly praying for a repeal of the vestry

[351] Journal, p. 11.

[352] Signed by about 175 persons, among them John Booker, Jr., Wm. Cross Craddock, Christian Ford, Edward Munford, James Jenkins, Stith Hardaway, Cho. Craddock, Edmd. Booker, John Wily, Abraham Lockett, Wm. Dyson, Christopher Hudson, Marston Green, Wm. Quinn, Thomas Nash, Henry Jeter, Thomas Jeffry, Richard Ward, Henry Buford, Matthew Waller, Peter Lamkin, Joseph Stephens, Thos. Overstreet, Wm. Stuart, John Archer, Wm. Worsham, etc.

law and for an alteration in the marriage law was drawn and committed to the hands of Rev. Reuben Ford to be presented to the next Assembly.

This memorial contains no allusion to assessment or incorporation.[353] It is as follows: "The memorial of the Committee of Several Baptist Associations, Assembled at Dover Meeting-House, the 9th day of October 1784 humbly sheweth.

"That your Memorialists still complain of a part of the Marriage Act, and Vestry Law, as grievous to Dissenters; for in the former, they are forbid going out of their Counties, to Solemnize the Rights of Matrimony, even among Members of their Own Societies, and Congregations, whereby the good purpose, which the Wisdom of your Honourable House intended by that Act, is disappointed. And in the latter, the property of Dissenters is taken from them, by those who are not their Representatives.

"Your Memorialists therefore humbly pray, that all Distinctions in your Laws may be done away, and that no order, or Denomination of Christians in this Commonwealth, have any Separate Privileges allowed them, more than their Brethren of other Religious Societies, distinguished by other Names; lest they Tyrannize over them.

"Your Memorialists have hoped for a removal of their Complaints, and the enjoyment of equal liberty; since it hath pleased your Honourable House to declare, that their Complaints are just, and their Petitions Reasonable; to you therefore they look up, that every grievous Yoke be broken, and that the oppressed go free; and that in every Act, the bright beams of equal Liberty, and Impartial Justice may shine, Your Memorialists shall ever pray.

WILLIAM WEBBER, Chairman.

On the same day, November 11th, the house went into the committee of the whole and held a long debate upon assessment. Madison and Henry spoke against each other. "The Generals on the opposite sides, were Henry & Madison. The former advocated with his usual art, the establishment of the Christian Religion in exclusion of all other Denominations. By this I mean that Turks, Jews & Infidels were to contribute, to the support of a Religion whose truth they did not acknowledge. Madison displayed great Learning & Ingenuity, with all the Powers of a close reasoner; but he was unsuccessful in the Event, having a majority of 17 against him."[354] It was probably on this occasion that Madison delivered the speech, the notes for which have been preserved.[355]

Henry advanced as his chief argument the relations of religion to the

[353] Semple, p. 95.
[354] Letter of Beverly Randolph. Letters to Monroe. MS., Library of Congress.
[355] I. Rel. not within purview of civil authority.
Tendency of estabg. Xnty— 1. to project of Uniformity. 2. to penal laws for supportg it.
Progress of Gen. Assest. proves this tendency.
Difference between estabg. and tolerating errour.
"True question—not Is Rel. necessy,—but
II. are Religs. Estabts. necesy. for Religion? No.
1. propensity of man to Religion.
2. Experience shews Relig. corrupted by Estabts.
3. Downfall of States mentioned by Mr. H.—happened where there was estabt.
4. Experience gives no model of Geni. Asst.
5. Case of Pa. explained—not solitary. N. J. See const. of it. R. I. N. Y. D. factions greater in S. C.

prosperity of the state, dwelling upon the evil fate of nations which had neglected religion and inferring therefrom the necessity of a religious establishment. Madison exposed this fallacy by stating that the true question was "not is Religion necessary,—but are Religious Establishments necessary for Religion?" He answered the question boldly in the negative, naming as examples the states in which religion was not established. Foote says of the debates on religion: "The true relations of Church and State was inquired into with patience, vigour, conscience, keenness, and judgment, in the exercise of great talents and eloquence." [356]

The committee finally reported a resolution "That the people of this Commonwealth, according to their respective abilities, ought to pay a moderate tax or contribution annually for the support of the Christian religion, or of some Christian church, denomination or communion of Christians, or for some form of Christian worship." The resolution passed by a vote of 47 to 32. In the affirmative were Samuel Sherwin, Nicholas Cabell, William Meredith, Thomas Edmunds, of Brunswick, Bernard Markham, Matthew Cheatham, Carter Henry Harrison, Edward Carrington, Joseph Jones, of Dinwiddie, Miles King, George Wray, Thomas Smith, Andrew Donnelly, Batte Peterson, Isaac Coles, John Coleman, Garland Anderson, Patrick Henry, William Norvell, John Scarsborough Wills, Philip Barbour, Joseph Jones, of King George, William Thornton, John Heath, William White, George Slaughter, Francis Corbin, William Curtis, Willis Riddick, William Armistead, John Kearnes, Daniel Sandford, Littleton Eyre, Thomas Gaskins, John

----

6. Case of primitive Xnty.
      of Reformation.
      of Dissenters formerly.
7. Progress of Religious liberty.
III. Policy—
   1. promote emigrations from State.
   2. prevent immig. into it, as asylum.
IV. Necessity of Estabt inferred from state of coy.
   True causes of disease.
   1. war ⎫
   2. bad laws ⎬ common to other States & produce same complts in N. E.
   3. pretext from taxes.
   4. state of administration of Justice.
   5. transition from old to new plan.
   6. policy and hopes of friends to G. Asst.
   True remedies not Estabt.—but, being out of war,
   1. laws to cherish virtue
   2. administration of justice.
   3. personal example— associations for R.
   4. By present vote, cut off hope of G. asst.
   5. Education of youth.
V. Probable defects of Bill.
   1. limited.
   2. in particular.
   3. What is Xnty? Courts of law to Judge.
   4. What edition: Hebrew, Septuagint, or Vulgate? What copy what translation?
   5. What books canonical, what apocryphal? the papists holding to be the former what protestants the latter, the Lutherans the latter what the protestants & papists ye former.
   6. In what light are they to be viewed, as dictated every letter by inspiration, or the essential parts only? Or the matter in general not the words?
   7. What sense the true one for if some doctrines be essential to Xnty those who reject these, whatever name they take are no Xn Society?
      [356] Foote, Vol. I, p. 339.

Thornton, Benjamin Lankford, William Mayo, Edward Bland, Thomas Walke, John Fantleroy, Bailey Washington, Carter Bassett Harrison, John Allen, Thomas Edmunds, of Sussex, Richard Lee, Joseph Prentis and Henry Tazewell.

Those in the negative were Wilson Cary Nicholas, Edward Carter, Zachariah Johnston, Robert Clarke, Moses Hunter, Archibald Stuart, John Nicholas, John Ward, Samuel Hawes, Jacob Morton, French Strother, Spencer Roane, William Gatewood, William Pickett, Samuel Richardson, Thomas Underwood, George Clendennen, Ralph Humphreys, Nathaniel Wilkinson, Benjamin Pope, Richard Bland Lee, Anthony Street, John Breckinridge, James Madison, Jr., Charles Porter, John Hays, Gawin Hamilton, John Hopkins, William Russell, James Montgomery, Nathaniel Nelson, and Thomas Matthews.[357]

Patrick Henry had mustered a clear working majority in the house, and the senate was strongly conservative in sentiment. An analysis of the vote shows that the division in the first instance upon the question of assessment was largely geographical. This first vote is important as indicating the real attitude of the delegates upon the assessment, or the measure of Patrick Henry's personal influence. In the later votes many changes occurred. Henry, reading the opinion of the conservative part of the State, proposed the resolution and put it through the house. The resolution, Madison states, "had early in the Session been proposed by Mr. Henry, and in spite of all the opposition that could be mustered, carried by 47 agst. 32 votes. Many Petitions from below the blue ridge had prayed for such a law; and though several from the presbyterian laity beyond it were in a contrary stile, the Clergy of that Sect favored it. The other Sects[358] seemed to be passive." Madison, in another letter, calls Henry "the father of the scheme."[359] He had promoted it with success, being supported by tidewater and southside Virginia, where the Episcopal church was still powerful. Midland Virginia was divided. The west strongly opposed assessment. This was the section of the State where Presbyterianism was the leading religious interest, as far as there was any religious interest, and there can be little doubt that the body of Presbyterians were opposed to assessment from the beginning. It is possible that the Baptists of the middle counties may have influenced some of the delegates from those counties who voted against assessment. The vote by counties for assessment was as follows: Amelia, Amherst, Brunswick, Chesterfield, Cumberland, Dinwiddie, Elizabeth City, Gloucester, Greenbrier, Greensville, Halifax Hanover, Henry, James City, Isle of Wight, Berkeley, King George, Lancaster, Louisa, Lincoln, Middlesex, Nansemond, New Kent, Norfolk county, Northampton, Northumberland, Pittsylvania, Powhatan, Prince George, Prin-

8. Is it Trinitarianism, Arianism, Socinianism? Is it salvation by faith or works also, by free grace or by will, &c., &c.

9. What clue is to guide [a] Judge thro' this labyrinth when ye question comes before them whether any particular society is a Xn society?

10, Ends in what is orthodoxy, what heresy.

    Dishonors christianity.

    panegyric on it, on our side.

Decl. Rights. (Writings of James Madison, Vol. II, pp. 88, 89.)

[357] Journal, p. 19.

[358] Works of Madison (Hunt), II, 113.

[359] Madison, Works, Vol. II, 94.

88

cess Anne, Richmond, Stafford, Surry, Sussex, Westmoreland and Williamsburg.

Opposed to assessment were Albemarle, Augusta, Bedford, Berkeley, Botetourt, Buckingham, Campbell, Caroline, Charlotte, Culpeper, Essex, Fluvanna, Goochland, Greenbrier, Hampshire, Henrico, Jefferscn, Loudoun, Lunenburg, Montgomery, Orange, Rockbridge, Rockingham, Washington, York, and Norfolk Borough.

The exceptions to the rule were Andrew Donnelly, of Greenbrier, Philip Barbour, of Berkeley, and George Slaughter, of Lincoln, all three of whom (though westerners) vcted in the affirmative; and Spencer Roane and William Gatewood, of Essex, Nathaniel Nelson, of York, and Thomas Matthews, of Norfclk Borough, who voted in the negative. These men fcllowed their inclinations, apparently without regard to the cpinions of their constituents. It is somewhat remarkable that both the delegates from Essex, an eminently conservative county, should have voted against assessment, but Spencer Roane was consistently radical on the religious question until that question went out of politics and into the courts in 1802.

Following the vote upon the resolution, a committee was appointed to prepare a bill providing a plan for a general assessment. It was fitting that Patrick Henry, who had brought in the resolution and carried it through, should be made chairman. The committee consisted of Henry, Francis Corbin, of Middlesex, Joseph Jcnes, of King George, Isaac Coles, of Halifax, William Norvell, of James City, George Wray, of Elizabeth City, Joseph Jones, of Dinwiddie, Carter Henry Harrison, of Cumberland, Henry Tazewell, of Williamsburg, and Joseph Prentis, of York. Speaker Tyler had taken no chances and had appointed a strongly conservative group to assist Henry in the work of drawing up the bill. The way was now clear for him. If the bill should be quickly prepared, it could be put through the house by an easy majority, and also through the senate. No organized opposition to assessment existed at this time and a majority of the people in the State favored it or were indifferent. Henry had behind him the delegates representing the most populous, intelligent and wealthy sections of the State.

The attitude of the Presbyterian church was made known to the Assembly by a memorial presented on November 12th.[360] The Presbytery of Hanover had met at Timber Ridge cn October 27, 1784. It formally approved of the petition drawn up by John Blair Smith in May, 1784. Smith and William Graham were appointed a committee to prepare a memorial for the fall session of the Assembly. The Presbytery the next day approved this memorial, "complaining of, and praying a redress of certain grievances," and ordered it to be carried to the Legislature by Messrs. John Tcdd, William Graham, John Blair, and Montgomery.[361]

The memorial, written by John Blair Smith, is a very able paper.[362] The bill for incorporating the Episcopal church is condemned on the ground that it made a distinction in law between clergymen and laymen. The Presbytery declined the privilege of incorporation because it made clergymen "independent of the religious communities to which they belong." In-

[360] Journal, p. 21.
[361] Foote, I, 335.
[362] Foote, I, 366.

corporation, furthermore, "would establish an immediate, a peculiar, and for that very reason, in our opinion, illicit connection between government, and such as were thus distinguished. The Legislature in that case would be the head of a religious party. . . . The principle, too, which this system aims to establish, is both false and dangerous to religion, and we take this opportunity to remonstrate and protest against it. The real ministers of true religion derive their authority to act in the duties of their profession from a higher source than any Legislature on earth, however respectable. Their office relates to the care of the soul and preparing it for a future state of existence, and their administrations are, or ought to be, of a spiritual nature suited to this momentous concern. And it is plain from the very nature of the case, that they should neither expect, nor receive, from government any permission or direction in this respect."

The principle of assessment was admitted, although in a qualified way. Religion, the memorial declared, did not need the support of the state, but the state needed the support of religion. "On this account it is wise policy in legislators to seek its alliance and solicit its aid in civil view, because of its happy influence upon the morality of its citizens. . . . It is upon this principle alone, in our opinion, that a legislative body has a right to interfere in religion at all, and of consequence we suppose that this interference ought only to extend to the preserving of the public worship of the deity, and the supporting of institutions for inculcating the great fundamental principles of all religion, without which society could not easily exist. Should it be thought necessary at present for the Assembly to exert this right of supporting religion in general by an assessment on all the people, we would wish it to be done on the most liberal plan. A general assessment of the kind we have heard proposed is an object of such consequence that it excites much anxious speculation amongst your constituents.

"We therefore earnestly pray that nothing may be done in the case inconsistent with the proper objects of human legislation or of the Declaration of Rights as published at the Revolution. We hope that the assessment will not be proposed under the idea of supporting religion as a spiritual system, relating to the care of the soul and preparing it for its future destiny. We hope that no attempt will be made to point out articles of faith that are not essential to the preservation of society, or to settle modes of worship, or to interfere in the internal government of religious communities, or to render the ministers of religion independent of the will of the people whom they serve. We expect from our representatives that careful attention to the political equality of all the citizens which a republic ought ever to cherish, and that no scheme of an assessment will be encouraged which will violate the happy privilege we now enjoy of thinking for ourselves in all cases where conscience is concerned."

The Presbyterian position in the assessment question has excited controversy and has been somewhat misunderstood. An inconsistency was observed between earlier and later petitions from Hanover Presbytery condemning assessment and this memorial of October, 1784, accepting it. As a matter of fact, the Presbytery never advanced beyond the position of accepting what was almost looked upon as a *fait accompli*. Foote states that Moses Hoge opposed the principle of assessment in the Presbytery and proposed a committee to draft a resolution to that effect, "and was dissuaded from pressing the matter by the assertion of an individual possessed of

90

information on the subject that some kind of assessment would be established, and he could only choose what kind he would have." [363] The individual "possessed of information" could be none other than John Blair Smith, the neighbor and friend of Patrick Henry, and there is little doubt that Henry had influenced him. Foote, in his account of the Presbytery, states that "There was a strong impression that some kind of assessment would be demanded by a majority of the citizens of the State. And it appears that, for a time, there was a leaning that way, in some, at least, of the members of the Presbytery." [364] A plan was introduced "agreeably to which alone Presbytery are willing to admit a general assessment for the support of religion by law." The plan states that religion as a spiritual system is not to be considered as an object of legislation, but it may be so considered in its capacity as a preservative of society, and public worship may be maintained by a general assessment for this purpose.

John Holt Rice, who was in a good position to know the facts, in 1826 published in his magazine a statement that "The general belief was that the measure (assessment) would be carried in spite of all opposition. Under this impression, the Presbytery resolved to attempt by remonstrance to the Legislature, so to modify the plan as to make it as harmless as possible. With this view they presented the reasoning contained in the latter part of the memorial." [365] And again: "It has been supposed from the latter part of the memorial now under consideration that the Presbytery of Hanover was in favour of an assessment of some kind, when in fact it was only their purpose, as before stated, to render a measure which they thought inevitable, as harmless as possible." This statement is confirmed by Foote's account of William Graham, in which he says that "When the bill for a general assessment was brought forward, with such an advocate as Patrick Henry, and with the Episcopal Church to support it, it was generally supposed that it would certainly become a law. To those who had been paying to support their own church and another foreign to it, this bill proposed relief; they were to pay only for the support of the church of their choice. As it was a relief from their former burdens, and as the Presbyterian congregations would not be called on to pay more for the support of their own ministers than they would cheerfully give by voluntary subscription, Mr. Graham was agreed with his brethren to send up the memorial which gives their sentiments on the subject of the support of religion, disclaiming all legislative interference; and, under the conviction that the law would in some form pass, proposing the least offensive form in which the assessment could be levied." [366]

Madison's evidence has usually been accepted as indicating the motives of the Presbyterian clergy in the assessment question. On November 14, he wrote to Monroe: "The Presbyterian Clergy have remonstrated agst any narrow principles, but indirectly favor a more comprehensive establisht." [367] On April 12, 1785, he wrote to Monroe that "The Episcopal people are generally for it (assessment) though I think the zeal of some of them has cooled. The laity of the other sects are generally unanimous on the other

[363] Foote, I, 557. Johnson, 105.
[364] Foote, I, 338.
[365] Literary and Evangelical Magazine, IX, 38.
[366] Foote, I, 455.
[367] Madison, Works, II, 90.

side. So are all the Clergy, except the Presbyterians who seem as ready to set up an establishment which is to take them in as they were to pull down that which shut them out. I do not know a more shameful contrast than might be found between their memorials on the latter and former occasion."[268] This is strong language and is an exaggeration. The mention of the Presbyterian petition in the journal of the house of delegates, which has been quoted by Rives, has further tended to a misconception of the Presbyterian position. "What is especially remarkable is, that in a memorial presented by the united clergy of the Presbyterian Church—a body which had hitherto distinguished itself by its zeal in favor of the principle of unlimited religious freedom—an opinion was now expressed, as cited in the journal of the house of delegates, that 'a general assessment for the support of religion ought to be extended to those who profess the public worship of the Deity.'"[269]

But the Presbyterians had made no such statement, as the petition itself shows. In this case, as in that of the petition concerning incorporation, the clerk of the house misstated the purport of the document. These misconceptions have passed down into history and have prejudiced the opinions of students not conversant with the manuscripts themselves and with the conditions affecting the Presbyterian church.

The religious struggle in Virginia has been misunderstood because generally it has been considered by itself, as a peculiar transaction, and with no reference to the social and political setting of the times. The controversy had a wider relation than to religion alone; it was a side of the Revolution. The study of a phase of a movement offers obvious advantages for treatment in detail, but the whole should be considered as well as the part, or misconceptions arise. Thus the agitation for the separation of church and state was a side of the great struggle begun before the war and culminating in the last years of the eighteenth century, the conflict between the forces of conservatism and democracy. Jefferson's war upon the existing institutions was waged in the interests of a general liberalism—political, social and religious. The revolution in thought did not end with the treaty of peace in 1783, but continued; democracy had yet much farther to go.

But in all revolutions there are reactions, and the reactions sometimes swallow up the revolutions. The reaction in the revolution in Virginia began in 1783, with the establishment of peace, and it had gained great strength by the fall of 1784. War had compelled the conservatives to make concessions they had not dreamed of in 1775, but the return of peace awoke the desire for an ordered and more or less aristocratic state of society akin to that which had existed in the colonial era. The conservatives, however, did not plan in a narrow and intolerant spirit. They simply lacked faith in democracy, and accordingly wished to return to former conditions as far as possible, making due allowance for the changes wrought by the Revolution. The establishment had been an important factor in the old social and political order, and the conservatives aimed at reviving it in a new and more liberal form, largely for the aid it would afford them in maintaining their threatened position. The evangelical sects had exerted a democratic influ-

---

[268] Madison, Works, II, 13, and Rives, I, 630.
[269] Rives, I, 601; Journal, p. 21.

92

ence in politics and society; the Revolution, with its denial of authority, had greatly encouraged the spread of liberal ideas. As a consequence, the mass of the population was tending to become alienated from the old political leaders and the old political and social caste, and to assert itself in political questions. The war, too, had brought about great social changes. Many eastern families had become impoverished and many had moved to western Virginia or to Kentucky. Overseers and other new men had come in to take their places. The conservative class, in such circumstances, could only hope to maintain its position of authority and influence by the strengthening of the powers of the state as against the growing tendency to individualism.

The reunion of church and state by a tax for religion afforded an opportunity to check the growth of liberalism—in a general way and also on the religious side. For one thing, the evangelical churches would be bridled. They would become a part of the establishment; they could no longer style themselves a peculiar people and enjoy the advantages of attack. Their crusading ardor would inevitably subside as they became parts of a system in which the Anglican communion would hold the chief place. The re-established church could oppose, with a better chance of success, the evangelical idea of religion, which was becoming more and more to be considered the only true Christianity.

The conservatives still controlled the eastern and southern counties, and some of the central—more than half of the representatives. This ascendency in 1784 was partially the result of traditional influence, but was still more the rule of merit. Men were returned to the house of delegates less because of wealth and position than because of education and fitness. The demagogue was as yet comparatively unknown.

The system of representation by counties instead of by population gave the conservatives an advantage, for the small eastern counties outnumbered the larger midland and western counties. The Cavalier element could thus count upon a more than proportional influence in the Legislature. The conservative reaction in 1784 included in its sphere of influence all of Virginia east of the mountains; and the influence was strong enough to create the feeling that the social and political power behind the movement was paramount and could not be successfully disputed. For this reason opposition to the assessment was silenced in eastern Virginia. No protests against it came from this section, although the question had been agitated from May to October, and the Presbyterian clergy contented themselves with an attempt to liberalize as much as possible the inevitable policy of the state. This was the attitude of the majority, at least; there may have been individuals among the Presbyterians who believed that the assessment would be a benefit and consequently were willing to accept it.

On November 17, the house again went into the committee of the whole on the religious question.[370] Resolutions were reported from the committee: "That so much of the petition of the Presbytery of Hanover, and of the Baptist association, as prays that the laws regulating the celebration of marriage, and relating to the construction of the vestries, may be altered, is reasonable" and: "That acts ought to pass for the incorporation of all societies of the christian religion, which may apply for the same."

[370] Journal, p. 27.

The first resolution passed. The second resolution was then put to the house and passed by a vote of 62 to 23.

The ayes were John Cropper, of Accomac; Samuel Shewin, of Amelia; Nicholas Cabell and William Meredith, of Amherst; Robert Clarke, of Bedford; Archibald Stuart and George Hancock, of Botetourt; Thomas Edmunds, of Brunswick; John Ward, of Campbell; Samuel Hawes, of Caroline; Jacob Morton and Thomas Collier, of Charlotte; Bernard Markham, of Chesterfield; Edward Carrington and Carter Henry Harrison, of Cumberland; William Watkins and Joseph Jones, of Dinwiddie; Miles King and George Wray, of Elizabeth City; Spencer Roane, of Essex; Thomas West, of Fairfax; Samuel Richardson, of Fluvanna; Thomas Smith, of Gloucester; Andrew Donnelly, of Greenbrier; Isaac Coles and John Coleman, of Halifax; Ralph Humphreys, of Hampshire; Garland Anderson, of Hanover; Patrick Henry, of Henry; John S. Wills, of Isle of Wight; Philip Barbour, of Jefferson; Joseph Jones, of King George; Benjamin Temple, of King William; John Heath, of Lancaster; Richard Bland Lee, of Loudoun; William Anderson, of Louisa; George Slaughter, of Lincoln; Francis Corbin and William Curtis, of Middlesex; Willis Riddick, of Nansemond; William Armistead, of New Kent; John Kearnes and Daniel Sandford, of Norfolk; Littleton Eyre and Bennet Tomkins, of Northampton; Thomas Gaskins and John Thornton, of Northumberland; Benjamin Lankford and William Dix, of Pittsylvania; John Clarke, of Prince Edward; Edmund Bland Lee, of Prince George; John Fauntleroy, of Richmond; Albridgton Jones, of Southampton; Nathaniel Nelson, of York; Thomas Matthews, of Norfolk City; Richard Lee, of Westmoreland; Bailey Washington and William Brent, of Stafford; Carter Bassett Harrison and John Allen, of Surry; and John Howell Briggs, of Sussex.

The handful in the negative were Wilson Cary Nicholas and Edward Carter, of Albemarle; Zachariah Johnston, of Augusta; John Trigg, of Bedford; Moses Hunter, of Berkeley; John Taylor, of Caroline; French Strother, of Culpeper; William Pickett, of Fauquier; Alexander White, of Frederick; George Clendennen, of Greenbrier; Nathaniel Wilkinson, of Henrico; Robert Marshall, of Isle of Wight; Benjamin Pope, of Jefferson; Anthony Street, of Lunenburg; John Breckinridge, of Montgomery; James Madison, of Orange; Gawin Hamilton and John Hopkins, of Rockingham; John Hays, of Rockbridge; John Taylor, of Southampton; Thomas Towles, of Spotsylvania; William Russell and James Montgomery, of Washington. A number of those who voted against the assessment resolution voted for incorporation. They were Robert Clarke, Archibald Stuart, George Hancock, John Ward, Samuel Hawes, Jacob Morton, Spencer Roane, Samuel Richardson, Ralph Humphreys, Richard Bland Lee, Nathaniel Nelson and Thomas Matthews.

The counties which remained opposed to incorporation after this defection were Albemarle, Augusta, Bedford (one delegate), Caroline, Culpeper, Fauquier, Frederick, Greenbrier, Henrico, Isle of Wight (one delegate), Jefferson, Lunenburg, Montgomery, Orange, Rockingham, Rockbridge, Southampton, Spotsylvania and Washington. John Taylor, of Caroline, was the only eastern delegate who voted against incorporation. The west, including Archibald Stuart, contributed a number of votes for incorporation; indeed the measure met with the favor of a great majority of delegates.

Committees were also appointed to draw up bills providing for changes in the marriage and vestry acts, and for the incorporation of religious bodies. The first committee was composed of Thomas Matthews, of Norfolk; Joseph Jones, of King George; Francis Corbin, of Middlesex; John Howell Briggs, of Sussex; William Brent, of Stafford; Carter Henry Harrison, Patrick Henry and James Madison, most of them conservatives. Carter Henry Harrison, Patrick Henry, Thomas Smith, William Anderson and Henry Tazewell, (all conservatives), were appointed to draw up the incorporation bill[371] Patrick Henry and his supporters were thus in complete control of the committees and might introduce such measures as they saw fit.

On the same day, November 17, an event came to pass which proved in the end to be the undoing of the conservatives. This was the election of Patrick Henry as governor—a veritable god-send to Madison and the progressives. It would be interesting to know what induced Henry to give up his position as the dominating force in the house (a position of the greatest power) to accept an office more honorable than influential and one which he had held before. He left the house at a moment when he had succeeded in gaining complete control, when it would have been possible for him to put through both the assessment and incorporation; and so gave his astute rival, Madison, an opportunity to defeat his work. Shortly after his election, Henry went home, leaving no man to take his place.

It may be that in going away Henry felt that he was no longer needed, that the conservatives were safely in control. The majority for the incorporation resolution was large enough to warrant this belief. But the incorporation policy as outlined in the previous bill did not pass unopposed. On November 18, the Presbyterian commissioners, John Blair Smith and John Todd, restated their views on the subject in a paper presented to the house.[372] They feared a misapprehension of the Presbyterian petition as relating to incorporation. "The Presbytery," they said, "suppose that the only incorporation which Government is adequate to, is of a civil nature, by which Societies in a collective capacity may hold property for any lawful purpose—and in this view to incorporate clergymen exclusively of the religious communities whom they serve would be in their opinion an unequal, impolitic and dangerous measure. As to the Incorporation of any order of men, or any religious Society by the State under the express idea of conveying to them any powers of Church Government, the Presbytery absolutely protest against it as inconsistent with the proper object of Legislation, and an unnecessary and dangerous measure. Unnecessary because all ministers by virtue of their office have an inherent right to meet and consult upon spiritual and ecclesiastical matters, when they please, provided they do not disturb the State. And dangerous because it would be to acknowledge the State as the indulgent parent of any class of citizens, whose consciences would permit them to become obedient children in spirituals; while others who should refuse submission in this respect, tho equally good citizens, might be treated with a partial coldness which would be undeserved." Smith from the first had opposed incorporation according to the plan proposed in May, 1784, and had stated his views clearly and forcibly on several occasions. Incorporation in a purely civil sense was not objected

[371] Journal, p. 27.
[372] Journal, p. 29.

to, but incorporation as giving the clergy of the old established church the right of property in the glebes and making them a distinct corporate body awoke the Presbyterian opposition.

Nothing was said of assessment. A majority of the people of the State apparently favored it, and the bill which should make it a law was being prepared. But assessment was destined to meet with opposition, and the first protest against it came from the west. On November 18, a petition was brought into the house from Rockingham county "in opposition to the scheme of a general assessment for the support of religion."[373] This paper reads as follows: "To the Honourable the Speaker and house of Delegates now Sitting The Petition of Sundry of the Inhabitants of Rockingham County—Sheweth—That while we pay the greatest Deference to so venerable a Body we may be permitted Submissively to say it is our Humble Opinions that any Majestrait or Legislative Body that takes upon themselves the power of Governing Religion by human Laws Assumes a power that never was committed to them by God nor can be by Man for the Confirmation of which Opinion we shall Cite no less authority than the Great Mr. Lock who says 'that the whole jurisdiction of the Majestrait reaches only to civil Concernments and that all civil power Right and Dominion is bounded and confined to the only care of promoting these things' which is so Pertinent that we need not Expatiate on it Onely say that if you can do any thing in Religion by human Laws you can do every thing if you can this year take five Dollars from me and give it to a Minister of any Denomination you may next year by the same Rule take Fifty or what not and give it to one of another or to them of all other Denominations—We think that where ever Religious Establishments hath taken place it hath been attended with Pernicious Consequences for Instance we shall go no further than New England for no sooner was their Religion Established their Ministers ample provided for than Fining Imprisoning Whipping Banishing, &c: Ensued part of which oppressions Continued untill as late as the year 1773 when Several Men were Imprisoned for Ministerial Tax about which time Sundry of their Ministers who had an opportunity to see the Consequence of such laws and practices appeared against them said to Connecticut Legislators. "The Affairs of the State are the proper province of civil Rulers as to the Church of Christ be content to let it stand on its own proper Gospel foundation Regulated by its own Laws and Guarded by its own Sanctions—and tho' she may appear weak and Feeble and Ready to fall yet the Interposition of worldly power to Establish her and civel Policy to Defend her will only jostle her foundations and sink her the Lower: To which we would add that it is certain Christianity was first planted and was propogated through the World for three hundred years by truth and love without and often against the use of Secular force can then the power thereof be more plainly denied in any way than by saying (as some does) that it would soon fail if not supported by Tax and Compulsion. For a further proof (if necessary) of its not failing without such human Support—Consider the State of Rhood Island which proved an Asylum for tne Distressed and Banished—The State of Pensilvania both of them hath been left intirely free in Religion even since their first planting one One hundred and forty the other one hundred years and the numerous

---

[373] Journal, p. 29.

Inhabitants in the Town of Boston hath enjoyed a like freedom these Ninty years last past. Now we would ask is Religion Lost in any of those places or whether there is not as much of it there as where thought to be well Guarded by human Laws we believe there is and that there are proofs enough to Shew that this Liberty hath greatly Contributed to their Wellfare both Civil and Religious and sure we are that there hath not appeared any thing amongst them more Contrary to the Spirit of true Christianity than what is before Related. We Beg Leave to Remark the Inequality of such Tax for considering peoples diferent Situations it can be but forcing one Mans Money from him and giving it for the Advantage or supposed Advantage of another and in which it is Impossible for himself to Share which is a Grievance we too long laboured under—Again we think it would Infringe upon what ought to be held most Sacred that is our Bill of Rights.

"Now if as above the power of Civil Government relates onely to Mens Civil Interests If whereever it hath been attended with pernicious Consequences If Christianity was first planted and propagated through the World for three Hundred years without and often against the Use of Secular force and that is plainly denying the power thereof to say it would soon fail if not supported by Tax and Compulsion If leaving States Intirely free in Religion hath Contributed to their Wellfare both Civil and Religious If a General sess to support Ministers would be Inequal therefore a Grievance And if it would Infringe on our Bill of Rights We humbly Beg that your Honourable house would take it into your Serious Consideration and leave us (as we have the Greatest Expectation you will that is) Intirely free in Religion or rather by a Law Establish us in the freedom we have Enjoy'd for some years past which Right the South Carolina Legislators (to their lasting Honor) hath confirm'd their Constituents in several years ago—As the original Design of Vestrys is now Ceas'd we desire that our Vestry may be Disolved and Overseers of the poor chosen in their Stead."[374]

This paper objected to assessment as a tax, and maintained the dissenter argument that religion can be supported without the interposition of the state.

---

[374] Signed by Silas Hart, Thos. Fulton, Henery Black, John Crawford, Isaac Crawford, James Crawford, Thomas King, Benjamin Garvin, William Hoghead, John Smith, Jas. Ramsey, William Smith, Ben Smith, John Alford, Ralph Lofftus, John Denison, Edward Wealden, Stephen Hansberger, John Divir, Joseph Smith, Robt. Harrison, Saml. Anderson, James Brown, Isiah Shipman, John Shipman, Isaac Henkle, John Edde, James Coohoon, Charles Muir, Christian Huyer, John Hemphill, Wm. Cravens, Jehen Yuun, Henry Henry, William Lane, John Guin, David Ralston, George Boswell, John Rash, Robert Davies, John Malcom, John Black, Joseph Douglass, William Hind, Uriah Gaston, John Huston, Geo. Huston, Bethuel Hering, David Taylor, Nathaniel Harrison, Henry Sellers, John Boyd, George Smith, Andrew Bogan, David Laird, James Laird, Thomas Care, Elyah Hooke, John Lingerfelt, John Hopkins, Jr., Derby Rogin, John Malcom, Felix Sheltman, Robt. Gregg, Charles Calichan, —— Snitz, Jacob Snitz, James Ralston, Andrew Erwin, Francis Stewart, Ellet Rugherford, John Craig, Daniel Harshman, William Hord, George Noull, Henry Kyzer, John Kite, David Berry, Nehemiah Harrison, John Miller, John Rice, Stephen Coonrod, Gasper Hanes, William Crup, Stepn. Eastin, William Devier, David Denison, Silas Hart, William Smith, John Chism, George Percy, Thomas Denison, Jas. Devier, John Runyon, George Doup, Ephriam Hopkins, Danl. Harrison, Hon. Shipman, Ezekikiel Harrison, John Reeves, Charles Donnely, John Harrison, Hugh Donaghe, William Bain, James Bruster, John Phearis, Samuel Gay, William Suntz, John Davies, Aram Bibb, Christian Kuns, Michel Kips, John Bane, Jesse Gum, John Wayt, Wm. Gilbert, John Henry, Robt. Harrison, Edward Collins, Matthew Myers, William Cravun, Jere Cravun, John Young, Edward Shanklin, Hugh Yum, Thomas Ceed, John Pickens, Richard Dictum, Randle Guin, Robert Craven, John Dicky, Peter Vanpalt, Isaac Keizer,

On December 1, another petition in opposition to assessment came in from Rockbridge.[375] It stated: "That your Memorialists hoped after the happy termination of a long and dangerous War all denominations of Christians in this State would have enjoyed equal Privileges both religious and civil free from the most remote attempt of any one Sect to gain legal advantages in distinction from the Rest—But to our great surprize before the wounds we received in our Country's Cause had ceased to bleed or the Arms with which we gained our Liberties began to rust The Episcopal Clergy come in and pray for distinctions incompatible with that political Equality which is the indoubted Privilege of every Christian in the Federal Union as the reward of the common blood and Treasure so freely spent by all—That every obstacle should be removed and every vestment taken of which may obstruct any Church in the exercise of their Religion is highly reasonable—But we hope the honourable House understand the objects of human Legislation and the design of civil Government too well to become the Spiritual Head or Source of influences to any Church—We hope they are two firmly atached to the common Peace and happiness of the State to create any such invidious distinctions which must be the Source of endless jealousies and discontent. "We have been also informed that it is in contemplation to have a Law passed this Session of Assembly to establish a general Tax for the Support of the Ministers of the Gospel of all Denominations, with this reserve that each Man may say to whom his quota shall be given—This scheme should it take place is the best calculated to destroy Religion that perhaps could be devised and much more dangerous than the establishment of any one Sect for whilst that Sect was corrupted by being independent of the will of the particular Societies or Congregations where they officiated for their Support the rest would remain pure or at least of Good Morals—But by a general tax all will be rendered so independant of the will of the particular Societies for their Support that all will be infected with the Common contagion and we shall be more likely to have the State swarming with Fools, Sots and Gamblers than with a Sober Sensible and Exemplary Clergy—Let the Ministers of the Gospel of all denominations enjoy the Privileges common to every good Citizen protect them in their religious exercises in the Persons Property and Contracts and that we humbly conceive is all they are entitled to and all a Legislature has power to grant. We are extreamly sorry to find our most essential Rights (after all the blood and treasure expended) tottering and uncertain and they still must be so whilst they have no better basis to rest upon than our present Constitution which at best we Consider but a temporary expedient formed and introduced without proper authority and from the Circumstances then existing made a compliance necessary. But as these Circumstances are now removed We pray the Honourable House (not in their Legislative capacity but as a respectable ba[n]d of Citizens) to call upon the People at large to choose a Convention for the express purpose of

---

Roger Dye, John Hicks, Danl. Denison, William Stephenson, Thomas McDowell, Michael Wullan, John Dyer, Thomas Gordon, Thos. Gordon Jun., Samuel Erwin, Thomas Scott, Philip Mayer, Joseph Noll. Jno. Robinson, Matthias Lar, James Hinton, Saml. Miller, Alexr. Muller, Ezekiel Miller, William Alford, Joseph Henton, John Hyde, and a number of other names in German writing.

[375] Journal, p. 29.

forming a Constitution that may define and secure the valuable Rights of the Citizens to them and their Posterity."[376]

It will be seen that in this paper assessment is mentioned as but a part of the complaint; the petition is a general indictment. The efforts of the Episcopal clergy to obtain an act of incorporation are "distinctions incompatible with political Equality." A general assessment is worse than the establishment of a single sect because its power of corruption is great. The occasion for the rise of such schemes lies in the nature of the constitution, which leaves "essential Rights * * * tottering and uncertain." The remedy is, of course, a new constitution.

Madison spoke of the Rockingham and Rockbridge petitions as the expressions of Presbyterian laymen. This statement is true to the extent that as far as religion went a majority of the petitioners were Presbyterians. But the petitions were written less from a religious than a political standpoint. They are primarily the protests of westerners against the conservative religio-political programme. The west had always been democratic and the Revolution was the triumph of its long-held opinions. As a matter of fact the Revolution had not gone far enough for the "back country," and at the end of the war appeals began to be made to the Legislature for a more liberal constitution than the constitution of 1776, which the west had never liked. Madison gave his weight to this agitation in the spring session of 1784,[377] but the conservative influence proved too strong. Agitation for a new constitution died down upon this defeat, but revived on a large scale a decade later, was renewed after the War of 1812, and finally triumphed in 1829, when a convention was called.

Men dissatisfied with the progress of events, harassed by the existing financial system, and anxious for a revision of the constitution so as to obtain for their section a larger representation, were not likely to take kindly to the eastern scheme for a new religious establishment, with its social and political influences, a plan devised for the purpose of strengthening the conservative power. The democratic west was jealous, rather on political than on sectional grounds, of a movement intended to check the liberty which had grown out of the Revolution and which seemed likely to partially reproduce the ante-bellum conditions. And largely on the rock of western opposition the assessment split, for the western delegates opposed it from the beginning, and in alliance with a part of the piedmont and southern representatives, succeeded in mustering a majority on the final vote in 1784.

But no other part of the State showed signs of moving. These two western protests against assessment were not followed by others. Indeed at the time the Rockbridge and Rockingham petitioners seemed isolated. On November 20, petitions from Lunenburg, Mecklenburg and Amelia

---

[376] Signed by John Davis, ——— Ligget, John Houston, Francis Fullin, John Kirkpatrick, William Wilson, John Wilson, William Davidson, Hugh Kirkpatrick, Thomas Crawford, William Burton, William Moore, William Login, James Moore, James Mall, James McNabb, James Hamilton, Thos. Wilson, John Link, David Leach, James Davis, James Harris, Edward Erwin, Moses Cunningham, Samuel Wilson, Patrick Vance, Sam Hougton, Saml. Ross, Henry Reed, ——— Reed, James Lyle. Joseph Lyle, Joseph Alexander, Alexr. Campbell, Duncn. Campbell, Go. Shreader, Jno. Finley, David Hay, John M. Kee, Thomas Harrison, Nathaniel Hall, John Thompson, Chas. Hays, John Caruthers, William Rumsay, John Galbraith.

[377] Rives, I, 555.

favoring assessment came into the house.[378] They employed the same arguments as the preceding petitions for assessment. Religion had been declining for years past, partly because of the war, "but chiefly by its not being duly aided and patronized by the civil Power." Religion is necessary for man's proper conduct in society, and for this reason "every Man should be obliged to contribute as well to the Support of Religion, as that of Civil Government; nor has he any Reason to complain of this, as an Encroachment upon his religious Liberty, if he is permitted to worship God according to the Dictates of his Conscience, and to join with & support that Church or Minister he prefers." The memorial furthermore asked for the incorporation of the Episcopal church in order to secure to it the property of the establishment and freedom of action.[379]

On December 1, similar petitions were presented from Dinwiddie and Surry. "We being fully pursuaded," reads the Dinwiddie paper, "that Religion and the sacred Institutions thereof, would have more Influence, and command a greater Respect, under the Smiles, & Support of Government, than they now have to, lay before you this our earnest Petition that Christianity may be, by a Law, made and declared to be, the established Religion of this Country."

The Surry memorial declared that "It is with the most heartfelt concern that your Memorialists see the countenance of the civil power wholly withdrawn from religion, and Mankind left without the smallest coercion to contribute to its support." Religion conduces to prosperity and the preservation of society. Consequently, "whatever is to conduce equally to the advantage of all, should be borne equally by all * * * The Experience of all governments has evinced that the compulsion of law is necessary to urge Mankind in general to a small sacrifice of private Interest for the promotion of the public good. And unless this principle is adhered to in the present instance, the worthy advocates of religion who feel its influence & see its necessity will be oppressed by a burthen which should be equally borne."

The great weight of opinion, as far as it had been expressed, was on the side of assessment. On December 2, 1784, Francis Corbin presented the bill for "establishing a provision for teachers of the christian religion."[380] The bill provided a certain tax, with rate left unfixed, upon all taxable property for the support of ministers, or teachers of the Christian religion, as they are named. Each taxpayer was given the privilege of designating the church which should receive this tax. In cases of refusal to name any

---

[378] Journal, p. 32.

[379] Signed by John Booker, Jr., Wm. Cross Craddock, Christr. Ford, Wm. Watts, Edwd. Munford, James Jenkins, Stith Hardaway, Chas. Craddock, Edwd. Booker, John Wily, Abraham Lockett, Wm. Pyson, Christopher Hudson, Marston Green, Wm. Quinn, Thomas Nash, Henry Jeter, Thomas Jeffry, Isaac Oliver, Richard Ward, Henry Buford, Matthew Wallis, Peter Lamkin, Joseph Stephens, Thos. Overstreet, Wm. Stuart, Thos. Hitower, William Wood, Robert Sneed, Robt. Foster, Joseph Wilkins, Luke Watson, Joseph Asborn, Edward Branch, Sewall Chapin, Liveston Thompson, Abraham Marshall, John Sturgis, Frans. Anderson, James Henderson, Rowlan Way, Jr., John Archer, Thos. Mitchell, Wm. Worsham, John Crawley, Joel Mottley, Jesse Woodward, Stephen Lockett, Abadiah Hendrick, Wm. Howlett, Lewellin Hudson, John Howison, Peter Ellington, Robert Hinton, John Chambers, John C. Cobbs, Daniel Stringer, John Bennett, George Belcher, Jno. Royall, Wm. Jennings, Stephen Cocke, Wm. Butler and many others.

[380] Journal, p. 51, and Virginia Historical Collections, X, 114.

church, the Legislature should apply the tax to some pious use. In its final form the bill left the taxpayer the option of giving his tax to education. The bill was read the second time on the next day and was referred to the committee of the whole.[381]

The conservatives seemed to have smooth sailing, but Madison noted a change in the house. On November 14, he had thought the bill would pass. "I think the bottom will be enlarged," he wrote, "and that a trial will be made of the practicability of the project."[382] But on November 27, he wrote as follows: "You, will have heard of the vote in favor of the Genl. Assesst. The bill is not yet brought in & I question whether it will, or if so whether it will pass.[383] A few days later, on December 4, his opinion was still stronger. "The bill for the Religious Asst. was reported yesterday and will be taken up in a Ccme. of the whole next week. Its friends are much disheartened at the loss of Mr. Henry. Its fate is I think very uncertain."[384]

The bill "to amend the several acts, concerning marriages," was brought into the house on December 10.[385] This bill, which placed the ministers of all denominations on an equal footing, formed, together with the incorporation bill and the bill for the dissolution of the vestries, the measures necessary to complete the disestablishment of the Anglican church. The bill "for incorporating the Protestant Episcopal Church"[386] was presented by Carter Henry Harrison. It gave the ministers and vestries of the respective parishes a title to the churches, glebes and other property, and outlined a method for the election of vestrymen, who were restricted to membership in the Episcopal church. Vestries were required to make an inventory of property in their charge to the county courts once in three years. Cases in which the revenue of parishes exceeded £800 were to be referred to the Assembly. All former laws in regard to the church were repealed and it was left to regulate its own ccncerns, subject to the provision that the regulation should be ccnducted in conventions consisting of two delegates from each parish, "whereof the minister shall always be one." The convention was empowered to remove unworthy ministers, and vestries were authorized to collect arrearages of the poor levies.[387] This bill when it became an act may be said to have completed disestablishment, because the title to ecclesiastical prcperty was vested in the church authorities, and those authorities were empowered to regulate church affairs without legislative interference. And yet at the same time, the civil authority maintained a certain hold on the church in requiring the making of reports to the courts, and in enacting certain rules for the conduct of external affairs. By the terms of the incorporation bill, separation of church and state was not entirely complete.

Two important bills on the religious question—for assessment and incorporation—were now before the house. The introduction of the latter bill before the settlement of the assessment question was a tactical mistake.

[381] Journal, p. 52.
[382] Madison, Works, II, 90.
[383] Madison, Works, II, 94.
[384] Madison, Works, II, 97.
[385] Journal, p. 65.
[386] Journal, p. 65.
[387] Hening, XI, 532.

It was a mistake to bring in a bill for the peculiar benefit of the Episcopal church when the general subject of civil support of religion was still under debate. The incorporation bill could have been drawn later, for the church was in no danger of spoliation with a conservative majority in the house. The incorporation act secured the title of the Episcopal church for a brief time, but it was premature and it alarmed the Presbyterian clergy, causing them to take a hostile attitude towards the whole conservative religious policy, and intensifying the naturally strong Baptist opposition. Yet Grigsby is probably right in his statement that since an expression of public opinion on the incorporation bill had been invited and had not condemned the bill, incorporation could hardly have been refused the Episcopal church.[388]

Only one petition—that of Hanover Presbytery—had opposed incorporation, and that had not opposed all forms of incorporation. The Presbyterians by no means conceded the right of the new Episcopal church to all the holdings of the old establishment, and, besides, they contended for a completer separation of church and state.

The committee of the whole debated the incorporation bill on December 18,[389] 20 and 21.[390] The bill passed on December 22, 1784, by a vote of 47 to 38. It will be seen that the conservative majority had greatly shrunk. In fact the opposition might have reduced the majority still further, but it was not Madison's policy to oppose incorporation at this time, and he voted for the bill. He conceded incorporation in order to defeat assessment. "The necessity of some sort of incorporation for the purpose of holding & managing the property of the church could not well be denied, nor a more harmless modification of it now obtained. A negative of the bill, too, would have doubled the eagerness and the pretexts for a much greater evil, a general Assessment, which, there is good ground to believe, was parried by this partial gratification of its warmest votaries." [391]

In the affirmative voted John Cropper and Thomas Parramore, Accomac; Samuel Sherman, John Booker, Amelia; Nicholas Cabell and William Meredith, Amherst; Bernhard Markham and Matthew Cheatham, Chesterfield; Edward Carrington and Carter Henry Harrison, Cumberland; James Pendleton, Culpeper; Joseph Jones, Dinwiddie; Miles King and George Wray, Elizabeth City; John Marshall, Fauquier; James Hubard, Gloucester; Peter Saunders, Henry; John S. Wills, Isle of Wight; Philip Barbour, Jefferson; Joseph Jones and William Thornton, King George; James Ball, Jr., Lancaster; Francis Peyton, Loudoun; William Anderson, Louisa; Samuel Goode, Mecklenburg; Francis Corbin and William Curtis, Middlesex; Willis Riddick and Godwin, Nansemond; William Armistead, New Kent; Daniel Sandford, Norfolk; Littleton Eyre, Northampton; John Thornton, Northumberland; James Madison, Orange; William Ronald, Powhatan; Edwin Ruffin, Prince George; Thomas Walke, Princess Anne; William Grayson, Prince William; Mann Page, Spotsylvania; William Brent, Stafford; Carter B. Harrison, Surry; Thomas Edmunds and John H. Briggs, Sussex; Richard Lee, Westmoreland; Nathaniel Nelson, York; and Henry Tazewell, Williamsburg.

[388] Virginia Historical Collections, X, 109.
[389] Journal, p. 75.
[390] Journal, p. 77.
[391] Madison, Works, II, 113.

102

The noes were Wilson Cary Nicholas and Edward Carter, Albemarle; Michael Bowyer and Zachariah Johnston, Augusta; John Trigg, Bedford; Moses Hunter, Berkeley; Archibald Stuart, Botetourt; John Nicholas, Buckingham; Samuel Hawes, Caroline; Jacob Morton, Charlotte; French Strother, Culpeper; Spencer Roane and William Gatewood, Essex; Alexander Henderson, Fairfax; Thomas Underwood, Goochland; George Clendennen, Greenbrier; Ralph Humphreys and Isaac Vanmeter, Hampshire; Garland Anderson, Hanover; Nathaniel Wilkinson, Henrico; Benjamin Pope, Jefferson; Richard Bland Lee, Loudoun; John Glenn, Lunenburg; Robert Sayres, Montgomery; John Kearnes, Norfolk; Charles Porter, Orange; Benjamin Lankford and William Dix, Pittsylvania; Richard Bibb and John Clark, Prince Edward; John Bowyer and John Hays, Rockbridge; Gawin Hamilton and John Hopkins, Rockingham; Isaac Zane, Shenandoah; John Taylor, Southampton; and James Montgomery, Washington.

In addition to the practically undivided western vote, the opponents of incorporation on this ballot commanded many southern and midland delegates, with a few easterners. The smallness of the majority may have acted as a warning to the conservatives to act quickly. It was evident that when the southern and midland delegates, now wavering between the east and the west and inclining to the latter, should array themselves with it, the game would be up. Henry's absence was greatly felt in this crisis, for he was especially influential with the delegates from the middle counties and the southside. No other man of the conservative party carried the same weight in the midland region, and the tendency to democracy naturally allied the central delegates with the mountaineers.

Promptly upon the passage of the incorporation act, the conservative leaders brought the assessment bill before the house. The debate extended from December 22 to December 23, and amendments were added. "In a committee of the whole it was determined by a majority of 7 or 8 that the word "Xn" should be exchanged for the word "Religious." On the report to the house the pathetic zeal of the late Governor Harrison gained a like majority for reinstating discrimination."[392] On December 23, the bill was engrossed by the close vote of 44 to 42.[393]

The engrossed bill came up for its third reading the next day, December 24. A motion was made to defer the reading "until the fourth Thursday of November next," that is, until the next session of the Assembly. The motion passed 45 to 38, by almost the same vote as upon incorporation, but reversed. The counties in the affirmative were Albemarle, Amelia, Amherst, Augusta, Bedford, Berkeley, Botetourt, Buckingham, Caroline, Charlotte, Culpeper, Essex, Fauquier, Greenbrier, Hampshire, Henrico, Jefferson, Loudoun, Lunenburg, Montgomery, Norfolk, Orange, Pittsylvania, Powhatan, Rockbridge, Shenandoah, Southampton, Spotsylvania, Stafford, Sussex, Washington and Norfolk Borough.

The counties in the negative were Accomac, Charles City, Chesterfield, Cumberland, Culpeper, Dinwiddie, Elizabeth City, Fairfax, Fauquier, Gloucester, Hanover, Isle of Wight, Jefferson, King George, Lancaster, Loudoun, Louisa, Middlesex, Nansemond, Norfolk, Northampton, Northumberland,

---

[392] Madison, Works, II, 114.
[393] Madison, Works, II, 99.

Prince Edward, Prince George, Princess Anne, Surry, Westmoreland, York and Williamsburg.

This vote shows that delegates who had not voted before in the religious question voted against assessment. In a word, the antis presented their full strength, won a few conservative votes and carried the day against their wavering opponents.

Following this vote, a resolution passed by a small majority "That the engrossed bill," establishing a provision for teachers of the Christian religion, "together with the names of the ayes and noes, on the question of postponing the third reading of the said bill to the fourth Thursday in November next, be published in hand-bills, and twelve copies thereof delivered to each member of the General Assembly, to be distributed to their respective counties; and that the people thereof be requested to signify their opinion respecting the adoption of such a bill, to the next session of Assembly."[394]

The postponement of the third reading of the assessment bill was a great victory for Madison. It was a victory of democratic policies over conservative, and of the progressives who wished to continue the work of the Revolution. But it was not a final triumph. Sentiment in the people at large was as yet unknown, and was supposed to rather favor assessment. The weight of petitions supported this conclusion.

It was therefore necessary for the progressive leaders in the house to begin what is called a campaign of education. A majority of the delegates in the house personally favored assessment. The western delegates almost unanimously opposed it, because the west was poor, new and radical, and as far as religion went, chiefly Presbyterian. A large element in the State, discontented with the weight of the existing taxes, would oppose the imposition of a new tax for any purpose. But there was a chance that the people might view the religious controversy apathetically, and consequently that the conservatives might be able to carry the day.

But the people were only seemingly indifferent, in spite of the fact that few anti-assessment petitions had been presented. "The only proceeding of the late Session of Assembly," Madison wrote to Monroe on April 12, 1785, "which makes a noise thro' the Country is that which relates to a Genl. Assessmt. The Episcopal people are generally for it, tho' I think the zeal of some of them has cooled. The laity of the other sects are equally unanimous on the other side. So are all the Clergy except the Presbyterians who seem as ready to set up an establishment which is to take them in as they were to pull down that which shut them out."[395] On April 27, he wrote that "The Bill for a Genl. Assesst. has produced some fermentation below the Mountains & a violent one beyond them. The contest at the next Session on this question will be a warm & precarious one."[396] Madison seems to have still doubted the outcome of the struggle. But already there was a drift against assessment. The next day Madison informed Monroe that "Our elections as far as I hear are likely to produce a great proportion of new members. In some counties they are influenced by the Bill for a Genl. Assesst. In Culpeper Mr. Pendleton a worthy man & acceptable in his

[394] Madison, Works, II, 113; Journal, p. 82.
[395] Madison, Works, II, 131.
[396] Madison, Works, II, 137.

general character to the people was laid aside in consequence of his vote for the Bill, in favor of an Adversary to it."[397] And again on May 29th, "But the adversaries to the assesst. begin to think the prospect here flattering to their wishes. The printed Bill has excited great discussion and is likely to prove the sense of the Comunity to be in favor of the liberty now enjoyed. I have heard of several Counties where the late representatives have been laid aside for voting for the Bill, and not a single one where the reverse has happened. The Presbyterian Clergy too who were in general friends to the scheme, are already in another tone, either compelled by the laity of that sect, or alarmed at the probability of further interference of the Legislature, if they once begin to dictate in matters of Religion."[398] Madison's spirit rose with time, as evidences came to him of a growing spirit of hostility to the assessment. "A very warm opposition will be made to this innovation," he wrote Monroe on June 21st, "by the people of the middle and back Counties, particularly the latter. They do not scruple to declare it an alarming usurpation on their fundamental rights and that tho' the Genl Assembly should give it the form, they will not give it the validity of a law." And he added on his own account, "If there be any limitation to the power of the Legislature, particularly if this limitation is to be sought in our Declaration of Rights or Form of Government, I own the Bill appears to me to warrant this language of the people." [399]

In July, 1785, Madison was drawn into a campaign which engaged his deepest interest. The necessity of a hostile criticism of the published assessment bill impressed itself upon the democratic leaders. George Nicholas, brother of Wilson Cary Nicholas, was the most insistent of these, and he, together with George Mason,[400] persuaded Madison to undertake the task. Nicholas wrote to Madison, on April 22, 1785, that "my brother informs me that he conversed with you on the propriety of remonstrating against certain measures of the last session of Assembly and that you seemed to think it would be best that the counties opposed to the measure should be silent. I fear this would be construed into an assent especially to the law for establishing a certain provision for the clergy, for as the Assembly only postponed the passing of it that they might know whether it was disagreeable to the people, I think they may justly conclude that all are for it who do not say to the contrary. A majority of the counties are in favor of the measure, but a great majority of the people against it, but if this majority should not appear by petition the fact will be denied. Another reason why all should petition is that some will certainly do it and those who support the bills will insist that those who petition are all the opposition. Would it not add greatly to the weight of the petition if they all hold the same language? by discovering an exact uniformity of sentiment in a majority of the country it would certainly deter the majority of the assembly from proceeding. I have been through a considerable part of the country and I am well assured that it would be impossible to carry such laws into execution and that the attempt would bring about a revolution. If you think

[397] Madison, Works, II, 142.
[398] Madison, Works, II, 145.
[399] Madison, Works, II, 146.
[400] Rowland's Mason, II, 87.

with me that it will be proper to say something to the Assembly, will you commit it to paper. I risk this because I know you are most capable of doing it properly and because it will be most likely to be generally adopted. I can get it sent to Amherst Buckingham Albemarle Fluvanna Augusta Botetourt Rock Bridge and Rockingham and have no doubt that Bedford and the counties Southward of it will readily join in the measure. I will also send it to Frederick and Berkeley and if it goes from your county to Fauquier Culpeper and Loudoun it will be adopted by the most populous part of the country." [401]

In accordance with Nicholas's suggestion, Madison wrote his "Memorial and Remonstrance." [402] This famous paper is an elaborate argument on the relation of religion to the state. It asserts in the loftiest spirit of freedom that religion is exempt from the cognizance of both society and the state. The principle of assessment was wrong; if it were lawful to establish Christianity as a state religion it would be lawful to establish a single sect, and if it were lawful to impose a small tax for religion, the admission would pave the way for oppressive levies. The assessment was not necessary for the support of the churches, which could stand on their own feet. The policy of ecclesiastical taxation would keep out foreigners. The interference of law in religion produced evil effects only, and an attempt to enforce by legal sanction a policy obnoxious to the majority of citizens would tend to enervate the laws and create a spirit of evasion. Madison put forth in this article for the benefit of the people of Virginia the arguments he had already used effectively in the Assembly. Several editions of the Remonstrance were printed (one by the Phenix Press of Alexandria) and copies were sowed broadcast. George Nicholas sent out the Remonstrance in July through the middle and western counties, [403] and it met with general approval. "One hundred and fifty of our most respectable freeholders," Nicholas wrote Madison, "signed it in a day." [404] The Remonstrance was printed in the Virginia Gazette, [405] and in every way the agitation was actively furthered. Mason sent the Remonstrance to his friends, among them George Washington. "As the principles it avows," he wrote, "entirely accord with my sentiments on the subject (which is a very important one), I have been at the charge of printing several copies to disperse in the different parts of the country. . . . If upon consideration, you approve the arguments and the principles upon which they are founded, your signature will both give the Remonstrance weight, and do it honor." [406] Washington replied: "Although no man's sentiments are more opposed to any kind of restraint upon religious principles than mine are, yet I must confess, that I am not amongst the number of those, who are so much alarmed at the thoughts of making people pay towards the support of that which they profess. . . . As the matter now stands, I wish an assessment had never been agitated, and as it has gone so far, that the bill could die an easy death; because I think it will be productive of more quiet to the State,

---

[401] Madison, Works, II, 183, note.
[402] Madison, Works, II, 183.
[403] Madison, Works, II, 184.
[404] Letters to Madison, V, xiv. MS., Library of Congress.
[405] July 30, 1785.
[406] Rowland's Mason, II, 88.

than by enacting it into a law, which in my opinion would be impolitic admitting there is a decided majority for it, to the disquiet of a respectable minority." [407]

Madison informed Edmund Randolph late in July that subscriptions to the Remonstrance were on foot in various counties and would be extended to others. He wrote Jefferson, on August 20th, that the opposition to the assessment was gaining ground and that at the instance of some of its adversaries he had written the Remonstrance. "It has been sent thro' the medium of confidential persons in a number of the upper Counties, and I am told will be pretty extensively signed." [408]

George Nicholas was the chief agent in the agitation which aroused middle and western Virginia and was destined to draw forth such an expression of public opinion as the state had never seen before. Nicholas was one of the ablest politicians Virginia evér produced. He served a number of terms in the Assembly and became an influential member. He was one of the chief powers in the convention of 1788, and apparently did as much as any other man to secure the ratification of the United States Constitution. "Clear as was the logic, convincing as were the ample and apt illustrations of Madison," Grigsby declares, "their effect was equalled, probably surpassed, by the exhibitions of Nicholas." [409] After the convention, Nicholas made the mistake of moving to Kentucky, where he was indeed prominent in local affairs, but where he was far from political centers. Yet he was made for a great career and he would no doubt have risen to a high place upon the national triumph of the Democratic party, if an untimely death had not taken him.

More important probably than the efforts even of Madison and Nicholas and their friends was the decision of the evangelical churches to oppose the assessment. The Presbyterians took action early in 1785. The memorial of October, 1784, had produced dissatisfaction amongst the Presbyterian laity, and when Hanover Presbytery met at Bethel on May 29, 1785, the Augusta congregation requested an explanation of the word "liberal," as used in the passage relating to assessment, and also the Presbytery's motive in sending the petition to the Assembly. [410] Moses Hoge and Samuel Carrick were directed to prepare an answer to the Augusta inquiry. The question was then put whether the Presbytery approved of any kind of assessment, and the vote was unanimously in the negative. Whatever may have been the private opinions of any members of the Presbytery, Fcote said, or the influence of Patrick Henry, Presbytery declared against all assessments. [411] A general convention of the Presbyterian church was arranged to meet at Bethel, Augusta county, on August 10, 1785.

Energetic efforts were made to secure a full attendance of delegates, and an advertisement was printed in the Virginia Gazette [412] requesting every church in the State to send representatives. The convention, when it

---

[407] Rowland's Mason, II, 89.
[408] Madison, Works, II, 163.
[409] Virginia Historical Collections, X, 286.
[410] Foote, I, 341.
[411] Foote, I, 341.
[412] June 4, 1785, et seq.

met, adopted a paper drawn up by William Graham, rector of Liberty Hall Academy. It differed considerably from the memorial of the previous autumn. All connection between church and state was strongly condemned, and the argument followed Madison's Remonstrance in part. The assertion of the divine nature of Christianity, and its primitive independence of the state and purity, soon to be repeated in a hundred petitions, was employed. An objection to assessment was found in the fact that the bill provided for no religion but Christianity, excluding Jews and Mohammedans. The assertion, however, that the bill "unjustly subjects men who may be good citizens, but who have not embraced our common faith, to the hardship of supporting a system they have not as yet believed the truth of, and deprives them of their property, for what they do not suppose to be of importance to them," is an exaggeration. The clause of the bill permitting the taxpayer to assign his tax to public education was expressly designed to meet this objection. The Bethel declaration more pertinently declared that the exclusion of any religion from the assessment plan changed its principle, and made what should have been a state support of morality for the benefit of society a discriminating religious measure. The act incorporating the Episcopal church was condemned in such language as shows that the incorporation had made impossible any unity of action between the Episcopal and Presbyterian churches.[413]

The possibility of such a union had always been remote, and it had now entirely passed away. Madison wrote in a rather cynical tone:

"The Presbyterian clergy, have at length espoused the side of the opposition, being moved either by a fear of their laity or a jealousy of the episcopalians. The mutual hatred of these sects has been much inflamed by the late Act incorporating the latter. I am far from being sorry for it, as a coalition between them could alone endanger our religious rights, and a tendency to such an event had been suspected." [414]

The Baptists took action at the same time. The general committee met at Dupuy's meeting-house, Powhatan, on August 13, 1785. Reuben Ford reported that he had presented the committee's memorial against the marriage and vestry laws and that the marriage act had been satisfactorily amended. Assessment was condemned by the committee,[415] and those counties which had not yet prepared petitions against it were urged to do so. Religion was of a divine nature and had no need of legal support. A memorial was drawn up and Reuben Ford was assigned the duty of carrying it to the Assembly.[416] This paper reiterated the statement that religion was a thing apart from the concerns of the state. The "Church of Christ 'is not of this world,'" from which it follows that "they cannot see on what defensible principles, the Sheriffs, County Courts and public Treasury are all to be employed in the management of money levied for the express purpose of supporting Teachers of the Christian Religion." This was a good hit at one of the objectionable features of the tax. Furthermore, it was sinful to "compel men to furnish contributions of money to support that Religion which

[413] Foote, I, 342.
[414] Madison, Works, II, 163.
[415] Semple, 95.
[416] Semple, 96, and James, 138.

they disbelieve and abhor." Here again, as in the Bethel memorial, the educational alternative of the assessment bill was ignored.

The Baptist petition enlarged upon the argument that Christianity was most powerful in its primitive and unsupported condition. "The Proud Greeks, the Stubborn Jews and the wild Barbarians were made to bow to the Sceptre of Gospel Grace." Establishments hinder rather than help Christianity. "Legislature will have sufficiently done its part in favour of Christianity when adequate provision is made for supporting those Laws of Mcrality, which are necessary for private and public happiness and of which it seems more properly the Guardian than of the peculiarities of the Christian Church."

The Baptist General Association met at Orange on September 7, 1785, and also adopted a remonstrance: first, that the civil power had no right to establish a religious tax; second, that the fear that religion would die without state support is "founded neither in Scripture, on Reason, on Sound Policy; but is repugnant to each of them"; third, that as the Assembly must be the judge as to the recipients of the tax, it would determine religious principles; fourth, that the Assembly which established all sects had the power to establish one; fifth, that the incorporation of the Episcopal church was inconsistent with human freedcm; sixth, that the reservation of the ecclesiastical property was a glaring distinction; seventh, that the indulgence granted Quakers and Menonites was an "open offense." The August declaration of the Baptist church had opposed assessment; the September resolutions opposed both assessment and incorporation. The Baptists were destined to become the strongest opponents of the latter measure, and it was largely due to their efforts that the Episcopal church was deprived of the glebes and churches.

The Protestant Episcopal church held its first convention on May 18, 1785, at Richmond. It was a distinguished body. Among the clergymen present were Devereaux Jarratt, James Madison and David Griffith, and among the lay members, John Page, Archibald Cary, John Tyler, Wilson Miles Cary, George Wray, Spencer Roane, Willis Riddick, Carter Bassett Harriscn, and Nathaniel Nelson. Twenty of the seventy lay deputies were members of the Legislature.

The counties represented showed that Anglicanism survived in the east and south. Seventy parishes in fifty counties sent delegates, while only two western counties (Frederick and Berkeley) were represented. Some of the central counties and three southeastern counties were not represented. James Madison, the future bishop, was elected president. Deputies were appointed to the general convention of the church at Philadelphia.[417] The convention drew up a constitution for the Episcopal church in Virginia, and issued a general address which was, in fact, a lament. "Of what is the church now possessed! Nothing but the glebes and your affections. Since the year 1776, she hath been even without regular government, and her ministers have received but little compensation for their services. Their numbers are diminished by death and other causes, and we have as yet no resource within ourselves for a succession of ministers. Churches stand in

---

[417] Hawks, Appendix, 5.

need of repair, and there is no fund equal to the smallest want." The whole tone of the address indicated a conviction that the times were out of joint and legislative aid uncertain. Yet the members felt hope, with the Revolution in the background and with the ecclesiastical property secured to the church. The new regulations were conservative. The vestries continued to hold the right of presentation. Courts consisting of three clergymen and three laymen were established to hear complaints against ministers. Complaints should be received only from the vestry of the minister complained of. Decisions of the lower court were referred to the convention for approval.

Edmund Randolph gave Madison his impressions of the Episcopal position in a letter of July 17, 1785: "I dedicate to you, as the patron of the protestant Episcopal Church, the enclosed journal. Between friends, my experience in the last convention does not make me anxious to step forward in another. We have squeezed a little liberality from them; but at a future day they will be harder than adamant, and perhaps credulous that they possess authority." [418] Madison replied with a criticism of the Episcopal constitution: "It may be of little consequence, what tribunal is to judge of Clerical misdemeanors or how firmly the incumbent may be fastened on the parish, whilst the Vestry & people may hear & pay him or not as they like. But should a legal salary be annexed to the title, this phantom of power would be substantiated into a real monster of oppression. Indeed it appears to be so at present as far as the Glebes & donations extend." [419]

The Assembly met on October 24, 1785. The membership had not changed very greatly. Wilson Cary Nicholas, Zachariah Johnston, Archibald Stuart, John Taylor, of Caroline, John Tyler, Benjamin Harrison, Miles King, James Jones, Spencer Roane, Alexander White, Charles Mynn Thurston, Richard Bland Lee, Littleton Eyre, James Madison, Carter Braxton, Henry Lee, Arthur Lee and Meriwether Smith were among the leading members.

The committee for religion consisted of Zachariah Johnston, of Augusta, chairman; William Norvell, John Tyler, Carter Henry Harrison, William Watkins, French Strother, Wilson Cary Nicholas, Bernard Markham, Samuel Sherwin, Robert Clarke, Thomas Smith, Henry Fry, Lewis Burwell, Carter Bassett Harrison, James Madison, William Curtis, Richard Bibb, Benjamin Harrison and Parke Goodall.

As soon as the session began petitions came into the house in such numbers as had never been known before. They were chiefly in opposition to assessment. "The steps taken throughout the Country to defeat the Genl. Assessment," said Madison, "had produced all the effect that could have been wished. The table was loaded with petitions and remonstrances from all parts against the interposition of the Legislature in matters of Religion." [420]

The anti-assessment petitions show, with few exceptions, the influence of Madison's Remonstrance. That paper had been circulated with a thoroughness, amazing in consideration of the sparseness of the population, the dif-

[418] Conway's Randolph, 163.
[419] Madison's Works, II, 152.
[420] Madison's Works, II, 216

ficulty of communication and the ignorance of a large part of the population. This wide range of circulation reflects great credit upon George Nicholas' talents for political managing. Many of the petitions indeed are copies of the Remonstrance; others are paraphrases. In other petitions the changes were rung upon Madison's phrases. The Remonstrance furnished the poor people of Virginia with an able argument against a threatened restraint of liberty and an additional burden. In the strength of the sentiment worked up throughout the State against assessment, the dissenters of the conservative tidewater counties now broke away from the traditional influences of their section and contributed largely to the protesting petitions.

The most popular argument in all these papers was the assertion, repeated in different terms in the Remonstrance and in the Presbyterian and Baptist memorials, that Christianity had grown and prospered in spite of the opposition of the State. A score of petitions declare that "certain it is that the Blessed author of the Christian Religion, not only maintained and supported his gospel in the world for several Hundred Years, without the aid of Civil Power but against all the Powers of the Earth, the Excellent Purity of its Precepts and the unblamable behaviour of its Ministers made its way thro all opposition. Nor was it the Better for the church when Constantine the great, first Established Christianity by human Laws true there was rest from Persecution, but how soon was the Church Over run with Error and Immorality."

Such was the dissenters' answer to the Anglican plea that religion could not exist without State support. To the argument that the church was suffering because of the prevailing license and skepticism, the petition answered that these evils did not spring from the want of an establishement—ministers should preach by their lives. "Let their Doctrine be scriptural and their Lives upright then shall Religion, if Departed, speedily return, and Deism with its Dreadful Consequences be removed."

A Botetourt petition of November 29, 1785, founded its argument against assessment upon the civic virtues of Greece and Rome, apparently in the belief that church and state were not connected in antiquity. The petition also found a grave dilemma in assessment—that is, if all Christian sects were aided by law, regardless of doctrine, the Assembly would find itself committed to the position of supporting heterodox opinions.

The Montgomery petition of November 15, 1785, asserted that religion was not absolutely essential to good morals. "Cannot it be denied that civil laws are not sufficient? We conceive it cannot, especially where the minds of men are disposed to an Observance of what is right and an Observance of what is wrong. And we Conceive also that Ideas of right and wrong, may be derived merely from positive law, without seeking a higher original." Assessment would not tend to improve morals, unless churchgoing should be enforced at the same time, but this would be tyrannical.

The Pittsylvania petitioners of November 7th feared that the sacrifices of the Revolution were to be disregarded and that the church of England was to be re-established "contrary to all Maxims of sound Policy."

So strong was the agitation against assessment that some of its former supporters changed sides. Thus a petition from Dinwiddie declared that the subscribers "are now as decidedly opposed to a General assessment as they were formerly in favour of it. * * * They reflect that it will be thought by this Honorable House and all Rational men much more consistent with a man's honour and his conscience publickly to renounce an erroneous Sentiment than by persisting in it to produce to Religion, to himself and to his country, consequences which he will forever have cause to lament."

Even the Quakers took the field against assessment. They denied that a provision was needed for educated ministers. "Christian knowledge is Immediately derived from the great author of the Christian Religion, and is no more dependent on human Literature or Pecuniary Provisions for learned Teachers, than that the Salvation of Souls depends on Human learning and knowledge."

The petitions came from every quarter of the State and from every class—Cumberland, Rockingham, Caroline, Buckingham, Henry, Pittsylvania, Nansemond, Bedford, Richmond, Campbell, Charlotte, Goochland, Westmoreland, Essex, Culpeper, Prince Edward, Middlesex, Henrico, Hanover, Brunswick, Powhatan, Fairfax, Stafford, Lunenburg, Frederick, Dinwiddie, King and Queen, Prince George, Mecklenburg, Albemarle, Orange, Northumberland, Louisa, James City, Amelia, Montgomery, Botetourt, Rockbridge, Chesterfield, Princess Anne and other counties.

Only one church presented petitions as coming from its members and that was the Presbyterian. Consequently it is impossible to estimate the strength of the various sects from the number of signatures. Many western petitions were simple indorsements of the Bethel memorial; these came chiefly from Augusta, Frederick, Berkeley and Rockbridge, as far as the counties can be determined. A special committee was appointed to consider the Presbyterian petitions.

The whole number of subscribers to the anti-assessment petitions was not less than 10,000, and the number may have been even larger. About 1,500 names were signed to the Presbyterian memorials, and, doubtless, other Presbyterians signed the undenominational protests. No estimate of the number of Baptists who signed can be made, but there can be no doubt that it was very large. Some Episcopalians and probably a good many Methodists subscribed. Besides these were the signatures of the people unconnected with any church or indifferent to religion and who consequently objected to a tax for church support.

While the opposition to assessment proved to be unexpectedly widespread, the sentiment in favor of it was also strong. A large part of the serious and cultured population of Virginia clung to the principle of state support of religion as to a familiar and beneficient policy. Innovations in religion always awaken deep alarm among conservatives, and they are almost always of concern to the state. Conservative Virginians were persuaded that such was the case in point, but the radical spirit had grown strong in the upper classes. But for this division of opinion, assessment would doubtless have been tried. An atmosphere of philosophic inquiry had existed in Virginia before the Revolution among the educated people. The Revolution spread this atmosphere of inquiry and unrestraint among all classes. Indeed the times were in many ways the freest and most inspiring in the history of the Commonwealth. Madison appealed to this spirit of intellectual and political freedom in his Remonstrance, and he was met with a notable response. The liberals who rallied behind him, and the evangelicals, gave him the victory over the great body of conservative political and social leaders. But the petitions show that there were many supporters of assessment, and, without doubt, many more never signed petitions. The conservatives were not equal to their opponents in energy and organization and the impression was produced that an overwhelming majority of the people of the State opposed assessment. It is difficult to find out, however, the strength of the opposing sides in the controversy. There were many decidedly for and against assessment, and at the same time a great part of the population had no definite views on the question at all. Furthermore, it is probable that the faint-hearted, who would have supported assessment under normal conditions, opposed it because of the hard times and the difficulty of paying taxes. The main argument of the conservatives was not new—that religion is necessary to the welfare of the State and the supervision of the State necessary to religion. Holding such an opinion, many good people considered the definite separation of church and state as a blow at the existence of religion.

They couched their petitions in the terms of concession. Ministers ought to have some assurance of a decent support; at present many of them lived very precariously. The assessment in no respect violated the spirit of civil and religious liberty, but tended rather to foster it. The Surry petition argued that the experience of mankind in both Christian and heathen nations testified to the benefits arising from the state support of religion. "In the most enlightened governments of Europe, the Religion of our Saviour has been countenanced and established by law." and further: "Should the great work of inculcating religious and moral truths be neglected, or in great measure confined to the most illiterate of mankind, the influence of religion must daily be impaired, and infidelity, enthusiasm and superstition with all the attendant follies and vices will proportionately increase among us." The experience of the past few years had taught that the most worthy ministers could not derive a support from voluntary contributions. Few men would undertake a laborious preparation for a career of starvation, but the proposed law made it possible for learned men to be preachers.

But the chief objection of the Surry petition to the entire separation of church and state was its novelty. "We cannot observe without concern that the United States of America exhibit to the world the singular instance of a free and enlightened government destitute of a legal provision for the support of religion. It is indeed with pleasure that we look up to the wisdom of our rulers for a more perfect constitution, both civil and religious, than has hitherto been known to mankind, yet we cannot indulge the vanity of supposing that the religious system of our country will be perfected on the principle directly opposed to the wisdom of all nations."

Pro-assessment petitions came in from Surry, Mecklenburg, Amelia, Pittsylvania, Lunenburg, Westmoreland, Amherst, Essex, and perhaps some other counties. Altogether about 1,200 names were signed to these memorials, which would make the supporters of assessment about one to eight. But this proportion is apparent only, as the conservatives made no especial effort to gain signatures, while their opponents labored hard. In the next year, 1786, when the repeal of the incorporation bill was threatened, petitions protesting against the repeal were signed by many more than 1,200 names. The weight of petitions settled the fate of the "Bill for Establishing a Support for Teachers of the Christian Religion." No mention is made of it in the journal of the house of delegates for this session, although it was considered in the committee of the whole. Foote affirms that "When the bill was taken up in the committee of the whole, Mr. Smith (John Blair Smith) appeared as one of the committee of the Presbytery of Hanover, and desired to be heard on a memorial from the Presbytery against the bill. Permission was granted, and Mr. Smith addressed the committee, and took part in the discussion which was continued for three days. When the question was called the bill was lost in the committee by a majority of three votes." [421] But Grigsby, in commenting upon this passage, points out that if the assessment bill had been rejected in committee as an independent bill a report would have been made to the house, the question would have been put, and the journal would contain a notice. He suggests, therefore, that the assessment bill was offered as an amendment to the bill for religious freedom and was rejected. [422] The statement is made elsewhere that Smith spoke in opposition to the assessment bill, [423] so it is likely that the president of Hampden-Sidney appeared before the committee.

The weight of the different influences which contributed to the defeat of assessment cannot be accurately determined. The poverty of the people had much to do with the energetic protests against the imposition of a new tax, for a bill to stay the whole tax collection for 1785 was narrowly defeated. Grigsby is right in naming the general poverty of the State as a cause of the defeat, but he lays rather too much stress upon it. After all, the separation of church and state was an ideal victory rather than a material one; it was an outcome of the spirit of the Revolution.

It is easy to see why the assessment bill quietly died in committee without being brought before the house; it is not so easy to understand the reaction which carried the "bill for religious freedom" through the Assembly. Undoubtedly the success of the summer's campaign and Madison's unrivalled ascendency in the house at this time had much to do with the counterstroke.

The bill for religious freedom was No. 82 in the list of bills in the Revised Code, which were to be presented to the house. [424] On December 14th, the "bill for establishing religious freedom" was brought up. The next day Alexander White reported to the house that the bill had been considered and amended in committee. [425] On December 16th the house considered the amendment, which struck out the preamble of Jefferson's bill and inserted the followings words: "Whereas, it is declared by the Bill of Rights, that religion, or the duty which we owe to our Creator, and the

---

[421] Foote, I, 431.
[422] Virginia Historical Collections, X, 124.
[423] Evan. and Lit. Mag., IX, 43.
It has been suggested that Reuben Ford may have appeared for the Baptists. (Virginia Historical Collections, IX, 125, note.)
[424] Journal, p. 93.
[425] Journal, p. 94.

114

manner of discharging it, can be directed only by reason and conviction, not by force or violence; and, therefore, all men are equally entitled to the free exercise of religion, according to the dictates of conscience, and it is the mutual duty of all to practice christian forbearance, love and charity towards each other." [426] The amendment was defeated, 38 to 66. Benjamin Harrison, John Tyler, Joseph Jones, Miles King, Alexander White, John Page, John S. Wills, Willis Riddick and Richard Lee were the most prominent men who voted in the affirmative.

A study of the vote shows that the conservative party was now pretty well broken up. It controlled votes from Accomac, Amherst, Brunswick, Charles City, Chesterfield, Dinwiddie, Elizabeth City, Frederick, Gloucester, Hanover, Greensville, Harrison, Isle of Wight, King George, Loudoun, Middlesex, Nansemond, New Kent, Norfolk, Northampton, Prince George, Princess Anne, Richmond, Southampton, Stafford, Surry, Westmoreland—most of the eastern counties with a sprinkling of central and southern. The rest of the State was lost.

The bill came up for the third reading on December 17th. A motion to postpone the reading until the following October was defeated, and the bill passed the house by a vote of 74 to 20. The conservative party on the religious question had now become a mere opposition. The twenty stalwarts were Thomas Claiborne, of Brunswick; Miles King and Worlich Westwood, of Elizabeth City; John Page, of Gloucester; Garland Anderson, of Hanover; Elias Wills, of Fluvanna; William Thornton, of King George; Francis Corbin, of Middlesex; Willis Riddick, of Nansemond; Daniel Sandford, of Norfolk; John Gordon, of Northumberland; Edward Bland, of Prince George, Anthony Walke, of Princess Anne; George Lee Turberville, of Richmond; William Garrard, of Stafford; John Francis Mercer; Carter B. Harrison, of Surry; Richard Cary and Wilson Miles Cary, of Warwick; and Richard Lee, of Westmoreland—representatives of the eastern counties now hopelessly outvoted in the house.

The senate adopted an amendment to the bill, striking out the first page and twenty-one lines of the second, and inserting the religious article in the Bill of Rights. [427] The house rejected the amendment, 35 to 56. The members voted in much the same way as on the former occasion. [428]

The bill was returned to the senate, which adhered to the amendment, sending the bill back on January 9, 1786, with a request for a conference. The house agreed and appointed Madison, Zachariah Johnston and James Innes as its committee. [429] The senate committee was composed of John Jones, Matthew Anderson, William Ellzey, Robert Rutherford and Walter Jones. The conference was held on January 12th. The next day the house adopted the amendment with amendments. [430] The senate amended this amendment to the amendment. [431] On January 16th, the house considered the senate's last amendments, which struck out a part of the preamble and inserted instead: "Almighty God hath created the mind free, that all at-

[426] Journal, p. 95.
[427] Senate Journal, p. 61.
[428] Journal, p. 117.
[429] Journal, p. 135.
[430] Journal, p. 139.
[431] Senate Journal, p. 90.

tempts to influence it by temporal punishments or burthens, or by civil incapacitations, tend only to beget habits of hypocrisy and meanness, and are a departure from the plan of the Holy Author of our religion, who being Lord both of body and mind, yet chose not to propogate it by coercions on either, as was in his almighty power to do; that the impious presumption of Legislatures and rulers," and made two other changes.[432]

The house accepted these amendments and the "bill for religious freedom," after so many delays and changes became law. Its passage came as a fitting epilogue to a drama already played out; separation of church and state in Virginia had been practically effected by the defeat of assessment. The act "for establishing religious freedom" added no new principle. In combining complete liberty of opinion and in forbidding taxation for church support,[433] the act merely expressed the results of the Revolution, but it served its purpose as a landmark and as an obstacle to any reversion to the past.

The senate amendments made no essential changes; they rather improved the preamble. Jefferson had begun the bill with the assertion: "Well aware that the opinions and belief of men depend not on their own will, but follow involuntarily the evidence proposed to their minds; that Almighty God hath created the mind free, and manifested his supreme will that free it shall remain by making it altogether insusceptible to restraint," which was elided into the memorable phrase: "Whereas Almighty God hath created the mind free." The senate also balked at the phrase: "That the opinions of men are not the object of civil government nor under its jurisdiction." There were also some minor changes. The Assembly, in this session, furthermore made a new provision for the poor. Counties were to be divided into districts, which should be under the jurisdiction of elected overseers of the poor, three to each district. These overseers should levy a tax upon all tithables for the poor relief. The powers of the vestries and churchwardens were transferred to the overseers, and settlements due from the vestries should be made to the overseers.[434] This act destroyed the last vestige of the establishment. Vestries were henceforth simply the servants of the church; they no longer rendered a service to the church on the one hand and to the State on the other. New civil officers, under the forbidding name of "overseers of the poor," replaced them.

And yet the divorce between church and state had not reached that absolute quality which Madison deemed so desirable. The incorporation act, with its regulations for the election and conduct of vestries, remained unrepealed. The Assembly, which passed the act "for establishing religious freedom," passed an act authorizing the election of vestries not elected within the time limit of the law of 1784.[435] There was yet something for the logical democrat to accomplish before the divorce of religion and the state would be complete.

---

[432] Journal, p. 143.
[433] Hening's Statutes, XII, 84.
[434] Hening's Statutes, XII, 27.
[435] Hening's Statutes, XII, 93.

CHAPTER VI

Repeal of the Incorporation Act

After the passage of the act "for religious freedom" the controversy entered upon another phase. That act marked the end of the conservative effort to check and control the growth of democracy and the spread of liberal ideas. The failure of the movement might seem to us a proper occasion for the cessation of political agitation on religious subjects, but the actors in the play thought otherwise. The general assessment had awakened irritation among the people who had most occasion to cherish resentment against the old establishment. Besides, the question of the existing relations of church and state had not been entirely settled, and the more practical question of the ownership of the church property had just begun to be debated.

The position of the parties in the religious controversy had changed in 1786. The Episcopal church had now definitely abandoned its attempt to rehabilitate itself by state aid. It was satisfied to hold what it possessed; it was on the defensive. The evangelical denominations had triumphed, and the most radical of them were prepared in turn to assume the offensive against the former establishment and to secure the repeal of the incorporation act of 1784.

The obnoxious features of this act were the reservation of the property of the establishment to the newly organized Protestant Episcopal church and the tentative control maintained over the church government by the regulations provided for it.

The Episcopal church had suffered a great blow in its failure to obtain civil support. The Anglicans had been bred up in a state church, and it was difficult for them to adapt themselves to the new conditions arising from the separation of church and state, especially at a time when money was scarce, ministers hard to obtain and the evangelical churches active and successful. The convention which met in Richmond on May 24, 1786, was attended by sixteen ministers and forty-seven delegates as against thirty-seven preachers and seventy-one laymen the year before; forty-three parishes were represented instead of the sixty-nine in 1785.

The convention ratified the constitution of the Protestant Episcopal church drawn up at Philadelphia in 1785. A committee, including John Blair, David Griffith, Archibald Cary, John Page and Carter Braxton, was appointed to draw up a memorial to the Assembly, protesting against the threatened repeal of the incorporating act. Finally David Griffith was elected Bishop of Virginia.[436]

The petition to the Legislature stated that: "Your petitioners have reason to apprehend that at your ensuing Session an attempt will be made

---

[436] Hawks, Appendix, 14.

to prevail with the General Assembly to repeal the law for incorporating said church. And altho no change of circumstances have intervened to require the repeal of an Act, which has been judged necessary; Yet lest the Silence of your Petitioners, amidst the various and zealous attacks with which they are threatened, may by any means operate to their prejudice, they think it not amiss to request that, altho as a church they have certain rights, which they enjoy independently of any human power, they may not be deprived of those conveniences, which the said act procures to them. Some have affected to consider the act here referred to, if not as an Establishment, as tending at least to an Establishment of the Episcopal Church; and strange fears have been excited for the safety and independence of the other Christian Churches without its pale. But how anything can look like an exclusive Establishment of a particular church, which the members of that church wish to see extended to the whole Fraternity of Christians, is a paradox your petitioners will not attempt to solve. They can safely appeal to the Searcher of Hearts for the truth of their profession, that however their opinion of the purity of their own church must naturally give them a degree of zeal for its support, yet that zeal is not embittered with any rancour against their Christian Brethren, who are all aiming at the same great object; and who, it is hoped, will all equally attain it in the end, by whatever different paths they may pursue it. Thus affected towards all denominations of Christians your Petitioners are not further from possessing, than from wishing to possess, any denomination or authority over others. They are anxious for nothing so much as for the true and genuine prosperity of their church, which may be promoted by the proper exercise of ecclesiastical, but would be lost by the assumption of temporal power. The Act in question gives however nothing of that kind. It enables indeed the Episcopal Church to accept donations to a certain extent, and by giving a sanction to the courts, which the said church may establish for the trial of misbehaving clergymen, removes a difficulty, which might perhaps otherwise arise respecting the Freehold or Glebe of a degraded clerk; to which he was entitled by the laws of the land. But from neither of these topics does it appear that danger can accrue to any. The enabling part of the law is pretty well guarded (as your petitioners can conceive) by the limitation annexed; and still more (as they have too much reason to fear) by the disinclination of her members (from whatever cause) to make even an adequate support to the church; and if to the incorporating Act she be indebted for the clear right of depriving a degraded clergyman of his Glebe, those who wish to have it otherwise ought not to expect to be considered in the light of candid opponents; since that wou'd be loaded with as much deformity as possible for the sake of exposing her the more successfully. Your petitioners trust that the moderation and unlimited charity of their disposition towards those Christians, who think themselves bound in conscience, or otherwise prefer, to withhold Communion with the Episcopal Church, will secure to them a similar return of Christian Forbearance; and thus by a continual interchange of friendly offices and brotherly love, render quite unimportant all the little differences of opinion, which may still keep them separate. But if contrary to this hope your petitioners shou'd meet with opposition from those, who wish to see an act repealed, which your

118

said petitioners think convenieht to the good government of their church, and which can affect the rights of no other, they leave to the consideration of the world, what church it is which has most reason to dread a tyrannous exertion of power, and a suppression of its dearest interests. Your petitioners therefore humbly pray such unreasonable interference may be rejected."

This mild appeal was not apt to weigh heavily in the balance against the vigorous efforts of the evangelical churches. They began their campaign in the summer. The Baptist General Committee, representing many churches, met in Buckingham county in August, 1786, and appointed a committee to draw up a petition asking for the repeal of the incorporation act and the sale of the glebes. Reuben Ford and John Leland were delegated agents to the Assembly.[437]

The petition adopted reads thus: "Representatives of Several Baptist Associations . . . Beg leave respectfully to address your Honourable House.

"When Britain with her cruel Usurpation over her Colonies in America, reduced them to the necessity of taking up Arms, to indicate their Natural Claims. A declaration of Rights . . . was made, by the good People of Virginia, Assembled in full and free Convention, as the Basis and foundation of Government. A Constitution so Liberal in Civil, and free in religious concerns, that we readily took the Oath of Fidelity to the State. From this principle we expatiated! for this free government we advanced our property and exposed our lives on the field of battle with our fellow Citizens; being often Stimulated with the harmonious Proclamation of equal Liberty of conscience, and equal claim of property.

"As hazardous as the Enterprize appeared, under the interposition of divine providence, by the prudence of our Ambassadors, the wisdom of our politicians, the skill of our Generals, the bravery of our soldiers and the aid of our Allies; after a seven years Contest, we obtained our liberty, and Independence with a vast empire added to us by the late treaty of peace.

"At this happy period, when America emerged from a bloody Obscurity to such a distinguishing figure of importance among the nations of the world; we felicitated our Selves with the enjoyment of every domestic, and Social blessing cf human Life: Nor were we willing to harbour a jealous thought of the Legislature, that the bill of Rights, would not be attended to in every particular.

"But to our great Surprize, in the Session of 1784, at the request of a few Clergymen, the members of the late established Church of England, were incorporated into a Society, called the "Protestant Episcopal Church," as a body Corporate and politic, and to the ministers & members of that Church, and their Successors were given, all and every Tract, or Tracts of Glebe Land, already purchased, and every other thing the property of the late established Church of England, to the Sole, and only use of the Protestant Episcopal Church.

"If Religion or the duty which we owe to our Creator, and the manner of discharging it, can be directed, only by reason and conviction; not by

[437] Semple, 98.

force and violence (so fully expressed in the XVI Art: of the bill of Rights, and the late Act for establishing Religious Liberty) we cannot see with what propriety the General Assembly could incorporate the Protestant Episcopal Church, give her a name, Describe the character of her members, modulate the forms of her government, & apoint the Time and place of her meeting. If this is not done by force, what force can there be in law? and to what lengths this may lead; and what violence it may produce, time only can discover, but we fear the awful consequences. The act appears a Bitumen to Cement Church and State together; the foundation for Ecclesiastical Tyranny, and the first step towards an Inquisition.

"New Testament Churches, we humbly conceive, are, or should be, established by the Legislature of Heaven, and not earthly power; by the Law of God and not the Law of the State; by the acts of the Apostles, and not by the Acts of an Assembly. The Incorporating Act then, in the first place appears to cast great contempt upon the divine Author of our Religion, whose Kingdom is not of this world, and Secondly, to give all the property of the State established church to one Society, not more virtuous, nor deserving than other Societies in the Commonwealth, appears contrary to justice, and the express words of the IV Art: of the Bill of Rights, which prohibits rewards or emoluments to any Man, or set of men, except for services rendered the State; and what services that Church has rendered the State, either by her Clergy or Laity, more than other Churches have done, we no not.

"If truth is great, and will prevail if left to itself (as declared in the Act Establishing Religious Freedom) we wish it may be so left, which is the only way to convince the gazing world, that Disciples do not follow Christ for Loaves, and that Preachers do not preach for Benefices.

"From the days of Edward the VI when the Liturgy was first framed to the year 1661 it was at several times Changed and revised by publick authority; This at once shows the fickleness of human Establishments, and while things are so mutable, it appears dangerous to religious Liberty for the Legislature to establish Rules and Directions for the Church, unless we were assured our Consciences and Sentiments would always acquiesce in the will of the Legislature.

"It is well known that Ecclesiastical Establishment is one part of the British Constitution, and therefore the Church of England is obliged to own the King of Great Britain to be her Head. Our declaration of Independence appears to have made every Son of Liberty in America a Dissenter from that church; but if that do not completely do it, has not the Protestant Episcopal Church since done it? in disapproving of a number of the old Articles, and forms of worship: If Dissenters therefore have no right to that Property, it seems That Church cannot lay a just claim to it.

"If the members of the Protestant Episcopal Church prefer Episcopacy to any other form of Government, they have an undoubted Right as free Citizens of State to enjoy it; But to call in the aid of Legislature to Establish it, threatens the freedom of Religious Liberty in its Consequences.

"And whereas the Incorporating Act appears to be pregnant with evil and dangerous to religious Liberty; your Petitioners humbly remonstrate against it; and trust that the wisdom of your Hon. House will repeal the exceptionable parts of the said Act, and apply the property to the use of the community, in such a manner as to you shall seem just.

WILLIAM WEBBER, Clk."

This petition advanced the claim that the Bill of Rights prohibited the regulation of ecclesiastical affairs by the Legislature, and consequently the latter had no right to make rules for the Episcopal church. The incorporation act might lead to establishment. The argument soon to be advanced by many people that the church of England and the new Protestant Episcopal church were different organizations and consequently that the latter was not the rightful heir of the former was well stated.

The Assembly met on October 16, 1786. Edward Bland, William Norvell, French Strother, Richard Bibb, Park Goodall, Thomas Smith, William Curtis, Alexander White, Thomas Underwood, Zachariah Johnston, Thomas Claiborne, Thomas Corbin, John Pride, James Innes and James Dabney composed the committee for religion.[438]

The fight for the repeal of the incorporation act began on October 31st with the presentation of petitions from Louisa, Henrico, Brunswick, Mecklenburg, Dinwiddie, New Kent, Gloucester, Lancaster, Nansemond, in favor of repeal, and of one from Westmoreland opposing it. The next day repeal petitions came in from King and Queen, Orange, Goochland, Spotsylvania and the Baptist church.[439] Other petitions came in later from Buckingham, Chesterfield, Louisa, Augusta, Powhatan, King George, Fauquier, Essex, Henrico, Albemarle, Hanover and a number which name no counties.

A fair estimate of the number of petitioners for the repeal of the incorporation act would be 5,000. The grant of religious liberty in the Bill of Rights is the underlying argument in nearly all the memorials, which construe the act as being a violation of the Bill of Rights, both of the fourth and sixteenth articles.

The Louisa petition of October 31, 1786, ran as follows: "The petition of sundry of the Inhabitants of the County of Louisa sheweth Whereas your honourable House has been pleased to make a Law incorporating the Episcopal Society, and vesting her with the Glebes, churches, surplus money and other Things, which we look upon to be the Property of the Publick; we do therefore most earnestly remonstrate against the sd Act. To take that Society into the Lap of the Legislature, and be at the Expence of supporting an Assembly (perhaps every year a long Time) to ratify her Decrees; is not only contrary to the 4th article of the Bill of Rights; but every way calculated to raise Jealousies in all other Societies, of alarming Consequences. If the Property vested in her hands, had been a free will offering of the People, we should forever hold our Peace, altho' we see cause to separate from her communion; but as it was procured by the Law of Injustice and Hands of Oppression, we think it reasonable and just, that said property should be put to publick use. It is not the wish of your Petitioners, that the Episcopal Society should have any Hindrance in the way of discharging her duty to God or Man; or that she should be deprived of any private Donation made her by her Friends but that whatever is

---

[438] Journal of House of Delegates, October 1786, p. 5.
[439] Journal, p. 15.

found in her Hands that is naturally publick Property, may be converted to the use of the publick, in such a way as the wisdom of your House shall direct; and that all Societies may be left to govern themselves, without the Expence of the publick or Sanction of Law."

The danger of arousing the jealousy of the other churches by the incorporation of one was perhaps the most distinctive argument in this paper. The Henrico petition complained that "When the Late happy Revolution Secured to the Citizens of this State an Exemption from British Control they hoped the Gloom of Injustice and Usurpation would have been forever dispelled by the clearing Rays of Liberty and Independence and that the Declaration of Rights which do pertain to them and their posterity would have been inviolably adhered to. But their hopes have been overcast with fearful Apprehensions when they find that Antient Distinction among the Citizens of the Commonwealth on account of Religious Opinions is still maintained by Legislature." This petition gives the most obvious argument of all—incorporation is a distinction and as such is opposed to the spirit of the Revolution. The Essex petition repeated the idea in similar words: "Let all Religious Societys stand on the same level and jealousies will cease, and Harmony abound. But if one Society has the particular Sanction and Direction of your Honorable House, it must be looked at by all others, as something alarming in its consequences, and repugnant to that liberal Principle to which they have reason to expect an invariable adherence in all your Publick Measures."

The Orange petition of November 1, 1786, declared that incorporation of the Episcopal church was "unprecedented in the New Testament and unwarrantabl. by the Bill of Rights, to say no more about it." The grant of the ecclesiastical property to that church was an injustice, because the property was provided by the people in general and therefore belonged to all; it was taken as taxes by force and ought to be returned; it was given to the Episcopal church as an emolument, while that church had dissented from the late establishment, disapproved of many of the articles of the establishment and had no more right to the property than any other sect of dissenters. According to the Bill of Rights, the Episcopal church had a right to regulate its own affairs, but not to claim the property or to expect the Assembly to legislate about it.

The King George petition of November 29, 1786, made a strong declaration of the State's right to the church property: "The Petition of Sundrie Inhabitants of the County of King George Sheweth, That, whereas it hath pleased your Honourable House to incorporate the Protestant Episcopal Church in this Commonwealth, and thereby have granted the said Society certain Profits and Privileges, that by the 4th Article of the Bill of Rights, no man, nor set of men are entitled to in this Commonwealth: Therefore, your Petitioners beg leave, respectfully to remonstrate against; and hope the wisdom of your House will resume the subject, and repeal the said Act. (That part excepted, which is a Repilation of former Acts Concerning the Protestant Episcopal Church, which were considered a necessary Releasement from certain Restraints that she was formerly under). For it is not the wish of your Petitioners that the Church should have any obstruction in the way of Discharging her duty to God or man; but at the same time cannot forbear expressing their Uneasiness at the preeminent distinction given that Society above all other Religious Denominations in this Commonwealth; nor can they see upon what defensible Principles Legislature can ground it. Let all Religious Societies stand on the same Level, and jealousies will leave and Harmony abound. But if one Society has the particular sanction of and Direction of your Honourable House, it must be looked at by all others, as something alarming in its Consequences, and repugnant to that liberal Principle, to which they have reason to expect an Invariable Adherence in all your Public Measures. And as to the Property Vested in the Protestant Episcopal Church, if it be the property of the citizens of this Commonwealth, they cannot see with what propriety it can be taken from them. For if it had been a voluntary free will offering they had formerly made to that Church, they would have held their Peace, and rested satisfied in her enjoyment of it, although they had seen Cause to depart from her. But as it was wrested from them by the hands of Injustice, it is but reasonable it should be restored. Therefore the Prayer of your Petitioners is that the Act incorporating the Protestant Episcopal Church may be repealed (excepting the part before excepted) and that the property vested in that Society, belonging to the Publick, be Sold, and the money applied to the use of the Commonwealth."

The Fauquier petition read: "The Peaceable Address and living Remonstrance'of the Several freemen of Virginia, Humbly Sheweth, That the Glebe Lands etc. Hitherto appropriated to the Sole use of one Denomination of Christmas which were procured at the expense of the Community in general, appears to us ought to be considered under our present happy constitution, as the Publicks at large and as Such ought to be put to any use, purpose, or purposes, that our Honorable Legislature Shall think proper, to promote the wellfare of this State. We hope therefore that our Honorable house will please to take this in Consideration at their next meeting or as soon as may be Convenient. We also fear the Act for Incorporating the Protestant Episcopal Church may prove dangerous to or destructive of our Liberty as a nation & for that reason Conscientiously think it ought to be Repealed; that so all denominations enjoying equal liberty both Civil and Religious may Cheerfully unite in Supporting the Common Peace, Freedom & Property of their Country. Your Compliance with this truly Loyal Request will lay us under a new obligation of Respect to you as the Patrons of Liberty & for you as such shall ever pray."

The Gloucester memorial affirmed that the Glebes and churches would be the undoubted property of the Episcopal church if they had been given as free-will offering, but since most of the glebes were the fruit of taxation they ought to revert to the State. Furthermore: "We look upon the Incorporation Act as an Innovation of the Bill of rights, we earnestly desire the said Act may be repealed."

The remarkable Chesterfield petition advanced the statement that the discrimination in favor of the Episcopal church tended to destroy the "fundamental compact" of society: "The humble petition of sundry Inhabitants of Chesterfield Sheweth That whereas during the Common Struggle with Great Britain, Your Petitioners were encouraged to sacrifice the tender ties of Blood and Treasure, under the Expectation of Equal and impartial liberty given to all the free Citizens of this Commonwealth indiscriminately, and without Distinction; our Bill of Rights clearly sets forth 'that no man or set of men are entitled to exclusive or separate emoluments or privileges from the Community but in consideration of public Service, which not being Descendable, and again 'That all power is vested in and consequently derived from the people. And for the Legislator to make the Episcopal Church their favorite, by the Incorporation Act; by which they enjoy the public Buildings in Convention, when on the Affairs of their Church, and all the Churches, Glebes, etc. The property of the whole Nâticn [Virginia nation?] which we humbly conceive, has laid the Foundation for Anarcy and Confusion, and tends to destroy the Fundamental Compact; if not Repealed. And for the Encouragement of Forbearance, Love and charity towards each other; We move your Honourable House, That you in your great Wisdom will repeal the Act above refered to; and that such Order be taken by you, with that property etc. as shall be for the Interest of the whole; As all claim an equal Right to it; first, because it was the fruit of their honest Industry, and the establishment being justly Exploded, it is but reasonable that every Religious Denomination should have their equal part. And again, because We bore an equal share in the struggle with Great Britain for Liberty and equally contribute to the present form of Government. If our Religious Opinions are no bar to our Civil Rights and if no man shall be compelled to support any religious worship place or Minister whatsoever, nor shall be enforced, restrained, or Burthened in his Bcdy or goods, nor shall otherwise suffer on acccunt of his religious Opinions or Belief (as is justly declared in the act for establishing religious Freedom) why then are these Emoluments Held and Injoyed by those we never gave it to? nor consented should be applied to their use. Tho' some affirm we gave it up; which never was the case, as you may see by our repeted Petitions, which some ccmplain of as being forever troubled with; which had all the Vestiges of Oppression and distincticns in matters of Religion been removed our Petitions would long since have ceased to have pesteied the Assembly; But Tuianny is not the better for being on this side of the Atlantic, her Iron Sceptre is still the same, to all that have not tamely become Beasts of Burden; Therefore trusting in your great Goodness, That this our most earnest and equitable request may be granted in some way that be just and equal."

The Essex petition maintained that the incorporation act cught to be repealed for the sake of liberty and harmony, and the Henrico paper expressed the apprehension aroused by the act: "When the late happy Revolution Secured to the citizens of this State an Exemption from British Controul they hoped the Gloom of Injustice and Usurpation would have been forever dispelled by the Clearing Rays of Liberty and Independence and that the Declaraticn of Rights which do pertain to them and their posterity would have been inviolably adhered to. · . . . But their hopes have been overcast with fearful apprehensions when they find that Antient Distinctions among the Citizens of the commcnwealth on Account of Religious Opinions is still maintained by the Legislature."

The Hanover petitioners asked for an abolition of preferences, distinctions and advantages. How much the Episcopal church might advance in dignity and influence, when aided by large sums of money, only time could show.

The Augusta memorial not only asked for a repeal of the incorporation act, but for an amendment to the constitution more nearly equalizing representation: "The Petition and Remonstrance of a number of the Inhabitants of Augusta County Humbly Sheweth That when the late happy Revolution was effected, we flattered ourselves, That the Blood and Treasure expended in bringing it to that happy Issue, would have been Rewarded with Equal and Impartial Justice to all the People, and that to extend to Life Liberty and Property, as well as to the free exercise of Religion according to the dictates of conscience. We also flattered ourselves That as "no man or set of Men are entitled to exclusive or separate emoluments, or privileges from the community, but in consideration of Public Services," so none should enjoy them; But we are sorry to observe that Our hopes have been disappointed. That what (under the former Government) was extorted from all, by the hand of arbitrary power, has been by our legislature applied to the sole use and benefit of the Protestant Episcopal Church, in exclusion of all other churches. We think it exceedingly plain, That what was procured at common expence should be applied to the benefit of all.

"We conceive, That the Act for Incorporating the Protestant Episcopal Church is highly exceptionable. It establishes an immediate a dangerous and unwarrantable connection between the Legislature and that Church. By that Act the Assembly must be considered as the Head of that church and peculiarly interested in its welfare: for from the Assembly it receives its authority to Act. Now if it is the prerogative of civil Rulers to authorize Religious Societies 'to regulate all their Religious concerns, Their Doctrine, Discipline and Worship, and to institute such Rules and Regulations as they may Judge necessary for the good Government thereof, and the same to revoke and alter at their pleasure,' Then indeed is every Religious Society in Virginia (the Protestant Episcopal Church excepted) exercising powers that do not belong to them, and the greatest indulgence they can expect is to be winked at by the Legislature in the exercise of the powers they have assumed, untill a convenient opportunity of suppressing them for the usurpation: Altho we conceived that our churches had sufficient authority for all necessary purposes from who hath said 'All power is given to me in Heaven and in Earth' . . . We conceive that giving a power to each Vestry of the Protestant Episcopal Church to lay up property clear of Taxation that will produce Eight Hundred Pounds neat yearly income, is unjust and dangerous: It is unjust Because That the Members of that Church have thereby a Privilege of supporting their Religion from the income of Property exempt from Taxes; while every other Denomination supprot their Religion from Property assessed for the Support of Civil Government: It is dangerous because it gives that church the direction of so very considerable a Fund without account, which may hereafter be used to the disadvantage of the other Sects.

"We therefore hope and earnestly request That you . . . will dispose of the Glebes which were purchased at common expence towards the lessening of our common Debt. That you will Repeal every part of the

Incorporating Act that we complain of And that as far as the Constitution and circumstances will admit you will Establish and maintain a perfect Political equallity amongst all the Citizens, and for this end you will so regulate the Senatorial Districts that the People may be equally Represented in that Branch of the Legislature."

The main contentions of the petitioners were that the incorporation act violated the Bill of Rights; that it continued the connection of church and state, and that it made the new Episcopal church the heir of the establishment to the prejudice of the other churches. The first objection would depend upon the construction of the Bill of Rights, and it was interpreted in more than one way. The incorporation act undoubtedly maintained the union of church and state, and was thus opposed to the doctrine of religious liberty in its absolute sense. The statement that the Episcopal church differed from the old establishment because some of its articles were not the same was hairsplitting. The Episcopal church was under the necessity of adapting itself to the political changes caused by the separation frcm England; but it continued to be a branch of the Anglican church in doctrine and discipline. Nevertheless, this argument was continually repeated and was not without effect.

The Episcopal church did not lack for defenders. Many petitions protesting against the repeal of the incorporation act came into the House of delegates from various counties—Leeds parish, Fauquier Trinity parish, Louisa, Christ Church parish, Middlesex, Stratton Major, St. Stephens and Drysdale parishes, Caroline, Littleton parish, Cumberland, Fredericksville parish, Louisa, Upper Nansemond Parish, Northfarnham parish Richmond, Charles and Bruton parishes, York, Petsworth and Ware parishes, Gloucester, Suffolk parish, Nansemond, and from Dinwiddie, Brunswick, Cumberland, Caroline, Lunenburg, Amelia, Mecklenburg, New Kent and Halifax counties. About 2,500 names were signed to these petitions, which were drawn up almost entirely in the tidewater and southside sections, where the Anglican church continued to exist in some strength.

The standing committee of the Episcopal church, appointed to defend its interests before the Legislature, presented a memorial on December 5, 1786: "The standing Committee appointed by the Convention of the Protestant Episcopal Church, beg leave to represent, that the said Convention, alarmed at the then apprehended Design of some·Christian Societies withholding from their Communion, to attack ye Act of Assembly for incorporating the said Church, prepared in opposition thereto ·a Petition which now lies before the Assembly. But your Memorialists are informed that ye mode of attack is either changed or extended; and that the greatest Efforts are now making to deprive the said Church of those Glebes, which have long since been purchased fcr the use of their ministers. In this situation, your Memorialists conceive it to be their Duty to make such a Representation against those Efforts, as they have no Reason to doubt the Convention would, if that Body was now siting. They think that ye Title under which this Church enjoys the said Glebes is the very same, by which every man in the State enjoys that Property which no one contests, and that it is a Right of which they cannot be deprived, but by violence, nor without annihilating public Faith, disturbing the Principles of all Government, and shak-

126

ing the Foundations of the State. Your Memorialists are sincerely desirous (and in this they are sure they speak the sense of the Convention, and they doubt not of their Society in general) of living in Harmony with their Fellow Christians of every Communion, and therefore unwilling to comment on the Designs of those who would disturb the Peace of the Episcopal Church; yet, they cannot but think, they would have done well to consider more maturely, what are likely to be the Feelings of a Body of Men, who compose so considerable a Part of the State, in being deprived, (If that can be supposed possible), of Rights of which they have never been accustomed to doubt; and whether in this Situation of Things, the full Accomplishment of their Plan be an object worthy of the s——— of those who profess to believe the Gospel of Peace. But your Memorialists beg Pardon, if in speaking of this subject, they have appeared, in the least Degree diffident of the result of your determination. They are not. They think themselves too well secured in their Rights by a Government whose primary object is equal Protection.

JAMES MADISON,
JOHN BLAIR,
JOHN BRACKEN,
JOHN PAGE,
HUGH NELSON,
Members of the Standing Committee."

The petitioners of Leeds parish, Fauquier, claimed that the repeal of the incorporation act would be legislation of a retrospective tendency and consequently was opposed to the principles of the constitution. "Your Petitioners look back with pleasure when they consider themselves individually instrumental in a revolution which has done honour to Humanity, a revolution founded on the broad Scale of equal liberty, declaring amongst other things the different modes of religious worship, to be free, and independent of each other,

"That they were highly pleased with such prospects of Justice, and promising harmony with their fellow citizens of different persuasions That revolutions happen in Church, as well as States, are nothing new; the Protestant Episcopal Church was the only established one before the revolution, which was then stript of every advantage, saving only the Churches and Glebes, a universal approbation of these measures, was the language of all denominations of Dissenters, That the Legislature, since which has been pleased to pass an act, Incorporating, the protestant Episcopal Church, at the request of its own members which we think proper, and reasonable, giving no just grounds of offense, to any other society of people, and in its tendency inoffensive and harmless. Your petitioners beg leave to represent, That notwithstanding the fair prospect of harmony, which there presented itself, That they are much alarmed at the frequent attempts, on the rights and interests, of the Episcopal Church, which they beg leave to enumerate, Firstly, the restless and growing disposition of the dissenters to repeal the incorporating act, for which purpose petitions are now on foot—Secondly, The same spirit exists, and a high fever rages, for the selling the Churches, and Glebes, And by a set of men in many instances, who were strangers to the building or paying one shilling for them, They conceive a spirit of persecution is more apparent, than the dictates of Justice, good order, and harmony, which ought to be studied and exercised, amongst all denominations of Christians. Your Petitioners most humbly hope that the incorporating act, may not be repealed, and that no countenance be shewn, by your Honourable Body, to any petition, praying the Sale of the Churches and Glebes, Because in the first instance it wou'd be disgraceful and savage, in the second unjust, because it will violently dispossess the present incumbents who hold possession under faith of Laws, the repeal of which, or otherwise destroying its operations must have a tendency to retrospect, and therefore contrary to the fundamental constitution of Government."

The Episcopalians of Trinity parish, Louisa, declared that they were driven to appeal to the Legislature by the many attacks made upon the incorporation act. Silence in the face of detraction might be harmful. They had no wish to assert authority over other denominations, and the incorporation act had no savor of temporal power. It merely enabled the Episcopal church to exert control over its ministers and to deprive "degraded" clergymen of their glebes.

The petition from Stratton Major, St. Stephens and Drysdale parishes is apparently in the handwriting of Edmund Pendleton.

"Your Petitioners Inhabitants of the Parishes of Stratton Major, St. Stephens and Drysdale, being inform'd that a petition will be offer'd to Your Hon'ble. House for repealing the Law of 1784, Incorporating the Protestant Episcopal Church, and for selling the Glebes, Churches, Plate &c. thereto belonging, and applying the money towards lessening Taxes, Humbly beg leave to represent to Your Hon'ble. House, that the sd. Law cannot be an Infringement of the sd. Article, as it only confirms to the church the Rights and Privileges saved and reserved to it by the Law of 1776, which grant'd Religious Liberty to all denominations and to appearance hath given content for ten Years past.

"But now to the astonishment of Your Petitioners, and we may venture to say of all peaceable & good men, those very Dissenters who in their petitions in 1776 held out the observance of Christian forbearance, Love & Charity, agreeable to the last Article of the Bill of Rights, have set up claims and ask'd for that, which your Petitioners conceive they have no right to in equity, or Law, the church holding very little if anything, which they contributed to procure; and in 1776 when by Law this contentious mite was sav'd and reserv'd to the church the Dissenters were perfectly satisfied; Which Law Your Petitioners, trust Your Honor'ble House will consider a Tenure of as Sacred a Nature as that which every man in the State holds, and has Secured to him his private property, and that you will reject all petitions tending to Disturb the tranquillity of the State, and in no wise repeal the sd. Laws."

The vestry and others of Fredericksville parish begged for a continuance of the incorporation act on the ground that it was necessary in the existing state of the church. Northfarnham parish exclaimed: "For what good Reason or under what Pretence the Enemies of the Church are become so implacable and persevering in their Endeavors totally to annihilate her, we are a Loss to conceive, for when she had the Ascendency in America at least, We know of no intollerant or persecuting spirit on her part towards any Denomination of Dissenters whatever—it never entered into our Heads that they, professing themselves Christians, would wish to erase the Foundations of our church and trample her Members under Foot."

Madison, George Nicholas, and a majority in the house of delegates favored the repeal of the incorporating act. Madison had voted for the act, but only as a means of defeating the assessment. He objected to the incorporation act because it was an admission of the power of the Legislature to interfere in religious matters; it had been passed at the solicitation of some members of the clergy and not of the body of the church, and it gave the clergy power to legislate for the laity and to regulate matters of faith; it made the removal of unworthy clergymen difficult, and, on the whole, was more injurious than beneficial to the Episcopal church.[440]

The committee of the whole discussed the petitions, and, on November 2, 1786, was discharged from further proceedings on them.[441] But the memorial of the Episcopal Convention was presented on December 5, and was referred to the committee of the whole, which went into session. Charles Mynne Thruston reported the following resolutions to the house.[442]

"Resolved, that it is the opinion of this committee, That an act ought to be passed to empower all societies formed for the purposes of religion, to hold such property as they are now possessed of, to acquire property of any kind, and to dispose thereof in any manner that may be agreeable to the said societies.

"Resolved, that it is the opinion of this committee, That so much of all acts of Parliament or acts of Assembly, as prohibits religious societies from forming regulations for their own government in any cases whatsoever, ought to be repealed; and that it ought to be declared that all such societies have full power to form regulations for their own government.

"Resolved, that it is the opinion of this committee, That the act "for incorporating the Protestant Episcopal Church;" ought to be repealed."

A committee, composed of Thruston, George Nicholas, John Page, Francis Corbin, Zachariah Johnston, Archibald Stuart, Isaac Zane, James Madison, John H. Briggs, and Joseph Eggleston, prepared the bill as ordered.[443]

On December 23, Charles Mynn Thruston brought in the repeal bill, which was entitled "to empower certain societies to hold lands and for other purposes." The bill was immediately read twice.[444] It passed the house on January 6, 1787, without a division, under the new title of "an act to repeal the act for incorporating the Protestant Episcopal Church and for other purposes."[445]

The senate amended the bill and passed it on January 8.[446] The house

---

[440] Madison's Works (Congress) I, 258. Draft of a petition in Madison's hand.
[441] Journal House of Delegates, October, 1786, p. 19.
[442] Journal, p. 87.
[443] Journal, p. 87.
[444] Journal, p. 120.
[445] Journal, p. 142.
[446] Senate Journal, p. 87.

refused to accept the amendments and the senate then receded from them."[47]

Madison informed Jefferson of the repeal in a letter of February 15, 1787.

"The act incorporating the protestant Episcopal Church excited the most pointed opposition from the other sects. They even pushed their attacks against the reservation of the Glebes, etc., to the church exclusively. The latter circumstance involved the Legislature in some embarrassment. The result was a repeal of the act, with a saving of the property."[48]

Thus, with no great struggle, the repeal of the incorporation act was carried. The result seems strange in view of the fact that the Episcopal party in the Assemblies of 1784 and 1785 had been large, almost dominant, and that it was still strong in 1786. The comparative ease with which the repeal bill passed denotes the completeness of the radical triumph. The defeated and hopeless conservative party had made a poor fight against the strong liberal tide. The progressives, too, had exceptionally able leaders in Madison and George Nicholas.

The repeal was a victory of the liberal party in the east. Assessment had been staved off in 1784 by the votes of westerners, but the west had comparatively little interest in the incorporation act, since the separation of church and state was practically complete beyond the Blue Ridge. Agitation for the repeal took place in the eastern counties, where the Episcopal church was strongest and had the most to gain by assessment. The petitioners for repeal were chiefly the dissenting and liberal elements in these counties, and the success of their agitation showed that the democratic party was now practically predominant in all parts of the State.

The repeal of the incorporation act definitely marks the separation of church and state in Virginia. All churches were now absolutely independent of the civil power as to doctrine, discipline and means of support. The Episcopal church for the first time stood on the same footing as the other churches in the State. The State had abandoned the effort to regulate society by means of religion; the principle of religious liberty was completely ascendant.

The question as to the ownership of the glebes, churches and other property of the old establishment remained open. The problem was one properly for the courts to decide rather than the Legislature, but the Legislature preferred to keep the matter in its own hands. Consequently the solution was reached as the result of a long and bitter political struggle instead of the calm reasoning of a legal argument.

---

[47] Senate Journal, p. 92.
[48] Madison's Works (Congress) I, 274.

CHAPTER VII

The Glebes

The religious controversy had now entered upon its last stage. Democracy was passing into radicalism and the forces of conservatism waned. The repeal of the incorporation act was a great blow to the Episcopal church; it had held together before, but it now began to decline with great rapidity. The church indeed was looked upon as the survival of another age. The tendency in religion was wholly evangelical, and in society and politics, irresistibly democratic.

The former dissenters, now predominant, prepared to follow up the victory of the repeal. They held that the Revolution, which had freed Virginia from British rule, given her a liberal constitution, and disestablished the church, should be pushed to its logical conclusion. The Revolution, according to this view, was not so much a development as a reformation; consequently the political system which had preceded the Revolution was partly wrong. The colony had unjustly taxed dissenters to furnish glebes and churches for the establishment; the remedy was the confiscation of the ecclesiastical property for the benefit of all citizens equally.

It was true that dissenters had been taxed for the support of the establishment, but they had actually paid little towards the purchase of glebes except in a few western counties. Few dissenters lived in Virginia prior to 1750, with the exception of Quakers, and most of the glebes in the old counties had been bought before this date. The dissenters in the majority of counties had merely contributed to the maintenance of existing institutions; they had little claim as individuals to the church property. The glebes belonged to the Anglican church both by law and custom.

But revolutions which overthrow ecclesiastical establishments usually result in an exaggerated idea of the rights of the state. It was so in this case. People overlooked the fact that the State was not the Colony; that it had not existed from the beginning. They forgot that the constitution and the laws supplementing the constitution had completed the old political era, and these laws had guaranteed the Episcopal church in the possession of the property. The radicals now wished to undo the audit and revive buried troubles. It is true, however, that they were partly justified in considering the disposition of the church property as an open question, in view of the attempt of the partizans of the Episcopal church to maintain a certain connection between church and state.

The State, in assuming the right to consider legislation concerning the glebes, claimed large powers. The political existence of Virginia indeed had been so continuous, in spite of the Revolution, that men failed to realize the exact significance of the break with the past. The house of delegates was the legitimate successor of the house of burgesses; the same delegates in large part, had sat in both. Consequently the adoption of a written constitution was hardly looked upon as the beginning of a distinctly new era as much as an important incident in a historic continuity. The Assembly did not regard the limitations of the constitution as final, nor the discussion of the ownership of the glebes as beyond its province.

The non-Anglican churches took advantage of this situation. The Presbyterians were the first to advance the theory that the ecclesiastical property, through the separation of church and state, reverted to the people. And, as a consequence, they began to advocate confiscation, but their natural conservatism prevented them from pushing the attack with much aggressiveness. The Baptists succeeded to the task and carried it to a successful conclusion by sheer insistence.

The Baptist General Committee, the executive junta of the church, met in Goochland, on August 10, 1787, and debated the status of the glebes and the position to be taken in regard to confiscation. The committee decided by a majority of one vote that the glebes were public property,[49] but it made no representation to this effect to the Assembly at the time.

The Presbyterians adopted a memorial at their convention on August 29, 1787, asking for the sale of the glebes. The old argument that the Episcopal church was not the same as the colonial church received reinforcement in the claim that the glebes had been bought by the ancestors of men who were Presbyterians, Baptists and Methodists; these descendants, therefore, should enjoy a part of the property paid for by their fathers.

"The petition and memorial of a number of the ministers and lay representatives of the Presbyterian Church in convention met, most respectfully sheweth—

"That your petitioners are sorry to be under the necessity of calling the attention of our political guardians to matters which may in some respects be considered of a peculiar nature, at a time when probably objects of great magnitude, and of general influence, not only to this state; but to the whole continent, may call for their deliberations. But actuated by the same principles which engaged us in, and carried us through the late glorious contest, a love of liberty and political equality, we think it a part of that duty which as freemen and citizens we owe to ourselves and posterity, again to address your honourable house: and whilst we acknowledge with all that gratitude which becomes good citizens, the attention given by your honourable body to the grievances which we formerly complained of, we cannot but express our sorrow to see how slowly and with what seeming reluctance, equal justice is done, and all denominations of christians in the state put in possession of their constitutional rights.

"We cannot enjoy that happiness, nor place that confidence in our government which we would wish, whilst we see our legislature in the face of human justice, and the inalienable rights of all the citizens, hold up a particular sect, or denomination of christians, as the objects of political favour. This we suppose is undenyably the case, in the exclusive appropriation of the glebes and churches to the protestant episcopal church, to the possession of which she has not the least shadow of a claim. As she differs

[49] Semple, p. 99.

from the Church of England, in the articles of her faith, the plan of her discipline, and the ceremonies of her worship; she is no more the same than the church of England is the same with the church of Rome: and has no pretext for identity, unless it be that the same persons compose her members, which composed the members of that ancient church, which is now no more in America. And therefore has no better right, than a great number of the Methodist, Baptist and Presbyterian churches, who can all plead the same; being once members of that church. These glebes and churches, were purchased with the common property of all the citizens of all denominations; and so far as there was any thing laudable in the institution which extorted this money it was that convenient places of worship might be provided for the people at large. Then to take what is common property, and designed for common benefit, and bestow upon this infant church, to the exclusion of a great majority of the community, is too glaring a piece of injustice to pass unnoticed, or be suffered to continue in a free country.

"We therefore pray the honourable house, to take the matter under their serious consideration, and adopt those measures which common justice must dictate. That the glebes be sold, and the money thence arising be divided, amongst the different denominations of Christians in each parish, in proportion to their number of tithes; to be by them applied to the religious uses of their respective communities. And that the churches with their furniture be so disposed of, that the people at whose expence they were procured, may enjoy the benefit of them in common for religious worship.

"This will give more general satisfaction, and be a better means of promoting Virtue & happiness, than any mode which a civil legislature, who have temporal things as their sole and immediate object, would by leaving the line of their duty devise. We should be happy to see our legislature confine themselves to the peculiar objects of their delegation, and exert their high authority in promoting virtue, & suppressing vice, by a vigorous and regular execution of the penal laws, and regular and virtuous example. This we are fully assured, will contribute more to the success of religion, and the happiness of the state, than by making any particular Sect the object of legislative regard.

"Whilst civil power is virtuously & regularly exerted, within the limits which its own nature, and reason has prescribed; and religion left to its own native beauty and energy, without discouragements on the one hand, or exclusive emoluments on the other, experiencing only common & equal protection, they will mutually conspire to promote the great ends of all government, Virtue, peace, good order, and happiness. We hope the wisdom & Justice of the honourable house will prevent the disagreeable necessity of our addressing you again upon this subject, and that in all future time, we may cheerfully contribute to the support and Strength of that Government, under which we live, and rejoice in the full possession of that equal Liberty for which we suffered, for which we fought. Signed agreeable to order of the Convention, at Bethel in Augusta, August 29, 1787, by John Brown, Chairman   Arch. Scott, Clerk."

The Assembly met on October 15, 1787. A committee for religion was appointed as from time immemorial, and it was still directed "to take under consideration all matters and things relating to religion and morality,"[450] but the act for religious freedom and the repeal of the incorporation act had now largely limited the functions of this committee to considering petitions for divorce.

Requests for the sale of the glebes came to the house from various quarters. The people of Tillotson parish, Buckingham, objected to the reservation of the glebes to the Episcopal church, desiring the sale of Tillotson parish glebe for the benefit of the inhabitants. Cumberland petitions asked for the sale of the glebe held by Christopher McRae and the giving of the proceeds to the parish poor. The vestry of Littleton parish at the same time protested.[451] Berkeley parish, Spotsylvania, also wished to sell its glebe for the sake of the poor.[452] The vestry of Saint James Northam, Goochland, applied for permission to sell the glebe, but in order to buy another in its place. Petitions from Orange and Chesterfield called for the sale of the churches and glebes in those counties, or their use in common by the various churches.[453]

The Presbyterian petition was brought before the committee of the whole on December 4, 1787.[454] John H. Briggs reported the following resolution from the special committee which had considered the memorial:

"Resolved that the glebe lands in the several parishes throughout this State, derived from the contributions of the people thereof, and in which there is no Episcopalian minister, be disposed of for public purposes, provided a majority of the parishioners shall consent thereto." It was lost, 45 to 62. The most prominent men voting in the affirmative were Zachariah Johnston, Archibald Stuart, French Strother and Isaac Zane. The great men were in the negative—George Nicholas, George Mason, Paul Carrington,

---

[450] Journal House of Delegates, Oct. 1787, 3.
[451] Journal, p. 33.
[452] Journal, p. 39.
[453] Journal, p. 59.
[454] Journal, p. 82.

The ayes were: Davis Booker, Zachariah Johnston, Archibald Stuart, John Trigg, James Turner, James Campbell, Joseph Cabell, Charles Patterson, John Clark, Charles Nevil Talbot, French Strother, Charles Chilton, Elias Edmunds, George Thompson, Samuel Richardson, John Early, Thomas Arthur, John Guerrant, Jr., Henry Banks, Ralph Humphreys, John Prunty, Thomas Cooper, John Pierce, Abner Field, James Dabney, William White, Green Clay, Charles Martin, Daniel Trigg, Joseph Cloyd, William M'Mahone, Archibald Woods, Hardin Burnley, William Ronald, Thomas Turpin, Jun., Theodorick Bland, Anthony Walke, William M'Kee, Benjamin Harrison, Andrew Cowen, Thomas Carter, Isaac Zane, John Dawson, Arthur Campbell, Samuel Edmiston.

The noes were: Edmund Custis, George Nicholas, Joseph Eggleston, William Cabell, Thomas Rutherford, Daniel Boone, Andrew Meade, Anthony New, Paul Carrington, Henry Southall, Benjamin Harrison, Matthew Cheatham, James Pendleton, Joseph Jones, William Watkins, Miles King, George Booker, James Upshaw, Meriwether Smith, George Mason, David Stuart, John S. Woodcock, Charles Mynn Thruston, Mann Page, Jun., Thomas Smith, Thomas Underwood, George Clendenin, Elias Poston, Isaac Vanmeter, Job Welton, Francis Boykin, Daniel Fitzhugh, Bernard Moore, James Ball, Jun., Josias Clapham, Richard Johnson, James Knox, Thomas Kennedy, Samuel Hopkins, John Jouett, Francis Corbin, William M'Cleny, Willis Riddick, Burwell Bassett, Cuthbert Harrison, James Webb, John Stringer, Abraham Beacham, William Lynch, Edmund Ruffin, Jun., Cuthbert Bullitt, Ludwell Lee, Walker Tomlin, Edwin Gray, James Monroe, William Fitzhugh, John Allen, Lemuel Cocke, John Howell Briggs, Thomas Edmunds, Richard Cary, Jun., and Samuel Griffin.

Benjamin Harrison, Meriwether Smith, James Monroe, the President, and Daniel Boone, the pioneer. Patrick Henry, then a member, was not present, nor was John Marshall, who would undoubtedly have voted in the negative.

The counties in the affirmative were Amelia, Augusta, Bedford, Buckingham, Berkeley, Campbell, Culpeper, Fauquier Fluvanna, Franklin, Goochland, Greenbrier, Hampshire, Harrison, Henry, James City, Jefferson, Louisa, Madison, Monongalia, Montgomery, Ohio, Orange, Powhatan, Prince George, Princess Anne, Rockbridge, Rockingham, Russell, Shenandoah, Spotsylvania and Washington.

In the negative were Accomac, Albemarle, Amelia, Amherst, Bourbon, Brunswick, Caroline, Charlotte, Charles City, Chesterfield, Culpeper, Dinwiddie, Elizabeth City, Essex, Fairfax, Frederick, Gloucester, Goochland, Greenbrier, Hampshire, Hardy, Isle of Wight, King George, King William, Lancaster, Loudoun, Lunenburg, Lincoln, Madison, Mecklenburg, Mercer, Middlesex, Monongalia, Nansemond, New Kent, Nelson, Norfolk, Northampton, Northumberland, Pittsylvania, Prince George, Prince William, Richmond, Spotsylvania, Stafford, Surry, Sussex, Warwick and Williamsburg.

This vote has no especial geographical significance. The question particularly affected the east, and democratic feeling then had not become radical enough to sanction the confiscation; only two eastern delegates voted for it. The majority of western delegates voted in the affirmative, but many were in the negative. The midland and southern sections were likewise divided.

This failure ended the attack upon the glebes for the session. The contest had centered about the Presbyterian petition, and the vote showed that a considerable party in the house favored the sale of church property, but the great democratic leaders were one with the conservatives in opposing a policy of confiscation. Mason and George Nicholas favored absolute religious liberty, but they refused to make a specific attack upon the Episcopal church after liberty had been gained.

The year 1788 was a quiet one in the annals of the religious struggle. The Presbyterians, having failed in 1787, put forth no more efforts for the sale of the glebes, and the Baptists had not yet decided to press the fight in the Legislature. Public interest was absorbed in the great contest over the adoption of the Federal Constitution. This debate indeed threatened to have a certain religious side, since Patrick Henry discovered a sinister intention towards religious liberty in the Constitution. John Blair Smith, writing to Madison on June 12, 1788, declared that "He has found means to make some of the best people here believe that a religious establishment was in contemplation under the new government. He forgets that the Northern States are more decided friends to the voluntary support of Christian ministers than the author, or at least warm abettor, of the assessment bill in this State."[455]

It seems that some Baptists opposed the Constitution on the ground that it offered no security for religious freedom, and that the Anti-Federalists, taking advantage of this sentiment, put forward John Leland, a Baptist preacher, as a candidate to the convention from Orange in opposition to

---

[455] Rives' Madison, II, 545, note.

.James Madison.[456] Leland, however, withdrew and thus avoided embarrassing
Madison. The adoption of the Constitution was fought out on purely political grounds.

The Baptist General Committee met in Goochland on March 7, 1787. It
decided to petition the Assembly for the sale of those glebes which were
vacant as public property,[457] a more moderate proposition than the Presbyterian request of the previous year. A committee was appointed to present
the Legislature with the memorial, which, however, appears not to have
reached the house at this session.

The General Committee met again on August 11, 1788, but no further
action was taken.[458] Little attention was paid to religious affairs at the fall
session of the Assembly, as the adoption of the Federal Constitution and
the adjustments to be made for the new system absorbed attention.

One religious case of some importance came up. Robert Dickson, minister of Lynhaven parish, Princess Anne, by his will made in 1774, bequeathed
some property in trust to the Lynhaven vestry for the benefit of his rela-
tives and for the endowment of a school. The vestry inquired whether it
had power to execute the trust since the repeal of the incorporation act and
asked to be constituted a legal successor of the former vestry by act of
Legislature.[459] An act was accordingly passed declaring the trustees
appointed to manage church property to be the successor of the former
vestries to the extent of holding property for the use of individuals or of
charities.[460] But in Norfolk county, the overseers of the poor asked to be
vested with property left for the benefit of the poor and the petition was
granted.[461] At the October 1789 session of the Assembly, the vestry of
Frederick parish, encouraged by the act giving the trustees the power to
manage church property, asked for the reinstatement of a suit for a debt
owed the parish, which suit the repeal of the corporation act had abated.[462]

The real war upon the glebes began in 1789, with the decision of the
Baptists to push the fight for confiscation. The General Committee of the
church met on August 10 at Richmond and drew up a memorial desiring
the sale of the glebes and the use of the churches in common, which was
presented to the house on November 14.[463] At the same time a petition came
in from Amelia asking that 100 acres of the parish glebe be appropriated as
a site for the county court house.[464] People of King William parish, Powhatan and Chesterfield, requested the sale of the unoccupied glebe for the
benefit of the parish.[465] William Norvell, on November 27, reported from
the committee for religion, which had been considering the Baptist petition,
that "the subject matter of the said remonstrance, praying that the glebe
lands may be sold, and that the churches heretofore used by the Episco-

[456] Sprague's Annals of the American Baptist Pulpit, 179, and James 155.
[457] Semple, 102.
[458] Semple, 103.
[459] Journal of House of Delegates, Oct., 1788, p. 87.
[460] Hening, XII, 705.
[461] Journal, p. 41.
[462] Journal of House of Delegates, Oct., 1789, p. 23.
[463] Journal of House of Delegates, Oct., 1789, 58.
[464] Journal, p. 65.
[465] Journal, p. 56.

palians, may be used in common by all religious societies, involves in it one of the great rights of the people; and justice, as well as policy, dictate that it ought to be acted on with the greatest deliberation, and that the sentiments of the good citizens of this Commonwealth, should be fairly collected on this important subject."[466]

The resolution provided that copies of the remonstrance and the resolution should be printed and distributed, as in the case of the assessment bill in 1785, and gave a brief outline of the origin of the glebes and of the action of the Assembly in 1776 in reserving the ecclesiastical property to the church of England, and, also, asserted that the Protestant Episcopal church was the same in rights as the former church.

The resolution concluded: "In order, therefore, to put an end to these disputes, it is declared and resolved by the General Assembly:

"1. That they will forever adhere to the act, 'concerning religious freedom.'

"2. That the contest for the glebes, churches and chapels, is not of a religious nature, but is to be decided by the rules of private property.

"3. That the grants aforesaid from the treasurer and company, and from the King of England, were to the followers of the church in each parish, forming one society, exclusively of all other persons whatsoever.

"4. That the transferring of the private donations, or any part of them, from the support of the Protestant Episcopal Church, to that of any other religious order, would be an unconstitutional invasion of right, and would in effect oblige the donors to contribute to the maintenance of tenets which they either did not foresee, or foreseeing, might not have approved.

"5. That all the glebes, churches and chapels, whether purchased or given, being vested in bodies which were capable in law of taking and holding them to their own use, and which actually did take and hold them to that use, it is against reason and the practice of every sect, that those who voluntarily depart from communion with them, should demand a share of their possessions.

"6. That it would be usurpation in the Legislature to convert the money arising from the sale of the glebes, churches or chapels, to public necessities.

"7. That the Legislative sanction for such a sale, would soon grow into a precedent for the constant intrusion of the State into all things which concern religion.

"8. That the stipulation and guarantee aforesaid, ought to be inviolably preserved."[467]

This is clearly and forcibly put and was probably inspired by Patrick Henry or Edmund Randolph, who were members of the committee for religion. The author skilfully turned the dissenter argument as to the wrongfulness of state interference in religion against the assailants of the glebes. The views of the conservative party in the Legislature could not have been better described than in these resolutions.

The house on December 9, 1789, decided to postpone further consideration of the Baptist memorial until the following March by a vote of 69 to 58.[468]

[466] Journal, p. 83.
[467] Journal, p. 83.
[468] Journal, p. 113.

Wilson Cary Nicholas, Henry Lee, Edmund Randolph and John Marshall voted in the affirmative. Patrick Henry again failed to be present.

The Baptists renewed their petition in 1790.[469] The General Committee this time fortified its request for the sale of the glebes and the use of the churches by all denominations with petitions from Goochland, Albemarle, Culpeper, King and Queen, Essex, Stafford, Richmond and Fluvanna.[470] The Baptist assault had now become formidable.

The discussion of the petitions came up in the house on November 13, 1790. The committee for religion made no further attempts to convince the people of the right of the Episcopal church to the property. The bold question was put to the house: "Resolved, That an act ought to pass, directing the sale of the glebe lands, excepting those which were private donations," and was rejected by the decisive majority of 89 to 52. The conservatives rallied and made the vote a very full one. Prominent among the members voting aye were Zachariah Johnston, French Strother, and Isaac Vanmeter, The leading conservatives were William Giles, Richard Bland, Richard Lee, Henry Lee, Patrick Henry and John Marshall.[471]

The counties in the affirmative were Albemarle, Augusta, Bedford, Botetourt, Campbell, Culpeper, Chesterfield, Fayette, Fauquier, Fluvanna, Franklin, Goochland, Greenbrier, Halifax, Hampshire, Harrison, Hardy, Henry, King George, Loudoun, Lincoln, Madison, Mercer, Monongalia, Nelson, Orange, Pendleton, Pittsylvania, Powhatan, Rockbridge, Rockingham, Russell and Washington.

In the negative were Accomac, Albemarle, Amelia, Amherst, Augusta, Berkeley, Brunswick, Buckingham, Caroline, Charlotte, Charles City, Chesterfield, Culpeper, Dinwiddie, Elizabeth City, Essex, Dinwiddie, Elizabeth City, Essex, Fairfax, Fauquier, Frederick, Gloucester, Greenbrier, Greensville, Halifax, Hanover, Harrison, Henrico, Isle of Wight, James City, King George, King and Queen, King William, Lancaster, Louisa, Lunenburg, Mecklenburg, Middlesex, Nansemond, New Kent, Norfolk, Northampton, Northumberland, Nottoway, Ohio, Prince George, Prince Edward, Rockingham, Russell, Shenandoah, Southampton, Spottsylvania, Sussex, Warwick, Westmoreland, Prince William, York, Williamsburg and Richmond City.

The vote on this occasion had more geographical significance than in the case of the Presbyterian petition of 1787. Then the western vote was greatly divided. In the present case eighteen western, eleven midland, two southside and one eastern county voted for the sale; in the negative were nine western counties, twenty-five eastern, seven midland, twelve southside, Williamsburg and Richmond. Only one eastern vote was cast for sale. The counties in the extreme west—now West Virginia—with the exception of Berkeley, Greenbrier, Harrison and Russell, were in the affirmative. The radical party was made up of western and midland members, in whose section the social changes had been greatest, and in which the Episcopal church had ceased to exist. This section, now imbued with radical feeling, made war upon the glebes as a vested interest and the survival of a past and hated system.

---

[469] Journal House of Delegates, Oct., 1790, p. 26.
[470] Journal, p. 27.
[471] Journal, p. 73.

The inevitable Baptist petition for the sale of the glebes was presented to the Assembly of 1791. A motion made to postpone consideration of the paper until the next October was defeated.[472] and the house debated the glebe question at length on December 6, 1791. The committee of the whole reported as follows: "Resolved, that it is the opinion of this Committee, that the memorial of the Baptist society for the sale of the Glebes, as it relates to private property, ought not to be decided on by the General Assembly."[473] A motion was again made to defer consideration of the glebe question until October but it was lost, 49 to 74.

A resolution was then offered in amendment to the first resolution, declaring that "Whereas there are within this Commonwealth great numbers of persons who have in times past, dissented from the Church heretofore established by law, who have been taxed for the purpose of purchasing lands and other property for its support; and it is contrary to the principles of reason and justice that any should be compelled to contribute to the maintenance of a church with which their consciences will not permit them to join, and from which they can therefore receive no benefit. And whereas the laws which have confirmed to the Protestant Episcopal Church the Glebe lands which have been so purchased are contrary to the spirit of our constitution, and in direct opposition to that article of the bill of rights which declares 'that no man or set of men are entitled to exclusive or separate emoluments or privileges from the community, but in consideration of public services.'

"Resolved, that the several Acts of Assembly which vest in the Protestant Episcopal Church Glebe lands which have been purchased with money arising from taxes levied on the citizens of this Commonwealth, ought to be repealed."

The question thus brought squarely to the issue was decided against the radicals. The resolutions failed to pass by a vote of 48 to 77.[474]

[472] Journal of House of Delegates, Oct., 1791, p. 79.
[473] Journal, p. 247.
[474] The ayes were: William Clack, Zachariah Johnston, John Tate, John Trigg, David Saunders, Martin M'Ferran, John Clack, Joseph Wyatt, Bernard Todd, Matthew Cheatham, William Madison, John Woodson, John Holcombe, William Pickett, John Early, Ashford Napier, John Guerrant, Jr., Hugh Caperton, Thomas Watkins, David Clack, John Haymond, John Mayo, Joseph Martin, Daniel Boone, Albert Russell, Samuel Taylor, Jacob Frowman, John Clopton, John Caldwell, Joseph Lewis, Thomas Barbour, Isaac Davis, William Patton, Matthew Clay, Thomas Tunstall, William Ronald, John Purnall, John Bowyer, William M'Kee, George Huston, George Baxter, Simon Cockrell, Isaac Zane, Robert S. Russell, Robert Brooke, William Tate, Robert Sayers and Joseph Kent.
In the negative voted John Wise, John Shepherd Ker, Francis Walker, Joseph Eggleston, Jr., Samuel Jordan Cabell, Andrew Waggener, John Waller, Charles Binns Jones, John Stith, David Bell, William Allen, John Hoomes, Sith Hardyman, David Patteson, Peterson Goodwyn, Miles King, George Booker, James Upshaw, George W. Smith, Roger West, Nicholas Fitzhugh, Matthew Page, Robert White, James Baytop, Mordecai Cooke, William R. Fleming, Benjamin Goodrich, John Winston, Thomas Tinsley, George Jackson, William Norvell, John Campbell, John Taliaferro, Woffendall Kendal, John W. Semple, Carter Braxton, Jr., James W. Ball, James Ball, Seven Powell, William O. Callis, John Overton, Thomas Todd, Edward Roysdale, Abraham Maury, Samuel Hopkins, Overton Cosby, Francis Corbin, John Evans, Willis Riddick, William Chamberlayne, John Cowper, Henry Guy, John Gordon, Francis Fitzgerald, Benjamin Biggs, Peter Hull, William Bentley, Willoughby Tebbs, Thomas Lawson, Robert Mitchell, Walker Tomlin, James Wilkinson, Edwin Gray, Francis Thornton, Travers Daniel, Jr., Robert Mercer, John Allen, James A. Bradby, Benjamin Wyche, John Mason, Hinde Russell, William Digges, Daniel M'Carty, Robert Shield, William Nelson, Robert Andrews and William Foushee.

In the following year the people of Prince Edward requested that the proceeds of the sale of the parish glebe and other effects be appropriated for some public use.[475] The vestry had been empowered in 1777 to sell the glebe and furniture, which produced a considerable sum of money. Part of this fund had been expended and the remainder was still held by trustees, as there was no legal object for its use. "Since the Act passed for the Dissolution of the vestry under the Establishment there hath been no vestry in this county neither do we know of any people that call themselves Episcopalians in the County." An act was passed in accordance with the petition directing the appointment of four trustees to receive the money raised by the sale of the glebe, which fund was to be appropriated to some public use by the county court, with at least twelve magistrates sitting.[476]

The Assembly thus sanctioned the miserable policy of frittering away the money raised by the sale of church property upon petty objects, such as the lessening of county taxes for a year, or in the most blundering and inefficient poor relief.

If some large and worthy object had been in the minds of the men who urged the sale of the glebes, the confiscation would have been more or less justified. In many counties, as in Prince Edward, the glebes had ceased to be occupied or claimed and they legitimately reverted to the public. They should have reverted to the State. If the State had collected in its treasury the money arising from the sales of the glebes, a fund would have grown up which might have materially affected the welfare of the people. Education would have been the best object for such a reserve. Jefferson was sighing and wishing for a system of public schools. Here he might have found the nucleus of a fund for its establishment. The scheme would have been worthy of Madison's best efforts. But the idea seems to have been firmly rooted in the minds of the people that the glebes were local possessions, instead of the property of the State, and in every community there were people possessed of some personal interest in the appropriation of the glebe money for local purposes.

The Baptists continued the contest in 1792 by once more addressing the Assembly. The glebe question was debated in the house again on December 7, 1792.[477] A motion made to postpone the subject indefinitely was amended by the following resolution: "Whereas there are certain tracts or parcels of land within this commonwealth, which have been purchased with money levied by taxes on the citizens thereof, and which have been appropriated to the support of the ministers of the Protestant Episcopal church; and whereas in many counties within this commonwealth, a great majority of the citizens have dissented from the said church, and have united themselves with other religious societies, and it is unreasonable that the property which they have been in such manner compelled to purchase, should be devoted to the support of a society with whom they cannot unite, without doing violence to their religious principles. Resolved therefore, That it is the opinion of this committee, that an act ought to pass directing some mode of collecting the opinions of the citizens of this commonwealth, respecting the sale of the said glebe lands, which have been purchased with money raised

[475] Journal of House of Delegates, Oct., 1792, p. 10.
[476] Hening, XIII, 555.
[477] Journal of House of Delegates, Oct., 1792, p. 177.

by taxes, and that in all parishes where a majority of the citizens desire a sale of such lands, the same ought to be sold, reserving to the present incumbent his right therein, and the money arising from the sale to be applied for the use and benefit of each parish respectively." The house was tied—56 to 56—on the motion and the speaker carried it for the affirmative.

The vote showed a great decline in the conservative party. The radical strength had not grown greatly but the conservatives had lost nearly all of their western votes, while still holding the eastern delegates solidly and a majority of the southside delegates. The western and midland counties voted together in the affirmative.

A committee was appointed to prepare the bill, which was presented on December 17, 1792, and called a bill "authorizing the sale of glebe lands." Possibly the committee may have gone beyond its instructions, and the title of the bill would seem to indicate this; at all events the bill was defeated for a second reading, and the attack upon the glebes thus failed once more.

The great year 1793 was a barren one in the controversy over the glebes. Other things attracted the attention of the legislators. A few unimportant petitions came to the Assembly, among them one from St. Anne parish, Essex, stating that the act authorizing the vestry to hold a lottery for the benefit of the glebe had proved ineffective, as the lottery tickets could not be sold, and asking permission to sell the glebe and buy another and better one.

The struggle was renewed the following year. The Baptist General Committee, on November 25, 1794, presented still another petition urging the confiscation of the glebes.[478] The house considered the petition on November 28 and a motion was made for the repeal of the guaranteeing act of 1776.[479] "Whereas there are certain tracts or parcels of land within this commonwealth, which have been purchased with money levied by taxes on the citizens thereof, and which have been appropriated to the support of the Ministers of the Protestant Episcopal church; and whereas in many counties within this commonwealth, a great majority of the citizens have dissented from the said church, and have united themselves with other religious societies, and it is unreasonable that the property which they have been in such manner compelled to purchase, should be devoted to the support of a society with whom they cannot unite without doing violence to their religious principles: Resolved therefore; That it is the opinion of this committee, that an act ought to pass repealing the fourth section of the act passed in the year 1776, entitled, 'An act exempting dissenters from contributing to the support and maintenance of the church as by law established, and its ministers, and for other purposed therein mentioned,' and so much of the act passed in the year 1786, intitled, 'An act to repeal the act for Incorporating the Protestant Episcopal church and for other purposes,' as guarantees unto the said Episcopal church the said Glebe lands, which have been purchased with money raised by taxes."

The resolution was lost—52 to 80. This vote shows that the relative strength of the conservative and radical parties on the religious question remained the same. The counties in the affirmative were Augusta, Bath,

---

[478] Journal House of Delegates, Nov., 1794, p. 39.
[479] Journal, p. 48.

Bedford, Botetourt, Buckingham, Campbell, Chesterfield, Fauquier, Fluvanna, Frederick, Franklin, Goochland, Greenbrier, Halifax, Hampshire, Harrison, Henry, Lee, Louisa, Montgomery, Monongalia, Madison, Orange, Pittsylvania, Patrick, Randolph, Rockbridge, Russell and Washington. Not a single eastern vote was cast in favor of the resolutions.

In the negative were Accomac, Amherst, Albemarle, Amelia, Berkeley, Botetourt, Caroline, Charlotte, Charles City, Dinwiddie, Elizabeth City, Essex, Fairfax, Frederick, Gloucester, Greensville, Hanover, Hardy, Henrico, Isle of Wight, James City, King and Queen, King William, Lancaster, Loudoun, Louisa, Lunenburg, Matthews, Mecklenburg, Middlesex, Monongalia, Nansemond, New Kent, Norfolk, Northampton, Nottoway, Pendleton, Powhatan, Prince Edward, Prince George, Prince William, Princess Anne, Stafford, Surry, Sussex, Warwick, Richmond, Shenandoah, Southampton, Spotsylvania, Westmoreland, Wythe, York, Norfolk, Norfolk Borough, Williamsburg and Richmond City. The conservatives obtained eight western votes—Berkeley (2), Botetourt, Frederick, Monongalia, Pendleton, Shenandoah and Wythe—all of the eastern votes, a good share of the midland and a majority of the southside votes. The majority against confiscation was still sufficiently large.

A number of petitions asking for the sale of particular glebes came before the Assembly of 1795. Halifax,[480] King William parish, Powhatan[481] and Chesterfield, and Louisa all petitioned. The Baptist General Committee, as a matter of course, addressed the house again, and the question was once more argued on November 27, 1795.[482] The committee of the whole reported a simple resolution: "That it is the opinion of this committee that the memorial of the Baptist general committee, praying that all acts and parts of acts, vesting in the Protestant Episcopal church, the glebe lands and other property formerly appropriated to the use of the said church, may be repealed, be rejected."[483] A motion was made to strike out the last words "be rejected" and insert "is reasonable," which was lost, 63 to 70. The counties in the affirmative were Augusta, Bath, Bedford, Berkeley, Buckingham, Campbell, Charlotte, Charles City, Chesterfield, Cumberland, Culpeper, Fauquier, Frederick, Franklin, Goochland, Greenbrier, Grayson, Halifax, Hanover, Harrison, Hardy, Henrico, Henry, Loudoun, Lee, Madison, Monongalia, Montgomery, Ohio, Orange, Pittsylvania, Powhatan, Prince Edward, Patrick, Randolph, Rockbridge, Russell, Shenandoah, Washington and Wythe. The radicals had gained votes from a number of counties, among them one from the east—Charles City.

In the negative were still Accomac, Albemarle, represented by Wilson Cary Nicholas, Amelia, Berkeley, Botetourt, Brunswick, Caroline, Charlotte, Charles City, Dinwiddie, Elizabeth City, Essex, Fairfax, Gloucester, Greenbrier, Greensville, Hampshire, Harrison, Isle of Wight, James City, King and Queen, King George, Lancaster, Lunenburg, Matthews, Mecklenburg, Middlesex, Nansemond, New Kent, Norfolk, Northampton, Northumberland, Ohio, Prince George, Prince William, Princess Anne, Pendleton, Randolph, Rich-

[480] Journal of House of Delegates, Nov., 1795, p. 15.
[481] Journal, p. 39.
[482] Journal, p. 47.
[483] Journal, p. 47.

mond, Southampton, Spotsylvania, Stafford, Surry, Sussex, Westmoreland, York and Williamsburg.

The conservatives held a few western votes, but had lost votes in other sections, and it was apparent that the two parties approached an equality as the democratic feeling in Virginia continued to rise. The conservatives, however, won a victory on December 16, 1795, when consideration of the King William and Southam parish petitions was postponed by a vote of 69 to 35. The Halifax petition received like treatment.

The dreary contest dragged on in the Assembly. of 1796. The petition of the Baptist General Committee, like an unfailing Thanksgiving turkey, was presented to the house. The radical spirit in Virginia had steadily risen with the development of the French Revolution, and the insistent annual attack upon the glebes had at length grown dangerous. The Episcopal church, in view of the situation, broke the silence of years and replied to the Baptist memorial. Both the Baptist and Episcopal petitions were referred to the committee of courts of justice, which had largely superceded the effete committee for religion. The committee made an exhaustive report, detailing the history of the glebes from the first reservations in the charters of 1606 and 1609; mentioning the grants of the king, private donations and the purchases of vestries; and asserting that the act of 1776 was a settlement of just claims "according to the true principles of the then new government."

"It further appears to your committee, that the Protestant Episcopal church of Virginia, which is the same in its rights with the former church of England, had from time to time been compelled to assert and vindicate those rights, against the pretentions of other religious bodies, distinct from itself in doctrine, discipline and worship.

"Resolved, That it is the opinion of this committee, that in order to put an end to these disputes, it ought to be declared and resolved by the General Assembly.

"1. That the contest for the Glebes, Churches, and Chapels, is not of a religious nature, but is to be decided by the rules of private property.

"2. That the grants aforesaid from the treasurer and company, and from the King of England and the glebes purchased by vestries were to the followers of the church in each parish, forming one society exclusively of all other persons whatsoever.

"3. That the transferring of the private donations or any part of them, from the support of the Protestant Episcopal Church, to that of any other religious order would be a unconstitutional invasion of right, and would in effect oblige the donors to contribute to the maintenance of tenets which they either did not foresee, or foreseeing, might not have approved.

"4. That all the glebes, churches and chapels whether purchased or given, being vested in bodies which are capable in law of taking and holding them to the use declared by law, and which actually did take and hold them to that use, it is against reason and the practice of every sect, that those who voluntarily depart from communion with them, should demand a share of their possessions.

"5. That it would be usurpation in the Legislature to convert the money arising from the sale of the glebes, churches or chapels, to public necessities.

"6. That the Legislative sanction for such a sale would soon grow into a precedent for the constant intrusion of the state, into all things which concern religion.

"And 7. That the stipulation and guarantee aforesaid, ought to be inviolably preserved."[484]

This was a reasonable and historical statement. The right of the Episcopal church to the glebes was placed upon the basis of possession, law and the intent of the makers of the constitution.

The radicals replied in a lengthy amendment setting forth their side of the case.[485] It was declared that the glebes were not vested in the parishes or vestries, but in the ministers. The original grantees of the glebes— the king, the people, individuals—were the trustees, and not the vestries, and the lands should revert to the donors when the object of the trust failed. The act of 1776 exempting dissenters from church taxes and reserving the glebes used the phrase "church as by law established," thus admitting that the Church of England "existed beyond the reach of a revolution, which had overturned the civil government of England." The act of 1779 repealing the act for the support of the clergy had destroyed the established church, and although the vestries were trustees, the object of the trust was annihilated and the property reverted to the donors. "A subsequent investiture of this property by the legislature in a particular sect, admits the failure of the trust, and the reversion of the property of the society, whilst it violates the 4th & 10th articles of the bill of rights."[486] The act of 1784 incorporated the minister and vestry and invested them with the church property. "If any previous investiture of this property had existed, such a law would have been unnecessary, and the interposition of the legislature first to incorporate and then to bestow, evidently discloses an opinion, that no corporate or individual title to the property existed; that it belonged to the public, and that therefore the authority constituted by that public, and not by a religious sect, had a right to dispose of it." The act of 1776 speaks of an established church; the act of 1784 of a "late established church," thus asserting the abolition of the establishment. Consequently the incorporating law and subsequent laws in favor of particular sects were "precedents claiming a power in the legislature to re-establish a national church." The act of 1786 repealing the incorporation law and reserving to churches the property formerly held by them secured only the property independent of the incorporation act, and consequently in 1788 trustees had been invested with the power of holding property formally enjoyed by vestries. From these acts and the acts passed for the sale of glebes in order to purchase others, it followed that the old method of investiture of the glebes had come to an end and the property right reverted to the people, "as representing the ancient grantees of Virginia—the king—the social compact previous to the revolution, and private donors in all cases wherein an heir should not appear."

The resolutions were therefore offered that all laws bestowing property upon the Episcopal church should be repealed, that all glebes not in

[484] Journal of House of Delegates, Nov., 1796, p. 167.
[485] Journal, p. 169.
[486] Journal, p. 171.

possession of ministers should be appropriated to the education of poor children, but that ministers possessed of glebes were entitled to hold them for life.[487]

This skilful but over-legal argument somewhat ignored the facts in the case. Nothing was said of the part played by the house of burgesses in ecclesiastical legislation and the position of the house of delegates as the successor of the colonial legislature. The laws passed after 1776 concerning religion were intended to secure old rights under another political system, and to speak of them as making a new establishment was a manifest distortion.

The house took no action at this time, contenting itself with tabling the conflicting resolutions.[488] The end of the religious controversy, however, was now rapidly approaching, as the radical spirit in Virginia reached its climax. The rise of radicalism followed the development of the French Revolution; it extended to religion, as well as to politics and society. It partly occasioned, or more probably was coincident with, a decline of evangelical religion. A spiritual reaction succeeded the emotionalism of the early Revolutionary period, and Virginia, through Jefferson, felt the French influence more deeply probably than any other American State. This characteristically British portion of America had changed with that thoroughness sometimes seen in naturally conservative communities. The Englishman turned Frenchman who was the Virginian of these years had lost his native interest in pedigrees, and he was frequently inclined to skepticism in religion by the too-heady liberal atmosphere.[489] Meade says that irreligion was rife. The "enlightened" boys at William and Mary amused themselves with such debates as "Whether there by a God?" and "Whether the Christian Religion has been beneficial or injurious to mankind?"[490] Hawks, in speaking of infidelity, said that "there never was, perhaps, a period in the history of Virginia when it was more prevalent than at this time."[491] It is true that the educated were infected with free-thinking to a considerable degree, but evangelical religion, in spite of its temporary decline in the years following the war, had taken too deep a hold upon the people to suffer more than a short eclipse. Much of the radicalism in Virginia was on the surface and disappeared with the national victory of the Democratic-Republican party in 1800. But it is true, nevertheless, that the French Revolution was approved in the commonwealth, and that conservatism was denounced as Toryism. The radical spirit so far prevailed in the Virginia Assembly in the last years of the century that it became more and more evident that the only hope of the Episcopal church for retaining the glebes lay in the withdrawal of the subject from legislative discussion and an appeal to the courts. Bishop Madison accordingly called a convention in December, 1797, and a committee was appointed to propose to the Assembly a trial of the case in the courts.[492]

[487] Journal, p. 174.
[488] Journal, p. 174.
[489] Meade, I, 142, note.
[490] Meade, I, 29.
[491] Hawks, p. 216.
[492] Hawks, p. 232.

The suggestion received the approval of the conservative party in the Assembly.

The annual memorial of the Baptist General Committee came before the house on December 9, 1797[493] On January 5, 1798, the debate once more opened. The committee of the whole reported resolutions stating that: "Whereas the constitution of the state of Virginia, hath pronounced the government of the King of England to have been totally dissolved by the revolution; hath substituted in place of the civil government so dissolved, a new civil government, and hath in the bill of rights excepted from the powers given to the substituted government the power of revising any species of ecclesiastical or church government in lieu of that so dissolved, by referring the subject of religion to conscience:

"Resolved therefore, That the several laws"—the acts exempting dissenters from supporting the establishment; repealing the act for the support of the clergy; the incorporation act; the act authorizing the election of vestries; the act repealing the incorporation act; the act giving powers to trustees—"ought to be repealed, as violating the principles of the constitution, and being inconsistent with religious freedom; and that the law intituled, An act for establishing religious freedom, ought to be declared to derive its obligation from its being a true exposition of the principles of the bill of rights and constitution." [494]

The conservatives offered the amendment "That whether the said religious society denominated the Protestant Episcopal church, under the words or principles of our constitution, be entitled to hold the said property or not, is a question of judicial and not of legislative decision." It was voted down, 52 to 99. An effort was then made to strike out of the resolutions the line "as violating the principles of the constitution and being inconsistent with religious freedom," but it also failed. The resolution passed by a vote of 97 to 51.

The radical party had consequently won the day on the glebe question. The radical interpretation of the Bill of Rights as completely severing the connection of church and state, first put forward by the dissenters during the war, now received legislative sanction.

By this interpretation the earlier Assembly which had passed laws bearing on the religious question had violated the constitution through ignorance. Needless to say, the majority of the framers of the Bill of Rights and constitution had never held this view, even though a minority would probably have claimed a wider authority for the declaration than was at first allowed. Constitutional interpretation can never be rigidly limited, and it was inevitable that at a time of radical ascendency a charter of rights should be looked upon as sweeping in its application.

The vote by counties was as follows: Ayes—Accomac, Albemarle, Amelia, Amherst, Augusta, Bath, Bedford, Berkeley, Brunswick, Buckingham, Campbell, Caroline, Charlotte, Chesterfield, Cumberland, Culpeper, Fairfax, Fauquier, Fluvanna, Frederick, Franklin, Goochland, Greenbrier, Greensville, Grayson, Hampshire, Harrison, Hardy, Henrico, Halifax, Henry, Isle of Wight,

---

[493] Journal of House of Delegates, Nov., 1797, p. 15. The Methodists had now joined the Baptists in the agitation. Massachusetts Historical Society Proceedings, 42, 346.

[494] Journal of House of Delegates, Dec., 1797, p. 73.

King and Queen, King George, Kanawha, Lancaster, Loudoun, Louisa, Lee, Matthews, Mecklenburg, Monorgalia, Montgomery, Madison, New Kent, Nottoway, Ohio, Orange, Powhatan, Prince Edward, Prince William, Patrick, Randolph, Rockbridge, Rockingham, Shenandoah, Southampton, Spotsylvania, Washington and Wythe.

The noes were: Accomac, Amelia, Berkeley, Botetourt, Charles City, Dinwiddie, Elizabeth City, Essex, Fairfax, Greenbrier, Greensville, Hanover, Henrico, James City, Lancaster, Lunenburg, Matthews, Middlesex, Nansemond, New Kent, Norfolk, Northampton, Northumberland, Prince George, Pendleton, Richmond, Russell, Southampton, Stafford, Surry, Sussex, Warwick, York, Norfolk Borough, Williamsburg and Richmond City.

The radicals were from the midland and southside and western counties, and a few from the eastern. Forty-one votes came from western counties exclusively. Most of the voters in the negative were easterners, although conservatives from all sections voted against confiscation. Miles King, of Elizabeth City, William Gatewood, of Essex, and Willis Riddick, of Nansemond, were three conservatives who had opposed the sale of the glebes for years.

In accordance with the resolution, the radicals reported a bill repealing all acts reserving the glebes to the Episcopal church. The house passed the bill on January 13, 1798.[495] The senate, however, amended it, and the house considered the amendment on January 20, 1798.[496] The bill read: "Whereas the Constitution of the state of Virginia, hath pronounced the government of the king of England, to have been totally dissolved by the revolution, hath substituted in place of the civil government so dissolved, a new civil government, and hath in the Bill of Rights excepted from the powers given to the substituted government, the power of reviving any species of ecclesiastical or church government, in lieu of that so dissolved, by referring the subject of religion to conscience. And whereas the several acts presently recited, do admit the church establishment under the regal government, to have continued so subsequently to the constitution; have bestowed property upon that church; have asserted a legislative right to establish any religious sect; and have incorporated religious sects; all of which is inconsistent with the principles of the constitution, and of religious freedom, and manifestly tends to the re-establishment of a national church," and repealing all the acts passed on the subject since the adoption of the constitution.

The senate amendment stated that the glebe question had agitated the public mind for many years, and "whereas the memorial of the Baptist society and others, has declared, that a repeal of all laws passed on the subject since the establishment of our present system of state government, would entirely satisfy their doubts and difficulties on the said question; and the convention of the Protestant Episcopal church, in order to have a final end put to the controversy, have been willing to submit it to the determination of the judiciary, whether the property aforesaid was not vested in them by laws passed antecedent to the establishment of the said constitution, and whether any thing contained therein can be considered as operating a

---

[495] Journal, p. 86.
[496] Journal, p. 95.

divestment thereof, which is the only constitutional mode by which the public can ascertain their right to the property claimed by others."

This amendment, which accepted the view of the unconstitutionality of the religious acts passed subsequently to the constitution, but maintained that the Episcopalian claim to the glebes was based upon acts passed prior to it, was lost by a vote of 31 to 79.[497] A second amendment directing the attorney-general to bring the glebe case before the courts and guaranteeing possession to the incumbents, the parishes and vestries, until decision should be rendered was also lost. The house remained steadfast in its opposition to the senate amendments when they were again referred to it,[498] and the bill failed to pass at this session.

The struggle was renewed at the next session of the Assembly. The perennial Baptist petition was presented on December 15, 1798.[499] Petitions from parishes asking for the sale of glebes also began to come in freely; the end was plainly in sight.

The repeal bill of the year before came into the house again on January 18, 1799.[500] The conservatives proposed a last amendment: "That whether the religious society denominated the Protestant Episcopal church, be or be not entitled to hold the Glebe lands, of which they are now possessed, is a question of judicial and not of legislative decision. It failed by a vote of 57 to 86.[501] A number of former conservatives voted against the amendment. The bill passed the house on January 23, 1799[502] and the next day the senate, seeing the uselessness of further resistance, acquiesced. The guarantees that the early revolutionists had given the Anglican church were withdrawn,[503] the glebes remained in the hands of the State, and the only question left for solution was the particular object of benevolence the Assembly might select for the bestowal of the church property.

Confiscation did not immediately follow, however. Nothing more was done at this session. In the following year a number of petitions asking for the sale of glebes for the benefit of schools and academies were presented.[504]

Similar petitions came in at the December 1801 session, and it was evident that the disposal of the glebes could not be longer postponed. The house, on December 15, 1801, considered a bill for the sale of the glebes and the use in common of the churches. The bill was amended[505] and passed the house on December 22d by the overwhelming vote of 126 to 39.

The senate did not immediately concur. It attached amendmendts to the bill which the house in turn amended. Finally the house accepted the amended bill on January 20, 1802.[506]

---

[497] Journal, p. 79.

[498] Journal, p. 98.

[499] Journal of House of Delegates, Dec., 1798, p. 24. The committee for religion had now gone out of existence. Divorces were considered by another committee. It was possibly felt that the existence of a committee for religion was inconsistent with the complete separation of church and state.

[500] Journal of House of Delegates, Dec., 1798, p. 83.

[501] Journal, p. 84.

[502] Journal, p. 98.

[503] Hening, XV, 149; Journal of House of Delegates, Dec., 1799, pp. 10, 26, 32, 46, 50.

[504] Journal of House of Delegates, Dec., 1801, p. 18.

[505] Journal, p. 32.

[506] Journal of House of Delegates, Dec., 1801, 214; Hening, XV, 314. The date usually given for the passage of the act is erroneous.

The act directed the county overseers of the poor to sell the glebes which were vacant or which might become vacant by the death of the incumbent. The overseers received a grant of large powers in conducting the sales and a percentage of the proceeds, which were to be appropriated for the benefit of the poor or for any other object which a majority of voters in each county might decide upon. Private donations made the Anglican church before 1777 were not to be sold, when "there is any person in being entitled to take the same under any private donor," and property obtained by the church since 1777 was not to be disturbed.

The act was stupid and bad in tendency, as confiscating laws usually are. As in the case of the suppression of the monasteries in England and similar sequestrations, the public profited little by the sale of the glebes. The act was passed in deference to popular demand, and it could hardly have made worse arrangements for the disposal of the church property. The glebes were turned over to the people of the individual parishes as the descendants of the original taxpayers. Instead of intrusting the sales of the glebes to the county courts, which might have conducted them properly, the act delivered them into the hands of the overseers of the poor, a usually incompetent class of officials. The returns from the sales would not have been large even if a fair value had been obtained for the property, but the whole, if kept together, would have yielded a nucleus for a fund which might have grown to be an important factor in public work. But such a disposition of the glebes, if thought of, would hardly have received popular approval, as too many people were interested in the sales from personal motives. As a consequence, the sale of the glebes, except in a few cases, was beneficial only to individuals and not to the public at large.

A final effort was made to save the glebes by an appeal to the courts. Turpin and other vestrymen of Manchester parish, Chesterfield, brought suit in the chancery court for an injunction to prevent the overseers of the poor of the county from selling the parish glebe under the terms of the act of 1802.[507] The vestrymen took the ground that the act of 1802 was unconstitutional, since the Episcopal church had a continuous identity with the church of England in Virginia, and the Assembly, in the act of 1776, had confirmed the right of the church to its property. The act was a "contemporaneous exposition of the new constitution, so as plainly to make the distinction between an establishment with power to create future burthens, and the rights of the Church of England to the property already acquired." The defendants replied that the complainants showed no title to the glebe, and that the act of 1802 was valid. Chancellor Wythe dismissed the bill and the plaintiffs took the case to the court of appeals.

The arguments of the counsel on both sides were able. From a historical point of view, the appellants made out a better case. They maintained that the church of England in Virginia was an independent colonial church, and that revolutions do not destroy existing social institutions. The fourth article of the Bill of Rights forbidding the grant of special privileges, did not apply to the church, the State had no claim to the property of social bodies and consequently the act of 1802 was unconstitutional.

---

[507] Virginia Reports, 6; Call, 113.

The defense affirmed that the Revolution had destroyed the established church, since the king of England was a component part of that church. Furthermore that the pretentions of the church were contrary to the Bill of Rights, as the revenues from the glebes were as much private emoluments as the ministers' salaries. A majority of the people at the time of the Revolution—according to Jefferson—were dissenters, and public property, under the Bill of Rights, could not be enjoyed by a minority. The Episcopal church was not identical with the establishment, as the petition of the church for incorporation in 1784 admitted. The vestry and church wardens had no estate in the land and could not maintain suits concerning it. The colonial church was not a corporation in that it lacked a name, seal, capacity to maintain suits and authority to buy lands; and if the church was not a corporation, the use of the land would have been vested in a minister and would have reverted to the public at the Revolution.

In the interim between the delivery of the arguments and the decision of the court, Edmund Pendleton, one of the judges, died. It is stated that he had prepared a decision pronouncing the act of 1802 unconstitutional. There can be little doubt that the great conservative would have given his decision in favor of a church whose rights he had always strongly championed.

Pendleton's death left the court tied—Tucker and Roane for constitutionality and Carrington and Lyons for unconstitutionality. Consequently Wythe's decision in chancery stood.

Tucker rendered an elaborately argued technical decision, declaring that the title to the glebe lands at the time of the Revolution was vested in the vestries and that the act of 1776 confirmed these titles. The judge found the end of the establishment in the incorporation act of 1784, which dissolved the old vestries, and there is much to be said in favor of this view. The new vestries elected after this act differed essentially from the old vestries in owing their existence and their rights to that act. These new vestries did not lose possession of the glebes by the repeal of the incorporation act, but were confirmed as trustees by the act of 1788. The act of 1798, however, dissolved these incorporated bodies, and as the glebes were not private property, the vestries no longer held a title. If the Assembly lacked the power to repeal the acts vesting the title of the glebes in the new vestries, it also had no power to pass the incorporation act of 1784, dissolving the old vestries and granting the property to new vestries. The incorporation act, in that it created exclusive rights, was repugnant to the principles established by the Revolution and so was unconstitutional. And even if constitutional, it had been repealed. But this act alone gave the Episcopal church a title, and as it was unconstitutional and had been repealed, the church no longer held any title to the glebes.

Roane's decision was also technical. He held that the title to the glebes was vested in the ministers and not in the vestries, and by the gift of the government, which acted not for itself but for the people. According to common law, the property reverted to the people as donors upon the dissolution of the corporations which had held them. The Episcopal church was not the same as the colonial church and therefore the ministers of the latter church were not the same as the pastors of the former church and not their successors. Thus for want of a grantee the lands reverted to the donors—the people. The acts of 1776 and 1784 vesting the glebes in the Episcopal church violated the Bill of Rights, which forbade grants of property to individuals except for public services, and so were unconstitutional. The act of 1802 had merely put aside the infractions of the constitution contained in these two acts.

Carrington and Lyons concurred in a brief and able decision. They claimed that the glebes had been vested in a church which was not the church of England but the church of Virginia. The Revolution did not destroy this title, as alterations in government do not affect private property. The sixteenth article of the Bill of Rights had not forbidden a continuance of the establishment, but related to emoluments and privileges which might be subsequently created. The act of 1776 confirming the church's title to the property was a contemporaneous exposition of the constitution and possessed the same force. The church had a right to the glebes at the time of the Revolution; nothing happened afterwards to affect the right, and thus the act of 1802 was unconstitutional.

This argument seems sound. The framers of the constitution, while making a grant of religious liberty, apparently had no intention of depriving the Anglican church of what it had held for so long a period.

Tucker's contention that the act of 1784 ended the establishment is convincing, but his inference that the act created a new establishment is perhaps not strong. The incorporation act was intended merely as an adjustment of old rights, made necessary by political changes, and not as the endowment of another religious establishment. The argument that the title to the glebes was vested in the ministers and their successors alone and consequently reverted to the public upon the failure of vestries to appoint ministers may be legally sound but it is not historically satisfying. The justice of history is real and not argumentative. The vestries were the truly component parts of the colonial church; they were the church government, the power, and to ignore their title to the glebes in favor of the ministers seems a strange claim. But neither ministers nor vestries existed for themselves, but for the church. The church was the entity. If the servants of the church held the glebes, they held them in trust for the church, and the moral title to them remained in the church as long as it continued to be the same body in doctrine and discipline.

The whole point turns upon the power of the Assembly to resume what it had formerly granted. If the house of burgesses could set up the establishment, or sanction its existence, was it possible for the Assembly of the State to take back what had once been given? The answer will depend upon the interpretation of the constitution. If the guaranteeing act of 1776 should be taken as supplementing or explaining the constitution, and this seems to be the case, it was a part of the constitution and the act of 1802 was unconstitutional. On the other hand, if the act of 1776 was not an explanation of the constitution but a violation of it, the act of 1802 was valid. But in any case it seems that some compensation should have been made the Anglican church for the loss of property which by custom if not by law belonged to it.

The confiscatory act of 1802 was the culmination of the radical spirit in

Virginia. The men imbued with the great ideals of democracy looked back with disapproval upon the colonial past under the British protectorate. They destroyed the relics of that past in the hope of obtaining a perfection of their ideas of government and life, and sometimes they committed an injustice in the process. The act of 1802 is a case in point. But, on the whole, society was greatly stimulated by the Revolutionary spirit, although the upper classes, poorer in property and prestige through the war, failed to produce another generation like the Revolutionary heroes. The loss was in large part made up by the general improvement in the condition of the people and by the inspiring spirit born of this liberal age.

CHAPTER VIII.

Fate of the Glebes.

Sales of glebes by the overseers of the poor began shortly after the passage of the act of 1802. Confiscation was limited to vacant glebes, as ministers of long residence were not disturbed, except perhaps in a few cases, but nevertheless the resistance of vestries on several occasions indicates that the law worked a good deal of hardship. Private donations were usually respected, though not always. In some cases the overseers of the poor were hindered in various ways in the attempt to discharge their functions, but the interference usually wore away, and it is estimated that most of the glebes had been sold by 1830.[507] Sales were usually not productive. "The purchasers of the glebes have, in every instance where a sale has been made, paid, as it were, almost nothing for them."[508] In some cases it seems that the overseers who conducted the sales derived the chief benefit from them. The money obtained from the glebes was devoted usually to lessening the poor tax for a year or so, providing a permanent fund for poor relief, and in education, but sometimes it went for other public purposes, such as the repair of roads. There was no concert whatever in the use of the funds, even in establishing schools; each county practically did what was right in its own eyes.

Besides glebes, church buildings, plate and furniture, some parishes owned slaves, and these seem to have been included in the sales. The overseers of the poor of Halifax, on December 21, 1802, asked for the dispossession of the incumbent of Antrim parish, Alexander Hay, and for authority to sell the parish slaves, which Hay had carried away. The glebe and churches of the parish were disposed of under the act of 1802. In 1803 the Episcopalians asked for an act incorporating trustees to hold property raised by subscription for the use of the church, but incorporation was then an anathema.

The unsatisfactory results of the sales of the glebes were partially due to the character of the men who conducted them—the overseers of the poor. Their office, unlike that of their predecessors, the vestrymen, was a rather unimportant local office and apparently not eagerly sought. Elections of overseers were sometimes badly conducted from lack of interest. In the election in King George county in 1804, it is stated that in one district a candidate was elected by three votes; in another district an overseer was elected by one vote.[509] Needless to say the duties of the office were often inefficiently performed. In some cases, after the sales of the glebes were made, the proceeds therefrom remained in the hands of the overseers without appropriation for any purpose.

---

[507] II Leigh. Selden et al. *v.* overseers of poor, p. 581.

[508] Hawks, 235, quoted from Lee's Review of Selden et al. *v.* overseers of poor of Loudoun county.

[509] Pet. December 8, 1804.

In Gloucester the principal obtained from the sale was consumed in part by the overseers, who sold the glebe on credit, received the money due in small payments and charged large commissions.[510] In King and Queen, a considerable sum was due from the sale of the glebe and from bequests, but the fund under the management of the overseers was of little advantage to the community and a petition was presented asking that it be vested in trustees.[511] The same thing had occurred in Stafford, where the overseers retained in their possession the proceeds of the sale of Overwharton parish glebe and a part of the Brunswick glebe.[512] The board of poor overseers of King William had difficulty in transacting business owing to the inattention of the overseers and the continual changes in office.[513]

A considerable part of the proceeds of the glebe sales went for education, but usually on a slip-shod and ineffective system, owing to the lack of schools to serve as models and the want of any central authority.· In some cases the principal was used; in others only the interest. Hanover parish, King George, asked that the balance of $4,248.96, due the parish from the sale, be established as a free-school fund, with special trustees to apply it. The people of Stafford petitioned for a similar use of their glebe fund, which in 1810 was still in the hands of the overseers of the poor. The people of St. Anne's parish, Essex, in 1821 made the same request. The glebe fund had likewise remained in the hands of the overseers. In some cases efficient schools were maintained or aided by the proceeds. Thus the Staunton Academy in 1853 was the beneficiary of a fund of $3,500, raised by the sale of 1802.[514] The income had been used for some years to lessen the county levy, and was then applied to the academy.

In a majority of cases the proceeds of the sales were used for poor relief, and sometimes poor houses were built from them. A few requests were made to appropriate the glebe fund for improving county roads and building bridges.

Private donations of glebes were usually respected and some glebes remained in possession of the Anglican church, or rather in the hands of vestries or trustees, for many years. These glebes, however, usually fell into decay and in most instances were sold sooner or later, as in the case of the King William glebe, Powhatan, which was a reservation granted by William III. The Nansemond glebe near Suffolk still remains in the possession of the church and is a valuable piece of property.

The use of the parish churches in common by all denominations, proved, as might have been expected, a failure. In some cases a single church secured possession by constant use for a long period. More often the churches gradually fell into disuse and were allowed to go to ruin, while the various sects built their own church buildings in the neighborhood. Occasionally there were sharp conflicts for the use of certain churches. Meade states that the Methodists and Baptists disputed the parish church of Prince Edward; in 1832 the Baptists obtained a title but did not refuse the

[510] Pet. December 16, 1813.
[511] Pet. December 21, 1815.
[512] Pet. December 12, 1810.
[513] Pet. October 21, 1814.
[514] Calendar of Petitions, A 1406.

Methodists the right to worship in the building.[515] In another case of dispute
the church was put up to the highest bidder.[516]

The case of Bruton parish church, Williamsburg, the most noted church
in Virginia, is interesting.[517] After the death of John Bracken, it appears
that Bruton church became a union church and was so used for many
years. The people of Williamsburg, without distinction of sect, repaired the
ruinous building, which was shared by the various sects until 1831. In that
year a Universalist minister visiting Williamsburg was refused the use of
the church and it then formally went back into the hands of the Episcopal
communion.

A number of law suits accompanied the sale of the glebes, in spite of
the decision in Turpin vs. Locket. The case of Selden vs. Overseers of the
poor of Loudoun was decided in 1840 as in the former case.[518]

Different in principle was the case of Claughton vs. Macnaughton.[519]
Duncan Macnaughton, minister of St. Stephen's parish, Northumberland,
applied in the chancery court for an injunction to restrain the overseers of
the poor of Northumberland from selling two glebes, which he claimed to
be private donations and of which he was the incumbent. The court
decided that the glebes could not be sold during the life of the incumbent,
and the court of appeals sustained the decision.

In the case of Terrett vs. Taylor[520] in 1815, the United States
supreme court decided that the Episcopal church of Alexandria had a
title to the Fairfax glebe as against the overseers of the poor of Fairfax
county. Justice Story delivered a very able opinion. He held that the
Revolution had not destroyed the civil rights of corporations, that the
guaranteeing act of 1776 was a contemporaneous interpretation of the
constitution and completed the title of the Episcopal church to the glebes,
and that the act of 1802 did not apply to Alexandria, since it had become
a part of the District of Columbia prior to this date. In 1824 the purchasers
of the glebe property, sold under this decree, brought suit to rescind the
purchase upon the ground of a defective title.[521] The supreme court decided
upon an appeal that the vestry of the Alexandria Episcopal church was the
successor of the Fairfax parish vestry and thus had a right to convey the
title.

Justice Story's decision in these cases rested more or less upon the
necessarily corporate character of religious bodies. The passing of the
danger of a state church together with the Revolutionary irritations, and
the many difficulties and inconveniences attending management of the
property of societies which had no legal existence brought about a change
in the attitude of the various denominations on the subject of incorporation.
Many petitions from a number of churches, including the Baptist, came to
the Legislature asking for the establishment of some system by which

[515] Meade I, 25.
[516] Meade I, 26.
[517] Petition of Robert Anderson, Mayor of Williamsburg, December 5, 1831.
[518] II Leigh, 581.
    Tucker's Commentaries, II, Appendix.
[519] 2 Munford, 513.
    A similar case decided in the same way was that of Young v. overseers of the poor of
Norfolk county. 2 Munford, 517.
[520] 9 Cranch, 43.
[521] Mason v. Muncaster et al. 9 Wheaton, 445.

property might be held by religious bodies. The difficulty was met by acts providing for the appointment of trustees to hold church property and granting members of churches the right to sue trustees for the proper execution of their trust.[522]

The separation of church and state, which had caused religious bodies these difficulties, did not injure the cause of religion in Virginia. Skepticism began to decline with the decline of French influence. It had probably never affected the mass of the people deeply and it largely disappeared as the evangelical churches renewed their energies. Evangelical Christianity indeed secured a notable triumph in Virginia, which became one of the most orthodox of countries and has remained so ever since.

The Episcopal church, when revived by bishop Meade, was revived in an evangelical spirit. Meade, a strong man and a thorough Puritan, left an impression upon his church which still continues. With the passing of the influence of the French Revolution, the democratic age began to wane. The national triumph of the Democratic Party carried with it a modification of its early tenets. In Virginia the past began to be looked upon with different eyes. It is probable that the complete overthrow of democracy in Europe after 1815 had an influence upon America at a time when foreign politics were followed with an interest inconceivable to the people of the present. The novels of Sir Walter Scott, which were exceedingly popular in Virginia, in their glorification of the feudal age, may have had some effect upon public sentiment. At all events the French Revolution was condemned by the generation following that which had approved it, and the colonial era was invested with the charms of imagination. The influence of slavery, although certainly not unrepublican, doubtless acted against the continuance of democratic ideals in society. The reaction found expression in politics by the rise of the Whig party, which at length divided Virginia with the Democracy. The problems of religion, however, were past. Religious questions no longer vexed politicians, and the churches, once hindered by state interference, grew in strength and influence with the passage of years. Separation of church and state in Virginia, instead of weakening Christianity, as the conservatives of the Revolution had feared, really aided it in securing a power over men far greater than it had known in the past.

---

[522] Pollard's Code I, 1396 *et seq.*

INDEX

158

160

162